Women and Careers

Dedication

Wayne Carlisle
1944-1991

Members of the Research Group on Women and Work dedicate this book to the memory of Wayne Carlisle as an expression of our love and respect. During the time we worked in collaborative research with Wayne, we found him to be a gentle, curious, generous man, a man who worked in supportive partnership with women and men and who sought to increase equality and opportunity in the world. We knew him to be the kind of man who changes the world through his example of balancing work and family, achievement and caring. Wayne demonstrated more than anyone else we know that work is love made visible. We will try to exemplify his spirit in our future work. We will seek him in what we do.

Women and Careers

ISSUES AND CHALLENGES

EDITED BY
Carol Wolfe Konek
Sally L. Kitch

SAGE Publications
International Educational and Professional Publisher
Thousand Oaks   London   New Delhi

For information address:

SAGE Publications, Inc.
2455 Teller Road
Thousand Oaks, California 91320

SAGE Publications Ltd.
6 Bonhill Street
London EC2A 4PU
United Kingdom

SAGE Publications India Pvt. Ltd.
M-32 Market
Greater Kailash I
New Delhi 110 048 India

Printed in the United States of America

Library of Congress Cataloging-in-Publication Data

Main entry under title:

Women and careers: issues and challenges / edited by
Carol Wolfe Konek, Sally L. Kitch.
    p.   cm.
    Includes bibliographical references and index.
    ISBN 0-8039-5262-7 (cl).—ISBN 0-8039-5263-5 (pb)
    1. Women—Employment—United States. 2. Women—Employment—
United States—Statistics. 3. Women—United States—Social conditions.
4. Women—United States—Attitudes. 5. Social surveys—United
States. I. Konek, Carol. II. Kitch, Sally.
HD6095.W672 1994   93-29476
331.4′0973—dc20   CIP

94 95 96 97 98 10 9 8 7 6 5 4 3 2 1

Sage Production Editor: Judith L. Hunter

Contents

Foreword

ELSIE R. SHORE

Like many people moving to Wichita, Kansas, I was surprised to find myself not in an agricultural community, but rather in an urban center with many large manufacturing companies and other corporations of all sizes. This discovery was especially pleasing, as it meant that I could pursue a research interest I had developed in graduate school: to study alcohol use and abuse among business and professional women. I had heard dire predictions that as women became "liberated"—that is, entered traditionally male areas of endeavor—their alcohol problems and alcoholism rates would increase, perhaps dramatically. These warnings, however, were accompanied by little or no supporting data. I wanted to see whether the predictions were coming true and whether steps could be taken to prevent business and professional women from following their male counterparts into problem drinking and alcoholism.

To conduct the primary prevention research project I envisioned, I needed a relatively large number of women, the majority of whom should not appear to have problems with alcohol. Selection bias was a recruitment issue. Women volunteering for a study of alcohol use and abuse could be expected to be recovering alcoholics, spouses of alcoholics, or others with vested interests in questions of alcohol use. I realized that a study of broader scope, in which alcohol use was only one part, would attract a greater variety of women. To this end, I spoke with colleagues at Wichita State University and found a number of faculty and staff interested in studying business and professional women. This was the beginning of the Research Group on Women and Work (RGWW). The group was diverse and inclusive, initially composed of 10 faculty, professional staff, administrators, and graduate students from four colleges at Wichita State University.

From the beginning, the members of the RGWW wanted to engage in a truly collaborative project. In addition to sharing the subject pool, we developed a shared vision of feminist research and worked together to establish and fund the group. We designed a comprehensive questionnaire dealing with each of our varied interests. Instead of taking our data back to our offices and working and publishing separately, we looked for connections and correlations among the areas we were studying.

This book contains results of the questionnaire distributed in April 1986 to 770 women, as well as some results of a third questionnaire returned by 238 of the same women in July 1991. Of those initial 770 women to whom questionnaires were mailed, 494 returned completed surveys, a response made more remarkable by the fact that the questionnaire was 29 pages long. Participants listed approximately 200 job titles. Among the respondents are engineers, business owners, accountants, attorneys, physicians, academics, administrators, and professionals in human services, medical care, advertising, banking, and manufacturing.

After the majority of our interdisciplinary group had analyzed our data from the questionnaire, we met in a series of meetings to discuss our findings and to share insights from our diverse training and experience. It is not an exaggeration to say that we were a community of scholars working in collaboration to discover coherent answers to questions we posed as diverse individuals.

The project employed a number of feminist strategies for the empowerment of the participants. The very length and breadth of the questionnaire communicated to participants the expectation of deep reflection and personal commitment to a joint venture in discovery. In addition to the interactive nature of the research design, it combined both quantitative and qualitative methods, resulting in both statistical and narrative data. It employed formative, as well as summative, strategies. Participants were encouraged to contribute responses to articles and columns in 12 newsletters entitled *Working Papers,* published over 2 years and funded by a grant from the National Institute on Alcohol Abuse and Alcoholism. Additional surveys occasionally were mailed to participants as inserts in the newsletter. Two requests for additional survey data produced good results. In addition, anecdotal information from participants suggests that they found the newsletter informative and entertaining.

We researchers were collaborating with each other across disciplinary and organizational boundaries as we were collaborating with our participants. We shared our results as they emerged, through the newsletter and in a number of public lectures and forums. We also sought additional information when participants called limitations and possibilities in our design to our attention.

The first RGWW project was undertaken to gain information about women's career experiences in the context of their lives, rather than from an organizational or male-comparative perspective. Feminist criticism of traditional social science research methods suggests that decreasing the distance between researchers and subjects, empowering subjects through interactive strategies, and revealing the results of research increases the status of "subjects" to that of participants, while giving them an investment in the social purposes of the research. Feminist criticism of traditional research methods also points to the limits of objectivity, as well as to the reductive, compartmentalizing effect of imposing narrow, disciplinary boundaries on the experience of individuals. We sought to overcome the limitations of such methods by acknowledging our awareness that disciplinary constraints often mask the biases, as well as the hypotheses, of researchers whose success depends on simulating neutrality or objectivity, rather than acknowledging that the very act of gathering and organizing knowledge has political implications and social outcomes.

Consistent with acknowledging our subjectivity, and our desire to interact with participants, we researchers not only shared our work with each other but also informed our participants of the results of the survey. We recruited participants primarily at meetings of various professional groups, and we told members at that time that they would receive questionnaire results. Women at the meetings I attended reacted favorably to that promise. We believe that our interactive, participatory design may have increased their interest in the study and contributed to our high return rate (65%).

Our continued involvement with participants in our study helped us maintain their cooperation when second and third surveys were sent and further enabled us to extend the project. Two follow-up questionnaires included some new topics not addressed in the first survey; they will result in longitudinal analysis and additional descriptive data and verify our interpretation of early results in the current study. We expect the Research Group on Women and Work to continue its contribution to increased understanding of women's careers and lives. Analysis of subsequent findings and expansion of research into additional areas of women's experience is forthcoming.

Acknowledgments

We welcome the opportunity to acknowledge the support, assistance, and contributions of our students. We were fortunate to work with a number of talented, intelligent, and dedicated graduate and undergraduate students, some of whom volunteered their time and efforts, and others who did not get paid what they were worth. They are Melody Embree, Kim Loudermilk, Marcia McCoy, Collette Hoglund, Michael Kauth, Sharon Pieri, Cindy Blanchat, Linda Farris, Selina Sanchez, and Jeanne Brown. Many other students generously helped on an as-needed basis, stuffing envelopes and making computers cooperate.

We also sincerely thank Steve Batt for his assistance with statistical analyses and computer programming and Lee Starkel for her technical assistance. Without guidance, many of us still would be at the data analysis stage.

This work was supported, in large part, by grants from the National Institute on Alcohol Abuse and Alcoholism. We value the commitment of that agency to the study of women and alcohol as much as we appreciate the funding that made such a large longitudinal project possible. In addition, we thank the various department chairpersons, deans, and administrators at Wichita State University for their individual and collective support of this interdisciplinary, feminist research.

Finally, we wish to thank Laurie Larwood for her encouragement and support.

1

Career Women in Perspective: The Wichita Sample

NANCY McCARTHY SNYDER

As an economist, who specializes in poverty, income distribution, and labor force issues, I have a professional as well as a personal interest in the economic status of women and children. Bureau of the Census statistics clearly indicate that the economic status of women and children in the United States has deteriorated over the last two decades. The design of policies to reduce poverty and inequality in the distribution of income therefore requires attention to the occupational choices and parenting choices of women.

When I discovered that the Research Group on Women and Work (RGWW) was in the process of analyzing the working lives of a group of successful women, I hoped that I could gain information from these women that might be used to improve the living standards of all women.

Trends in Female
Labor Force Participation

Interest in the working lives of women has grown with increases in labor force participation by women. Although it is true that women have always "worked," until recently the economic role played by women was concentrated in "work that could efficiently be combined in the

1

Table 1.1
Female Labor Force Participation Rates, United States, 1900-1990

AGES	1900	1920	1930	1940	1950	1960	1970	1980	1990
16-19 *	26.6	28.4	22.8	18.9	22.6	23.9	25.5	51.5	51.8
20-24	31.7	37.5	41.8	45.6	42.9	44.9	56.3	69.2	71.6
25-34	19.3	23.7	27.1	33.3	31.8	35.2	45.2	66.2	73.6
35-44	15.7	19.2	21.7	27.2	35	42.6	50.6	66.5	76.5
45-54	15	17.9	19.7	22.5	32.9	46.7	52.9	61	71.2
55-64	13.2	14.3	15.3	16.8	23.5	35	42.4	41.1	45.3
All ages	21	22.7	23.6	25.8	29	34.5	39.9	51.8	57.5
Ages 20-64	19.7	22.9	25.4	29.4	33	40.6	49.2	61.5	70.8

SOURCES: Smith, J. P., & Ward, M. P. (1984). *1900-1970: Women's wages and work in the twentieth century.* New York: Rand.
Department of Labor. (1981, January). *Employment and earnings.* Washington, DC: Bureau of Labor Statistics.
Department of Labor. (1988, January). *Employment and earnings.* Washington, DC: Bureau of Labor Statistics.
Department of Labor. (1992, January). *Employment and earnings.* Washington, DC: Bureau of Labor Statistics.
*NOTE: Before 1950 this group includes those aged 14 to 19.

home with child care" (Bergman, 1986, p. 7). Consequently the vast majority of female labor was allocated outside the market exchange of supply and demand. It has been only in the postwar period in the United States that women have entered the labor market in large numbers.

Changes in the work patterns of women have been sudden and marked. In 1900, 21% of all women were employed outside the home. In 1950, that number was 29%, but by 1990, the female labor force participation rate was 57.5%. Participation rates for women aged 20 to 64 show even greater growth, from less than 20% in 1900, to 33% in 1950, to over 70% in 1990. Women now make up over 45% of the total labor force (see Table 1.1). Interestingly the labor force participation of men has been falling (from 86.6% in 1948 to 76.1% in 1990). Much of this decline can be explained by improved retirement benefits that have encouraged early retirement. The increase in female labor force participation has offered male workers more flexibility. Changing female labor force behavior has been most marked among women of childbearing age, with most of the increase taking place since 1960. Between 1960 and 1990, the participation rate for women aged 25 to 34 more than doubled, from 35.2% to 73.6%. For women aged 35 to 44, the rate grew by nearly 30%, from 42.6 to 76.5%.

Most of the change in labor market attachment can be explained by changes in the behavior of white women. Between 1900 and 1990, the participation rate for white females aged 20 to 64 more than quadrupled, while that of nonwhite women less than doubled. African American women have always had higher labor force participation rates than white women, due mainly to economic necessity. Only since 1970 have rates of whites approached those of nonwhites. In 1990 the participation rates for African American and white females were nearly equal. Participation rates for other minority women were slightly lower.

Social and economic institutions have been slow in recognizing the changing labor market status of women. Wages, hours, setting, and other working conditions still are set on the assumption that the typical worker is male with no family or household responsibilities. As recently as 1950, 70% of American households were male-headed with a one-salary income. By 1990, roughly less than 15% of families in the United States fit this model. In 1973, 47% of the wives in 25- to 34-year-old married couples worked. By 1985, two thirds of all young wives were employed (Levy & Michel, 1986).

Although women have entered the labor force in very large numbers in recent years, their labor force behavior still differs significantly from that of men. Women are more likely than men to work part-time. In 1986 over 20% of women aged 24 to 64 who were employed worked fewer than 30 hours per week. For men in that age group, the comparable figure was only 6%. In addition, of the women who worked more than 30 hours per week, 13% had worked fewer than 40 weeks in the previous year (Fuchs, 1989). Even among professional women, differences in hours worked are significant.

Among white married women with 18 years or more of schooling and at least one child under age 12 at home, only 1 in 10 works more than 2,250 hours per year. By contrast, half of their husbands do, and one third of these men work more than 2,500 hours (Fuchs, 1989, p. 31).

Women are also more likely than men to move in and out of the labor force. Historically women worked for a period after education completion, married, raised children, and may or may not have entered the labor force. That trend is changing. More and more women are staying in the labor force after they marry and have children. By 1990, 59.4% of married women with children under age 6 and over half of women with children under 1 year of age were in the labor force.

Occupational Segregation

This past lack of permanent labor force attachment is used by some to explain another dominant feature of labor force behavior: Women workers tend to be segregated into a very few occupations that often are designated as "women's work" and that are among the lowest paid (Becker, 1981; Mincer & Polachek, 1974; Polachek, 1979).

Barbara Bergman (1986) analyzed occupational segregation by ranking 335 occupations that employed 25,000 or more in 1984 by the percentage of women they employ. Just about half of the women (49.87%) were in the first 54 occupations, all of which were more than 76% female and employed only 3.94% of the men. The 131 lowest ranking occupations, which employed 49.41% of the men, were all more than 83% male and employed only 4.76% of the women. The relatively well integrated occupations—those with 30% to 50% women—employed about 17% of the workers of each gender (Bergman, 1986, p. 7).

Economic explanations for occupational segregation are based on the human capital theory. In its simplest form, this theory explains differences in labor productivity and, hence, wages by differences in investment in and depreciation of human capital (e.g., education, training, on-the-job experience). Polachek (1984) argued that because women plan to move in and out of the labor force more often than men, they can maximize their lifetime earnings by choosing occupations characterized by low depreciation and low training costs. These theories, in general, have not been confirmed with empirical evidence (Bergman, 1986; England, 1984).

Fuchs (1989), however, speculated that the preference of many women for part-time work contributes to occupational segregation because female-dominated occupations offer greater opportunities for part-time work. Evidence shows that the greater the proportion of both men and women in a given occupation who work part-time, the larger the proportion of women employed in that occupation. These findings are confirmed by Shelton (1992), who identified a negative relationship between the number of children a woman has and the hours she spends in the paid labor force. She found that women with no children spend 85.4% as much time in paid labor as men with no children but that women with two or more children spend 75.5% as much time in paid labor as comparable men.

There are alternative explanations of why women workers are concentrated in a very few occupations relative to men and why these occupations tend to be female dominated. One explanation is the strong forces of socialization and sex-role norms. Children learn at a very early age that certain jobs are identified with either men or women. Although the forces involved in the socialization of sex-role stereotypes are changing quite rapidly, the pressures on young females to choose careers traditionally deemed appropriate for women are still significant. Thus studying the professional lives of women who have opted for nontraditional careers should offer some insight into the career selection process.

Occupational segregation has been used to explain low female earnings. The crowding-out hypothesis asserts that because certain occupations are dominated by women and because the number of these occupations is small relative to the number of occupations available to men, women "crowd" these occupations, increasing the supply of labor and depressing the wage. Likewise, because women are not free to easily enter certain male-dominated professions, the supply of labor to these jobs is kept low and wages are inflated. The obvious result is low wages for women relative to men.

Occupational segregation remains a significant feature of the female labor force. In 1989, 95% of all secretaries, stenographers, and typists still were women (Moen, 1992). Nevertheless the 1970s and 1980s were marked by a significant reduction in the level of segregation. For example, between 1967 and 1985, the percentage of female physicians more than doubled, from 7% to 14.6% of all physicians; the proportion of female engineers increased from 1.2% in 1950 to 7.9% in 1989; and the proportion of female lawyers and judges increased from 4.1% in 1950 to 19% in 1989 (Reskin & Roos, 1990). Younger entrants to the labor market were far more likely to choose traditionally male careers, although this integration was much more marked in professional and managerial jobs than in the blue-collar fields. Today women make up 25% of all new MDs and MBAs and over 33% of law school graduates. Consequently measures of occupational segregation are higher for older groups of women than for younger.

Because younger women are opting for more continuous labor force attachment, the job experience of all women workers is increasing more rapidly than for men. Education levels of women workers also are increasing faster than for men. "This is partly due to increased college attendance by women; but also, in recent years, female work force participation rates have increased much faster among the more educated" (Smith & Ward, 1989, p. 17).

The labor force experience of women is, thus, increasingly similar to that of men. These trends bode well for future narrowing of the wage gap. Nevertheless there are reasons to believe that work experience and career development of women will remain different from those of men for some time (Gutek & Larwood, 1987, p. 10).

Career Paths

Study of career development has paralleled closely research in human development. Until recently (within the past 20 years), the major focus of professional development research was on males. Young men were expected to choose a career and to remain in that career throughout their working lives. The emphasis of research was on the process of occupational choice.

Women were not expected to choose a career in the same way. It was assumed that most women would elect homemaking, but the process was complicated because specific plans depended on whom they would marry and at what age. Consequently women invested little in education and took jobs they expected to hold only until they married or had children. In general, women did not expect to advance in their work, and employers did not expect women to be long-term employees (Gutek & Larwood, 1987).

Originally research on women who did not follow this path assumed that they were "inferior in some way, frustrated and dissatisfied" (Gutek & Larwood, 1987, p. 8). Research in the late 1960s and early 1970s finally refuted the notion that women in nontraditional careers were deviant, but it was not until the mid-1970s that changing views of human development began to incorporate career considerations.

Adulthood is no longer considered to be a static period. Consequently careers also can be viewed as changing and developing throughout the entire adult stage of the life cycle.

A career can include a series of related jobs within an organization or different jobs within various companies. Career development implies that the series of jobs represents some progress—for example, up the hierarchy, an increasingly large salary, increasing recognition and respect from one's colleagues, or more freedom to pursue one's own interest or to select one's projects. The more one's career progresses in these ways, the more it is judged to be successful (Gutek & Larwood, 1987, p. 9).

Research on the career development of women is relatively new, and most of it assumes a male norm of occupational choice and career development against which women are compared. Women are socialized to place their primary energy into nurturing roles. Career roles have, until recently, been considered as secondary by most women.

In a recent survey of the literature on women's career development, Esther Diamond (1987) cited several studies that argue that women experience the same initial occupational choice variables and motivation as men but that the choice of actual jobs is more complicated for women and is limited by a number of demographic, institutional, and economic considerations (e.g., income, convenience, flexibility of hours, home responsibilities, husband's attitudes). A number of studies make the point that the process of female occupational choice is a reciprocal one. Earlier theories that assumed vocational choice was one-way—that is, a function of interindividual differences and preferences—are considered to be incomplete by those studying the professional careers of females. In the case of women, individuals select occupations, but organizations also select in the sense that they accommodate or fail to accommodate the family responsibilities borne by most women employees.

According to Rix and Stone (1984), "As long as it is women who are the ones to step off the fast track and meet family responsibilities, they will be at a competitive disadvantage in career advancement as it is presently structured" (p. 210). This statement appears to be especially true of women in managerial careers, simply because the prime childbearing/rearing years are also the key years for traditional career advancement.

Larwood and Gattiker (1987) studied the differences in career paths of successful men and women. They anticipated that those they studied would show career movement toward increased professional status, line positions as opposed to staff positions, and higher positions. They expected to see progressive advancement and that such advancement would be positively correlated with hierarchical organizational success. They also expected to find women "systematically delayed, relative to men, in the development of their careers" (p. 134) because many women do not expect organizational success and thus do not pursue it and because many employers do not expect women to achieve success and thus limit opportunities. To test these hypotheses, Larwood and Gattiker studied 215 individuals who were defined as successful by 17 major corporations in California.

In general their hypotheses were confirmed. The major exception was that individuals did not move toward line and away from staff positions. Overall, men had higher professional standing and higher positions within their departments than women. Progress is less regular for women. These findings confirm earlier findings that early success is helpful to later hierarchical success. The authors also found evidence suggesting, but not proving, sex discrimination.

Older women are still substantially behind older men, whereas younger women are nonsignificantly behind younger men. Instead the pattern may indicate that external forces outside her control are more important to a woman's success in her career than to a man's success in his (Larwood & Gattiker, 1987).

The failure of the institutional structure of work to accommodate work-family conflicts has clearly influenced the career development of professional women. Using a representative sample of employed women in the Los Angeles area, Valdez and Gutek (1987) found that a larger-than-expected proportion of women in managerial positions were divorced or separated, an indication that marriage and family responsibilities have different effects on men and women. Other findings about career development for women indicate that marriage and children affect work and career opportunities more than work affects women's families (Laws, 1979). In other words, accommodation is not symmetrical.

Wichita

The sample of white-collar women on which this book is based was drawn in Wichita, Kansas. A brief description of demographic charac-teristics of the community provides background for assessing the appli-cability of these findings to other populations. Wichita is the largest city in Kansas, with a 1990 population estimated at 304,011. In 1990, 51.4% of the city's population was female and 48.6% was male. Similarly, the national population was 51.3% female and 48.7% male. The age com-position of the population was also similar to other urban areas in the United States; that is, it is slightly younger than average. The median age in Wichita in 1980 was 28.8 years, compared with 30.1 years for Kansas and 30.0 years for the United States. Likewise, a lower percent-age of Wichita's population was above age 65—11.8%, compared with 12.6% for the United States.

Nontraditional female labor force patterns are not unusual in Kansas. Women in Kansas historically have had higher labor force attachment than those in the nation as a whole. In 1986 the participation rate for all women in the United States was 55.3%; in Kansas it was 58.2%. Participation rates for local economies are not available between census years. In 1990 the labor force participation of women in the United States was 57.3%; in Wichita it was 60.9%.

The lack of more recent data merits some discussion. Detailed eco-nomic data for local economies is reported only by the decennial census. Even as we write in early 1993, detailed information from the 1990 census is not available in many variables. Consequently very little current information on the Wichita population and economy (except for the industrial composition of employment and personal income) is available. For example, no recent information is available on the characteristics of the local female labor force. Obviously, analysis based on 1980 data becomes less and less reliable, the longer the elapsed time from its collection. Unfortunately there is no alternative. For that reason, characteristics of the working women in Wichita are compared with those in the rest of the United States at a common point in time—1980. The more recent statistics that do exist (e.g., personal income data) suggest that Wichita has not had economic and other trends significantly different from those of the nation as a whole. The differences that do exist have been moving Wichita closer to national averages.

The industrial composition of the Wichita economy offers one explanation for above-average female labor force participation: Wichita is heavily dominated by manufacturing. Employment in these industries as a percentage of total employment is well above national averages. In June 1988, over 25% of Wichita's labor force was employed in manufacturing, compared with only about 20% nationally. The dominance of manufacturing and periodic tight labor markets have offered women opportunities in relatively high paying blue-collar occupations. Above-average reliance on manufacturing also helps explain Wichita's relatively high incomes. In 1990, per capita income in Sedgwick County, which includes Wichita, was $14,555, only slightly above the United States average per capita income of $14,387.

Another factor contributing to higher than average female labor force participation has been the relatively high divorce rates. Throughout the 1980s, Kansas reported a divorce rate above the national average.

In addition, educational attainment in Wichita and Kansas are above national averages. A comparison of years of schooling of citizens of Wichita and citizens of the United States reveals that the mean years of schooling in Wichita in 1980 was 12.7 years; for Kansas, 12.6 years; and for the United States, 12.5 years (see Table 1.2). Males uniformly have slightly higher educational attainment than females, but as noted earlier, the gap is narrowing. It also is known that occupational segregation is inversely correlated with years of education (Fuchs, 1989). Thus better educated women are less likely to be segregated into all-female occupations. Of the population over age 25 in 1980, 64.9% of the women in the United States were high school graduates. In Kansas

Table 1.2
Comparison of Educational Attainment

	High School Graduate	College 1-3 years	College 4 or more years	Median Years of Education
1990 U.S. Population (25 years & older)	%	%	%	
Female	78.5	37.3	17.4	12.7
Male	78.2	41.3	21.9	12.8
Total	78.4	39.3	19.5	12.7
1980 Kansas Population (25 years & older)	%	%	%	
Female	73.2	17.4	13.7	
Male	73.5	16.8	20.7	
Total	81.3	22	21.1	12.6
1980 Wichita Population (MSA) (25 years & older)	%	%	%	
Female	74.5	18.4	14.4	
Male	77.5	20.1	23.9	
Total	81.9	23.5	22.7	12.7

SOURCE: U.S. Census of Population. (1980). *Detailed population characteristics.* Washington, DC: Bureau of the Census.

that percentage was 73.2%; in Wichita, 74.5%. These statistics indicate that fewer Kansans attend college but that a higher proportion graduate. In the United States, 12.5% of women attended college four or more years; in Kansas, 13.7%; and in Wichita, 14.4% of women attended college four or more years.

The occupational mix of women workers in Wichita is reasonably close to national patterns (see Table 1.3). Not surprisingly, due to the heavy emphasis on manufacturing, women in Wichita are more likely to be in blue-collar, technical, sales, and administrative support jobs, particularly precision production, than women in the nation as a whole, but are slightly less likely to be managers and professionals.

In the professions, Wichita has proportionately twice as many women engineers but only 29% as many women lawyers and 87% as many women judges as the nation as a whole. The large number of engineers is explained by the presence of aviation manufacturing in Wichita. Boeing, Cessna, Beech, and LearJet all employ relatively large numbers

Table 1.3

Comparison of Female Labor Force Participation by Occupation and
Income, Wichita and the United States, 1980

Occupations	Percentage of Female Labor Force (employed females 16+)				Median Income (non-indexed 1980)		
	% Wichita	% U.S.	Wichita as % U.S.		Wichita	U.S.	Wichita as % U.S.
Managerial Occupations:							
Executive, Administrative & Managerial	6.76	7.37	0.92		12,776	12,783	1
Self-Employed Managers & Administrators	0.34	0.36	0.94		7,867	8,107	0.97
Professional Occupations:							
Engineers	0.28	0.15	1.87		16,166	16,725	0.97
Teachers, Post-Secondary	0.43	0.55	0.78		18,901	16,626	1.14
Teachers, Elementary & Pre-Kindergarten	3.96	4.55	0.87		12,549	12,610	1
Teachers, Secondary	0.94	1.15	0.82		12,327	13,122	0.94
Lawyers & Judges	0.05	0.17	0.29		13,019	18,503	0.7
Physicians	0.11	0.14	0.79		23,735	22,585	1.05
Registered Nurses	3.21	2.92	1.1		15,208	14,898	1.02
Technical & Administrative Support Occupations:							
Technicians & Related Support Occupations	3.68	3.13	1.18		11,655	11,641	1
Administrative Support (Clerical)	32.22	31.22	1.03		10,281	10,074	1.02
Secretaries, Stenographers, Typists	11.06	11	1.01		10,213	10,127	1.01
Service Occupations:							
Service, except Protective & Household	15.93	16.14	0.99		7,338	7,418	0.99
Precision Production	4.28	1.82	2.4		12,553	10,439	1.2
Operators, Fabricators & Laborers	10.26	11.71	0.88		10,912	8,841	1.23

SOURCE: U.S. Census of Population. (1980). *Detailed population characteristics* (Tables 219 and 278). Washington, DC: Bureau of the Census.

of engineers. The small number of women attorneys is more difficult to explain. Part of the reason is that Wichita has relatively few government agencies, which often have large legal staffs. Another possible explanation is that the legal profession in Wichita was slower to admit women than it was in other parts of the country.

Characteristics of the Sample

Researchers in the Research Group on Women and Work intended to develop a sample of white-collar career women who were willing to participate in a longitudinal study conducted by a team of researchers investigating diverse aspect of the lives of professional women. The most significant feature of the sample is that it is made up, for the most part, of women in nontraditional careers.

In that sense, the sample is representative neither of all working women nor of women in the professions. As was shown in Table 1.3, women in the professions have been concentrated in elementary and secondary education and in nursing. The recruitment of the sample thus deliberately excluded professional organizations of teachers and nurses.

Identification of occupation for members of the sample was quite difficult in some cases. Three individuals indicated they were retired but included no previous job title. Others indicated job titles so generic that placement in a specific occupation was difficult. For example, nine women said they were counselors; it was unclear whether they were educational, personal, or financial counselors. In such cases they were classed in the "Other Professional" category. That category also includes accountants, social workers, occupations associated with communications and public relations, and miscellaneous other occupations.

A few members of the sample appear to be employed in more traditional clerical professions. Nine reported that they were secretaries, and seven that they were administrative assistants. A total of 37 women fall into this "other" category, which includes bank tellers, cashiers, and some others. This group represents 7% of the entire sample. Occupation is unknown for an additional 30 members of the sample.

Managers and executives make up the single largest occupational category (see Table 1.4). The second largest occupational category is associated with post-secondary education; this is a weakness. Women in higher education have higher educational levels and more flexibility than do women in other professions. In the total professional female labor force, higher education accounts for less than 4%. But the overrepresentation of certain occupational groups is not limited to higher education. The fact that very few nurses and teachers are in the sample means that the occupational distribution will overrepresent other occupations relative to their numbers in the overall female labor force. Physicians, for example, made up less than 1% of the female labor force in the United States in 1980, yet they are over 5% of the sample.

Table 1.4
Comparison of Occupational Distribution of Sample (1987)
With U.S. Female Labor Force in Managerial and Professional
Occupations (1980)

Occupations	U.S.		SAMPLE	
	#	%	#	%
Managerial Occupations:				
Executive, Administrative & Managerial	3,168,857	30.16	171	40.3
Self-Employed Managers & Administrators	1,153,349	10.98	19	4.5
Professional Occupations:				
Engineers	233,152	2.22	7	1.7
Teachers, Post-Secondary	233,045	2.22	76	17.9
Teachers, Pre-Kindergarten, Elementary & Secondary	2,412,924	22.96	18	4.2
Lawyers & Judges	74,037	0.7	15	3.5
Physicians	57,966	0.55	25	5.9
Registered Nurses	1,232,544	11.73	10	2.4
Other Health Professions	267,777	2.55	19	4.5
Other Professional	1,674,059	15.93	64	15.1
Total	10,507,710	100	424	100
Other			37	
Unknown			30	
Retired			3	
Total			494	

SOURCE: U.S. Census of Population. (1980). *Detailed population characteristics: Part 1. United States summary* (Table 276, p. 166). Washington, DC: Government Printing Office.

The unusual occupational distribution is the result of a deliberate attempt to study and analyze women in nontraditional careers. Because demographic characteristics of the national female labor force are not

broken down by occupation, it is impossible to compare the characteristics of the sample with those of other female professionals (see
Table 1.5).

A large proportion of the participants are in the mid-years of their
careers: 38% are in their 30s, and 27% are in their 40s. Only 15% of the
population are in their 20s, 12% in their 50s, and 7% are over 60 years
of age.

The sample is overwhelmingly white (96%). Minorities, which include
African Americans, Asians, Hispanics, and American Indians, make up the
remaining 4%. This breakdown is interesting because the racial composition of Sedgwick County is very close to that of the nation as a whole. In
1980 Sedgwick County was 84.3% white, while the United States was
84.9% white. This lack of minority representation is clearly a weakness in
the sample that efforts to identify and recruit minority women did not
succeed in correcting. It is also true that minority women still are underrepresented in most professional occupations.

A large majority (65%) of the respondents are married; 15% are
single, and roughly the same number are divorced or separated; 2% are
widowed; and only 1% of the sample reported living-as-married. In
contrast, figures for the national female labor force show a lower
percentage married (55.3%) and a much larger percentage (24.9%)
single. Part of this difference can be explained by the fact that the
national figures include all females aged 17 and over. The sample
includes no one under age 20, and very few under age 25. Because most
of the population between ages 16 and 20 are single, it would be
expected that the local sample would show a lower proportion of single
women. In addition, although Kansas has a higher than average divorce
rate, it also has a higher than average marriage rate, which would leave
the number of never-married women low, compared with the rest of the
nation. There is virtually no difference between the sample and the national
female labor force in the proportion of women who are divorced, separated,
or widowed.

Almost 36% of the sample are childless; 18% have one child, 29%
have two children, 11% have three children, and 6% have four or more
children. Less than half of the sample reported they currently have
children living at home; 14% of those have at least one child under 5;
9% have a child between 5 and 11; 19% have at least one child between
12 and 17; and 5% have a child 18 or over living at home.

It would be expected that a sample of professional women would have
above-average levels of education. Sample statistics confirm this

Table 1.5
Characteristics of Research Group on Women and Work Sample,
1987 (*n* = 494)

	% of Sample		% of Sample
AGE		**RACE**	
20s	15.2	white	96.4
30s	38.3	black	1.3
40s	26.9	Hispanic	.6
50s	12.3	native American	.4
60s	7.3	Asian	1.1
		other	.2
MARITAL STATUS		**EDUCATION**	
married	65.1	high school graduate	99.2
single	15.4	some college	96.4
separated	1.0	college graduate	56.1
divorced	14.6	masters	29.4
widowed	2.4	JD, MD, PhD	15.6
cohabitating	1.4	none	11.1
CHILDREN		**AGE OF CHILDREN AT HOME** (at least one child in these age groups)	
0	35.7	under 5	14.0
1	18.4	5-11	8.5
2	29.0	12-17	18.6
3	10.8	18 and over	4.9
4 or more	6.1	none	54.0
INDIVIDUAL INCOME		**FAMILY INCOME** (only 63% reporting)	
less than $10,000	6.8	less than $20,000	1.9
10,000-19,999	19.4	20,000-29,999	4.2
20,000-24,999	21.8	30,000-34,999	5.5
25,000-29,999	18.7	35,000-39,999	5.5
30,000-34,999	13.0	40,000-44,999	12.2
35,000-49,999	12.5	45,000-49,999	8.0
50,000 and over	7.7	50,000-54,999	14.5
		55,000-59,999	11.3
		60,000 and over	37.0

hypothesis. Over 99% are high school graduates, 96% have some college, and 56% are college graduates. Almost 30% have a master's degree, and 16% report holding law, medical, or doctoral degrees.

Consistent with the high level of educational attainment, the incomes of the sample are relatively high. In 1987 the median income for full-time year-round women workers in the United States was under $16,000, yet three quarters of the sample earn over $20,000. Median family income in the United States in 1986 was $29,459, but 94% of those reporting have family incomes in excess of $30,000.

A sample of career women is, by its very nature, atypical of the entire labor force, but this study was designed to examine the lives of women engaged in nontraditional occupations. Research on the working lives of entrepreneurial, managerial, and professional women can, however, help raise relevant research questions for the study of other groups of working women.

It is apparent that more and more young women are opting for more education and for professional and managerial careers. Measures of occupational segregation are significantly lower for younger women than for older women (Fuchs, 1989). This difference means that findings based on the experiences of the current generation of professional women will have increasing significance in the future. In addition, evidence is growing that the United States will experience major labor shortages in the near future. It is expected that two thirds of new entrants into the labor force through the year 2000 will be women (Hudson Institute, 1987). High demand for labor will ensure that many of these women will be needed in what traditionally have been considered "men's" jobs.

Research that can help facilitate productive working lives for these employees will be of major significance. Many of these women will be of childbearing age. Employers are rapidly beginning to recognize that policies that can help ease the strain between work and family responsibilities will be essential to their operations. Because professional women have been more likely than other women workers to maintain continuous labor force attachment, their experiences should be of some assistance to those who will follow.

Although it is important to use caution in generalizing from this sample to the general population of career women, the women in the sample are representative in some important respects. The major purpose of this chapter is to provide an economic and demographic perspective for the sample of career women who participated in this study. Comparisons of the demographic characteristics of the female labor force in Wichita with those of the United States are limited because the current study (1989) is so far removed from the 1980 decennial census, the only source of many data series. Nevertheless, by most measures, Wichita is a typical mid-sized community. Occupational characteristics and median incomes of women workers are quite similar to the national statistics. If anything, women in Wichita have a longer history of labor force participation than in other parts of the country.

The validity of Wichita as a sample community is confirmed by its common use as a test market for new products. The pricing policy of Sears, Roebuck & Co., initiated March 1, 1989, in a highly publicized national campaign, was tested in Wichita during the fall of 1988 (Schwadel, 1989). In addition, during the 1988 presidential election, ABC television used selected Wichita precincts in its national sample to project election returns.

There is ample evidence that Wichita is a reasonably representative community. No evidence exists that there are significantly more or fewer impediments to the economic progress of women here than in most other communities. The evidence garnered from a survey of professional women in Wichita should, therefore, have valid implications for working women everywhere.

References

Becker, G. (1981). *A treatise on the family.* Cambridge, MA: Harvard University Press.

Bergman, B. R. (1986). *The economic emergence of women.* New York: Basic Books.

Department of Labor. (1981, January). *Employment and earnings.* Washington, DC: Bureau of Labor Statistics.

Department of Labor. (1988, January). *Employment and earnings.* Washington, DC: Bureau of Labor Statistics.

Department of Labor. (1992, January). *Employment and earnings.* Washington, DC: Bureau of Labor Statistics.

Diamond, E. E. (1987). Theories of career development and the reality of women at work. In B. A. Gutek & L. Larwood (Eds.), *Women's career development* (pp. 15-27). Newbury Park, CA: Sage.

England, P. (1984). Explanations of job segregation and the sex gap in pay. *Comparable Worth: Issue for the 80's* (pp. 54-64). Washington, DC: U.S. Commission on Civil Rights.

Fuchs, V. R. (1989). Women's quest for economic equality. *Journal of Economic Perspectives, 3*(1), 25-41.

Gutek, B. A., & Larwood, L. (1987). Introduction: Women's careers are important and different. In B. A. Gutek & L. Larwood (Eds.), *Women's career development* (pp. 7-14). Newbury Park, CA: Sage.

Hudson Institute. (1987). *Workforce 2000: Work and workers for the 21st century.* Washington, DC: U.S. Department of Labor.

Larwood, K., & Gattiker, U. E. (1987). A comparison of the career paths used by successful women and men. In B. A. Gutek & L. Larwood (Eds.), *Women's career development* (pp. 129-156). Newbury Park, CA: Sage.

Laws, J. L. (1979). *The second X: Sex role and social role.* New York: Elsevier.

Levy, F. S., & Michel, R. (1986). An economic bust for the baby boom. *Challenge, 29*(2), 33-39.

Mincer, J., & Polachek, S. W. (1974). Family investments in human capital: Earnings of women. *Journal of Political Economy, 82*(2), S790-S801.

Moen, P. (1992). *Women's two roles.* New York: Auburn House.

Polachek, S. W. (1979). Occupational segregation: Theory, evidence and prognosis. In C. Lloyd, E. S. Andrews, & C. L. Gilroy (Eds.), *Women in the labor market* (pp. 000-000). New York: Columbia University Press.

Polachek, S. W. (1984). Women in the economy: Perspectives on gender inequality. *Comparable Worth: Issue of the 80's* (pp. 34-53). Washington, DC: U.S. Commission on Civil Rights.

Reskin, B. F., & Roos, P. (1990). *Job questions, gender questions: Women's inroads into male occupations.* Philadelphia: Temple University Press.

Rix, S. E., & Stone, A. J. (1984). Work. In S. M. Pritchard (Ed.), *The women's annual* (p. 210). Boston: G. K. Hall.

Schwadel, F. (1989, March 1). The "sale" is fading as a retailing tactic. *Wall Street Journal,* p. B1.

Shelton, B. A. (1992). *Women, men, and time.* New York: Greenwood.

Smith, J. P., & Ward, M. P. (1984, October). *1900-1970: Women's wages and work in the twentieth century.* New York: Rand.

Smith, J. P., & Ward, M. (1989). Women in the labor market and the family. *Journal of Economic Perspective, 3*(1), 9-23.

U.S. Census of Population. (1980). *Detailed population characteristics.* Washington, DC: Bureau of the Census.

U.S. Census of Population. (1980). *Detailed population characteristics: Part 1. United States summary.* Washington, DC: Government Printing Office.

Valdez, R. L., & Gutek, B. A. (1987). Family roles: A helping or a hindrance for working women? In B. A. Gutek & L. Larwood (Eds.), *Women's career development* (pp. 157-169). Newbury Park, CA: Sage.

2 "We're All in This Alone": Career Women's Attitudes Toward Feminism

One participant in our study stated, "While feminism runs the spectrum from anti-male extremes to the conservative, 'all I want is my fair share,' I think, for myself, feminism is a movement that strives to point out and correct inequities in social, economic and political arenas with the ultimate goal of a egalitarian society." Another participant said, "Feminism is the seeking of equality for women as human beings."

These positive reports contrast to such negative perceptions of feminism as "resulting in reverse discrimination" by women who "would call themselves humanists or civil libertarians if they were concerned for all people," and another respondent's observation that a feminist is "a woman who is very defensive about her actions, work and thoughts; feels she is self sufficient—doesn't need anyone else."

In many respects, feminist concepts have come to represent divisions between women, as well as connections between women in contemporary society. In this chapter Sally Kitch frames her consideration of rhetorical and perceptual differences between career women who identify as feminists and those who do not in the concept of *backlash* articulated by Susan Faludi (1991). Kitch points out that although the majority of women in this study are self-identified feminists, more women in this study accept the goals and policies of feminism than accept its label (of 64% of these participants who consider themselves to be feminists and 90% who recognize that sex discrimination exists in the workplace, 83% of the sample continue to believe that a woman's individual hard work will ensure her career success). Kitch composes a provocative examination of some contradictions between women's appreciation of feminist accomplishments and disapproval of feminists from participants who reject the feminist label.

Similarly, although large majorities of both feminists and nonfeminists in the study agreed that the workplace is male oriented, the large majority also agreed that career women must be prepared to compete on the same terms as men. In other words, a feminist consciousness among these respondents has revealed to them the structural barriers to women's success embedded in the institutions of work and family, but it has not led them to seek typically collective and woman-centered feminist solutions. Instead of envisioning actions that address the structural barriers, these respondents imagine "pulling themselves up by their bootstraps" and overcoming obstacles by individual effort. Kitch considers the limitations of the feminist beliefs of women in the study and reflects on implications for career women's future.

SALLY L. KITCH

T he decade of the 1980s may well become known as one of the most contradictory periods in American history.[1] Its political rhetoric of "feel good" was accompanied by the exponential increase of misery on many fronts: poverty, unemployment, drug abuse, crime, corruption. At all governmental levels, the more money we spent, the fewer services and necessities we had. While politicians touted the United States as the greatest society on earth, it became, for the first time, the world's greatest debtor nation.

Looking back on the decade with the help of social commentators such as Susan Faludi, we now can see that feminism was an important site of the decade's contradictory messages. Women's modest demands for justice and equal opportunity, though only minimally heeded, were blamed for all manner of social ills, including the very ones women were struggling to correct. Indeed the word *feminism,* which originally connoted simply the achievement of basic civil rights for women, was demonized during the 1980s to the point that even women who favored such rights (and much more) were willing to disavow the term. In surveying 236 "twenty somethings" in 1990, Paula Kamen discovered that although men and women alike recognized sexism as a continuing problem and supported women's rights and the women's movement, "what was generally missing in their thinking was a sense of connection and commitment to feminism itself. Most didn't identify with feminism or want to be associated with it on a personal or political level" (Kamen, 1991, pp. 23-24).

Faludi's *Backlash: The Undeclared War Against American Women* (1991) revealed the extent to which paranoia about feminism was orchestrated by the media in perhaps unwitting collusion with the conservative administration that dominated politics in the 1980s. Faludi filled almost 500 pages with tales of the misrepresentation of various social science studies about attitudes and gender differences, as well as of the blatant manufacture of "trends," based on little or no supporting evidence, that created the antifeminist backlash the media pundits allegedly were reporting. Fueling the media blitz against feminism, according to Faludi, was the age-old threat to masculinity that even minuscule advances for women apparently have represented. In addition, as women began to feel abandoned by the media, the government, and their families, many took the path of least resistance: When

> keeping the peace with the particular man in one's life becomes more essential than battling the mass male culture[,] saying one is "not a feminist" (even while supporting quietly every item of the feminist platform) seems the most prudent, self-protective strategy. Ultimately in such conditions, the impulse to remedy social injustice can become not only secondary but silent. (Faludi, 1991, p. 58)

Among the many examples of the media's antifeminist, self-fulfilling prophecies was the popularization of the "cocooning" image manufactured by self-styled "consumer authority" Faith Popcorn and reported, with thinly disguised glee, by newspapers and magazines across the country. That image, based primarily on TV shows, best-sellers, *People* magazine, and Popcorn's unproven theory that styles repeat every 30 years, was used to characterize the trend of the 1980s—the abandonment of careers by well-educated and ambitious women in favor of traditional roles at home. Faludi demonstrated that the media's methods of data collection in support of the cocooning trend were almost as inadequate as Popcorn's had been. Yet, despite the facts—the drop-out rates of men and women from the work force were roughly equal, and women's labor force participation rose steadily in the 1980s (from 51% to 54% for all women and to more than 70% for women aged 25 to 44), for example—the damage was done. The media blitz against feminism had taken its toll; women responded to the reports as if they were facts. By 1987 the proportion of women applying to business schools dropped for the first time in a decade. By 1989 almost half of the women in a *New York Times* poll on women's status said they "feared they had sacrificed too much for their gains" (Faludi, 1991, pp. 82-86, 59).

In 1985, when the Research Group on Women and Work (RGWW) study began, the dynamics that Faludi, Kamen, and others have now explained were not immediately obvious. Like many feminists, I was beginning to believe that despite what I saw among my students and read about in women's studies texts, women themselves (instead of those who could profit or otherwise benefit from it) were instigating a trend away from feminist identification even as they were enjoying the fruits of feminism's labors. I remembered vividly a remark that Betty Friedan (who delighted the backlash media by criticizing feminism in her 1981 book *The Second Stage*) had made at the Women's Decade Conference in Houston in 1976. She told the story of her daughter, then in law school, who announced that she was not a feminist. The look on Friedan's face as she recounted the tale said it all: "How sharper than a serpent's tooth. . . . " But her response to her daughter was what stuck in my mind. She told the younger woman that she must always remember that she had gotten where she was not only by her own talents and charm but also by the hard work and struggle of her foremothers. She must now "pay her dues" to those who had gone before by not disavowing them and their identities.

When given the opportunity to participate in the research group study, I wanted to test participants' identification as feminists and to determine whether they would call by what I considered their proper name—the benefits of feminism—their own employment and educational attainments. I wanted to see whether this group of achieving women, many of whom were in professional or managerial roles undreamed of a decade earlier, would be willing to pay their dues to the women who had struggled before them to break down barriers in graduate schools, corporations, and financial markets. Perhaps somewhat pessimistically, I hypothesized that many more of them would support feminist issues than would admit to being a feminist.

At the same time, I wanted to test the impact of feminism on these women's lives. I wanted to know what messages of feminism they had internalized. I was interested particularly in whether the collective message of feminism—the legacy of consciousness raising and the rhetoric of "the personal is political"—had endured as these women attempted to solve problems in their personal and professional lives. Would they, I wondered, seek alliances with other women in the ongoing battle to achieve their own success, self-determination, and justice in the worlds of work and family? My association of collective action with feminist identity is supported by the work of Elizabeth Cook and others who define the components of feminist consciousness as "the development of a group identity, politicization, and the development of support for organized action" (Cook, 1989, p. 72).

Despite the antifeminist media blitz, which affected me too, I was not ready to concede defeat for feminism. I designed my part of the questionnaire to provide evidence for what my own experience was telling me: Women were living their lives as if feminism mattered, as if the goals and struggles of the women's movement were important to them. I was not sure exactly what feminism meant to them or whether they would embrace it as a label for their beliefs, but I felt strongly that they would prove supportive of the issues and goals that legitimately could be categorized as feminist.

Feminist Identification and Beliefs

A study of feminist attitudes and identifications is not a simple matter. Complicating it is the complexity of the term *feminism* itself. Coined in 1895 to denote the advocacy of women and the support of women's political rights, today, almost 100 years later, the term connotes a wide variety of views. Contemporary texts on feminist theory identify as feminist at least 10 theoretical positions, some of which contradict others. Feminism can be modified legitimately with such terms as *liberal, radical, marxist, existential, postmodern, psychoanalytic, cultural, separatist,* and *eco-,* among others, and feminists belonging to various schools of thought debate the origins of women's oppression, as well as the appropriate means for achieving gender justice.

The most typical feminist positions in the United States historically have been the liberal, radical, and cultural positions. *Liberal feminists* advocate the redistribution of persons throughout the existing social system. *Equality* is a watchword of the liberal position and an outgrowth of the Enlightenment views that spawned the American Revolution. Liberal feminists consider all but a few sexual differences the result of social forces. The focus for change in liberal feminism is on society's laws and public policies, but liberal feminists basically support the American economic system and government; they simply demand that democracy live up to its promises for all people, including women. In contrast, *cultural feminists* celebrate differences of values and temperament between the sexes, which most believe to be innate, and support social change based on the infusion of feminine values into the social system. *Radical feminists* share cultural feminists' advocacy of characteristics they attribute to women but identify patriarchy, a system of male domination entangled with most known governments and economies that systematically disempowers and/or disparages women, as the root of the problem. They believe that such patriarchal systems must be overhauled or eradicated, rather than modified, and women put into positions of power. They advocate the redistribution of rewards among persons in a completely redesigned social system.

Evidence suggests that such nuances among types of feminism are not commonly understood, even among women who identify themselves as feminists. According to Kamen's study (1991), for example, young women who support feminism offer a pastiche of theoretical positions under the term, without noticing subtle differences that threaten consistency. Kamen's young feminists said, first and foremost, they support equal rights, meaning equal opportunities for employment and education as well as legal rights—a liberal position. Issues mentioned in connection with feminism in that group, however, reveal both liberal and cultural tendencies: violence against women, abortion rights, equal pay for equal work, child care and health needs, racism, tolerance for women's choices in the family, and greater support for motherhood. Greater support for motherhood acknowledges gender differences that some liberals would disavow by demanding that men and women should "mother" equally. The eradication of rape and domestic violence has radical overtones in the creation of women-only or women-centered institutions, such as rape crisis centers and battered women's shelters. Such measures transcend the limited concept of equal opportunity. They also reveal the limitations of the liberal feminist position.

Downing and Roush's 5-stage developmental model (1984) suggests that some variations in feminist positions may be related to stages in women's feminist identity formation. According to the model, self-identified feminists in the second stage (the stage after nonidentification) are "sensitized to women's oppression" and respond to it with "anger and guilt." Feminists in the third stage have discovered sisterhood, are immersed in women's culture, and prefer socializing with women to the exclusion of men. Feminists in the fourth stage have transcended traditional sex roles, have recognized the positive aspects of being a woman and have learned to "evaluate men on an individual basis." Stage five feminists are committed to social change and have learned to translate their feminist identities into "meaningful and effective action" (Bargad & Hyde, 1991, pp. 183, 185).

Most studies designed to test large populations for feminist identification have begged the question of feminist diversity and developmental differences. They tend to equate support for feminism with support for specific public issues that have been labeled as feminist, with support for a general, undefined women's movement or with the expression of certain attitudes—such as the equality of men and women—that obscure or ignore such differences. In general, research into the topic can be said to promote the liberal strain of feminism. Researchers tend to identify feminist views with the advocacy of sexual equality and to equate issues involving work and public policy with both feminism and the women's movement. That feminism—as a system of ideas—sometimes exists apart from political activism—the women's movement—rarely is addressed by the research.

Several studies of feminist attitudes indicate that the most salient demographic factor in a woman's support of issues considered to be feminist or in her development of a feminist viewpoint or consciousness is educational level. The higher her educational attainment, the more likely a woman is to espouse feminist viewpoints (Cook, 1989; Gruber & Bjorn, 1988; Morgan & Walker, 1983; Thornton & Freedman, 1979). A major exception to that finding concerns African American women of low educational attainment, who tend to be more feminist in outlook than their similarly educated white counterparts (Ransford & Miller, 1983).

On other measures, the effect of race on feminist outlook is unclear. One study found virtually no differences in attitudes toward feminist issues between African American and white women (Ransford & Miller, 1983). A 1986 *Newsweek* poll (How women view work, 1986, p. 56) found slight differences. Although only 70% of white women supported the women's movement, 74% of nonwhite women did. On a similar measure in a 1989 *New York Times* poll (Women's Lives, 1989), the results were more dramatic: 85% of African American women, 76% of Hispanic women, but only 64% of white women agreed that the United States needs a strong women's movement.[2] In studying African American women alone, however, Wilcox (1990) reported that only 46% of African American women were feminists or potential feminists; significantly, most of those favored collaborating with white women in the feminist struggle. (The variety of questions asked in various studies undoubtedly accounts for some disparities in results.)

Marital status also has a mixed effect on women's support for a feminist viewpoint. Although married women are generally less feminist in outlook than are never-married women (Agassi, 1979; Gruber & Bjorn, 1988; Morgan & Walker, 1983), divorced women are not consistently more feminist in outlook than the married or never-married (Agassi, 1979; Thornton & Freedman, 1979). The influence of age is similarly inconsistent. On some items, younger women appear more feminist; on others, older women do. For example, when asked in the *Newsweek* poll whether they thought the women's movement had improved their lives, 88% of women age 18 to 29 replied positively, while 73% of those age 30 to 44 and only 60% of those over 45 did so. In contrast, a study of autoworkers in Michigan revealed that age and job seniority promoted feminist viewpoints. Younger women tended to arrive at feminist viewpoints only after having had negative job experiences, such as sexual harassment or overt sex-based discrimination (Gruber & Bjorn, 1988). Kamen (1991) reported that older feminists believe that women become more radical with age, as their need to impress men lessens and as their lives present them with radicalizing experiences. Gloria Steinem identified those experiences as "entering the paid labor force and discovering how women are treated there; marrying and finding out that it is not yet an equal partnership; having children and discovering who is responsible for them and who is not; and aging, still a greater penalty for women than for men". Both Steinem and Anna Quindlen, a feminist journalist, believe that younger women actually have more power in society because of their status as sex objects than older women do. (Kamen, 1991, pp. 111-112)

Elizabeth Cook's research (1989) may provide one key to this inconsistency. She reported that, after 1984, the youngest age group in her study (18 to 24) exhibited "a slightly lower level of politicized feminist consciousness" than the second youngest group (25 to 39) (p. 82). The younger women, probably influenced by the media backlash of the early decade, may have been ignorant of the efforts involved in achieving the gains they took for granted and become less supportive of feminism than those engaged directly in the struggle.

Income levels of women in the labor force apparently have little effect on women's support of the women's movement. According to the *New*

York Times poll (1989), there was no difference in level of support (67%) between women at the lowest (under $12,500) and the highest (over $50,000) income levels. The highest level of support (71%) occurred among women in the middle range ($25,000 to $34,999).

Few scholarly studies address the question of overt feminist self-identification in the population at large. Therefore the best sources for this information are the popular news media. The *Newsweek* poll (1986) mentioned above asked directly whether respondents considered themselves to be feminists. *Newsweek* discovered that 56% of all women (55% of whites, 64% of nonwhites, 59% of working, and 48% of nonworking women) said yes; 28% of all women said no; only 4% of all women identified themselves as antifeminists. No mention is made of the missing 12% of all women; (How women view work, 1986, p. 51). A small study of Ohio State University students (Dill, 1990) found widespread, but qualified, feminist identification. Most of the 18 respondents (age 18 to 41) considered themselves to be feminists, but only 3 did not add qualifiers to the term. Researcher Kim Dill concluded that equivocating respondents associated feminism with gender deviance. Many saw full-fledged feminists as being "off the deep end," "punky," or "totally out there." Rather than interpreting this equivocation as a disclaimer, however, Dill interpreted the qualifiers as generally supportive of feminism. The students' opinions reflect a calculation of the costs (gender norm violations) and benefits (positive outcomes on issues) of feminist identification. Dill's work, coupled with the larger *New York Times* survey, suggests that women perceive the benefits of feminism in their work lives but worry about its effects on their personal lives.

The demonization of the term *feminist* in the 1980s is evident in the fact that even women who report themselves in solidarity with feminist causes express dislike for the label. Some young women in Kamen's study (1991), for example, supported feminist causes but disavowed the term as promoting a "narrow" agenda apparently separate from "larger" issues that concerned them, such as trade unionism. Others believed feminism to be a trap that, like an obsession with racial justice, can consume too much of a person's identity. Still others found the word too radical and the label too hazardous professionally. Some regarded the term as outmoded, indicative of an older generation that has now been discounted. Some women of color preferred the term *womanist,* based on Alice Walker's phrase that connects African American women with their historical roles of taking charge, asking questions, and acting in solidarity with other women of color around the globe (Walker, 1984).

The women Kamen interviewed who were not sure of their feminist identification worried (in roughly this order) that feminists want to play the same roles as men, to focus entirely on their careers, to deny what is feminine, and to identify as lesbians. In addition, this group thought that feminists hate men and want to rule them. Some among them did not see the struggle for women's rights as relevant to themselves or did not see themselves as activist enough to be feminists. They believed that feminism can be taken too far.

In Kamen's study (1991) 103 nonfeminists provided the terms that constituted the negative stereotype of feminism in the 1980s: "bra-burning, hairy-legged, amazon, castrating, militant-almost-antifeminine, communist, marxist, separatist, female skinheads, female supremacists, he-woman types, bunch-a-lesbians, you-know-dykes, man-haters, man-bashers, wanting-men's-jobs, want-to-dominate-men, . . . bizarre-chicks-running-around-doing-kooky-things" (p. 23). Yet, according to Kamen, even those nonfeminists tended to support women's rights in general and to appreciate the basic goals and principles of the women's movement. What further evidence is necessary to prove that the 1980s was a time of contradiction?

Description of the Study

The first part of "Section 4: What Do You Think?" of the RGWW questionnaire was designed to test participants' levels of support for various issues considered to be feminist, as well as their willingness to identify themselves as feminists. Participants were asked to rate a set of 20 statements on a 5-point Likert scale. (Because of small cell sizes in extreme categories, and in order to reduce complexity in reporting and analysis, the 5-point scale was collapsed into two categories, agree and disagree. Neutral answers are noted where significant.) With the goal of expanding the study of feminism beyond the usual equation of feminism with equality, the 20 questions concerning feminist issues targeted several categories of American feminist thought: (a) support for women's economic, political, and personal rights to both opportunities and outcomes (a liberal position); (b) recognition that various social institutions, such as work and the family, are structurally sexist and that such institutionalized sexism cannot be overcome solely by individual hard work and self-sacrifice; and (c) the appreciation of female solidarity and support for collective advocacy of women. Beliefs in (b) and (c) are evident in liberal, radical, and cultural positions. Some questions in category (c) asked explicitly about the merits of the women's movement. The association by several researchers of feminist consciousness with group identification, power discontent, system blaming, and a collectivist orientation supports the use of such categories (Cook, 1989; Wilcox, 1990).

Items designed to test support for sexual equality included "Men and women should receive equal pay for equal work" and "Women's special duties in the family require them to commit less time and energy to their careers than men do." Items designed to test for recognition of the women's movement included "Women's activist groups have helped to improve things for working women." Those designed to test for women's solidarity included "Career women have very little in common with full-time homemakers." Other items were designed to determine participants' recognition of structural barriers to women's success, for example, "The biggest problem a career woman faces is the structure of the organization in which she works . . ." and "When all is said and done, a woman will succeed in her career if she is willing to work hard for that success." (As indicated earlier, for the purposes of reporting the results, categories have been collapsed so that completely and partially agree responses have been reported as agreement, and completely and partially disagree responses have been reported as disagreement. With a few exceptions, neutral responses have been disregarded.)

Frequencies were run on responses to the 20 statements. Responses then were cross-tabulated and correlated (using Pearson's r's) with various demographic data, including age, marital status, and income and educational levels, and with self-identification as a feminist. Cross-tabs also were run on the leadership data from "Section G: Women and Leadership" of the questionnaire.

Participants were asked to respond to: "Do you consider yourself to be a feminist?" (yes or no); "If you have answered 'no,' do you know any women who define themselves as feminists?" (yes or no). Essay questions asked for a definition of feminism and a description of a feminist. Essay answers were analyzed by two researchers to determine participants' definitions of, and positive and negative associations with, feminism. Recurring key terms were tabulated and ranked. Participants also were asked to list organizations they belonged to. Those were tabulated and analyzed for evidence of affiliation with feminist groups.

Results: Correlations, Cross-Tabulations, and Self-Identification as a Feminist

Participants' support of feminism must be divided into overt and covert categories. Feminist responses to most of the 20 statements can be considered as covert support because few of the items contain the word *feminism* or ask for direct assessment of issues' relationship to feminism or the women's movement. The overt level has been measured by the responses to the direct question "Do you consider yourself to be a feminist?" and to the more obvious statements among the first 20.

In general, as expected, more covert than overt support for feminism was found among the participants. However, a surprising amount of overt support was found: 298 respondents, or 64% of the entire sample, identified themselves as feminists. That figure is higher than the *Newsweek* poll (1986) result of 56% of women who so identified themselves. In the RGWW survey, 167 respondents, or 36% of the sample, did not consider themselves to be feminists. That result is also higher than the 28% of women in the *Newsweek* poll who did not consider themselves to be feminists. In the RGWW survey, 7 respondents failed to answer or indicated that they were unsure whether they were feminists.

The two most important variables associated with feminist self-identification in the RGWW survey are marital status and education. That education is the only statistically significant variable associated with feminist self-identification is consistent with other studies.

Still the effect of marital status on self-identification should be noted: 58% of the married women called themselves feminists, compared with 100% of separated women, 73% of divorced women, 73% of widowed women, 71% of those "living as married" ($n = 7$), and 69% of single women (8% of whom have children).

Differences are more dramatic among the various educational levels (Figure 2.1): 23% of those with a high school education or less identified themselves as feminists, while 76% of those with MAs and MSs and 68% of those with JDs, LLDs, MDs, PhDs, and EdDs so identified themselves; 67% of those with bachelor's degrees considered themselves to be feminists.

The drop in self-identification as a feminist between master's level and doctoral level participants resulted primarily from the lower rate of self-identification among the medical doctors and lawyers (JDs, LLDs, MDs) included in that group. Only 57% of each of those groups answered yes to the self-identification question. The highest rate of self-identification as a feminist (79%) occurred among PhDs and EdDs.

Figure 2.1
Feminist Self-Identification by Education Level.

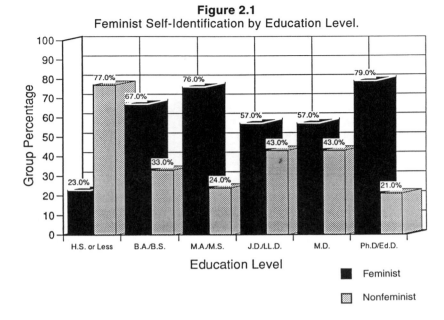

Other demographic variables had little effect on participants' self-identification as feminists. Neither individual nor joint income levels were
significant to self-identification. Family size and age of respondents were
also insignificant. With low numbers of racial minorities in the sample, the
results by racial or ethnic group were also statistically insignificant. It is
interesting to note, however, that these inconclusive results reflect other
studies in which African American women demonstrate higher levels of
support for feminism than whites. African American women in the RGWW
study ($n = 6$) identified themselves as feminists at the rate of 83%, whereas
only 63% of white women were self-identified feminists.

Feminist Issues

Levels of covert support for issues that can be classified as feminist
were higher in the RGWW study than the levels of self-identification
as a feminist. (In these results, as opposed to the responses to the direct

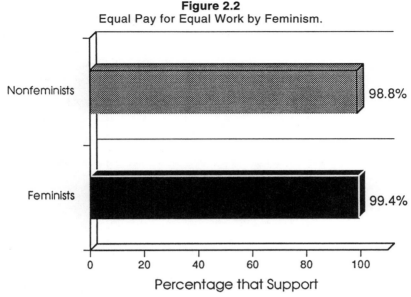

Figure 2.2
Equal Pay for Equal Work by Feminism.

NOTE: Feminism *p* < .005.

questions about feminist identification, age and other variables besides education played an important part.) In fact, 99% of the entire sample supported the concept of equal pay for equal work, with an almost equal rate of support among self-identified feminists (99.4%) and self-identified nonfeminists (98.8%) (Figure 2.2). (Hereafter, the self-identified feminists will be called feminists, and the self-identified nonfeminists will be called nonfeminists.) Similarly high rates of support for comparable pay for work of comparable worth also were found among feminists (93.2%) and nonfeminists (90.4%) (Figure 2.3).

More surprising, the recognition that most women have been subject to sex discrimination, whether they know it or not, was high among both feminists (95.3%) and nonfeminists (82.5%). In fact, on this question, as on several others, age was a more significant—but inconsistent—variable than self-identification as a feminist (Figure 2.4). Women over age 45 were most aware (92.4%) of the presence of sex discrimination. In contrast, age had the opposite influence on respondents' rating of the statement "Women should be able to obtain education in any field and to enter any field in the work world" (Figure 2.5). Although 98% of the

Figure 2.3
Comparable Pay for Work of Comparable Worth.
by Feminism and Age Groups

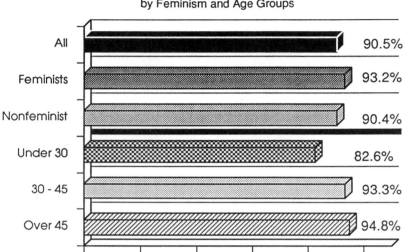

NOTE: Feminism p = NS; Age Groups $p < .05$.

entire sample agreed with this statement, no one under age 30 disagreed or was neutral about equal educational and employment opportunity. Similarly, women over age 45 were less opposed (58.6%) to the assignment of jobs by sex than were women between ages 30 and 45 (75.9%) or women under age 30 (84%) (Figure 2.6). These findings reflect the inconsistencies in feminist responses by age reported in other studies.

American Cultural Traditions

Although some feminist positions unite the views of both feminists and nonfeminists, certain traditional values of American culture remain immune to feminism. Those traditions include marriage, motherhood, and self-reliance, or individualism. Self-identification as a feminist does little to weaken support for these deeply embedded American values, especially individualism. The intransigence of the latter value,

Figure 2.4
Most Women Have Been Subject to Sex Discrimination.

by Feminism and Age Groups

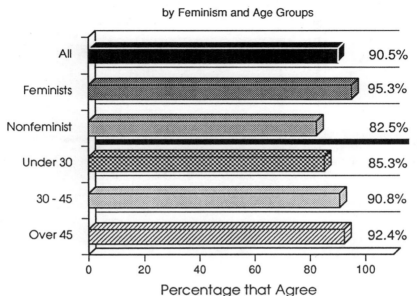

Percentage that Agree

NOTE: Feminism $p < .000$; Age Groups $p < .05$.

which is also consistent with a liberal worldview, represents a barrier to the collective identification and preference for collective action that characterize feminist identity.[3]

Support for marriage was strong among both feminists and nonfeminists. Neither group thought a career woman would be better off if she never married (Figure 2.7): 68.7% of nonfeminists and 61.9% of nonfeminists disagreed that women should forgo marriage in favor of career. A respondent's marital status was more important than her self-identification as a feminist on this question. The clearest opposition to the idea of forgoing marriage for career came from married feminists and nonfeminists (68% and 70%, respectively). Singles and formerly married women of both groups were somewhat less opposed, but their support for motherhood was even stronger. Neither feminists nor nonfeminists supported the idea of sacrificing motherhood to a career (Figure 2.8); 81.5% of feminists and 79.1% of nonfeminists disagreed that a career woman would be better off if she did not become a mother,

Figure 2.5
Equal Educational and Work Opportunities for Both Sexes.
by Feminism

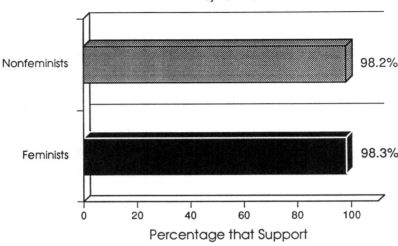

NOTE: Feminism *p* < .000.

statistics that show a stronger support among these working women for motherhood than for marriage. Mothers were only slightly more opposed to the sacrifice of motherhood for career than were nonmothers: 82% of mothers, compared with 77.7% of nonmothers, opposed that sacrifice. The group most opposed to the sacrifice of motherhood for career were the single feminists; 86% of them disagreed that a woman should sacrifice motherhood for a career. That group valued the motherhood experience, which they may not have had, more than twice as much as they valued marriage and 4 percentage points more than mothers did.

Strongest was participants' support for the concept of *individualism*—the reliance on one's own efforts to succeed: 82.8% of the entire sample (88.5% of nonfeminists and 79.9% of feminists) agreed that a woman's hard work will ensure her career success. This belief persisted despite almost universal (90%) recognition of the existence of sex discrimination (Figure 2.9). Participants were unwilling to abandon the idea that anyone can make it in American society if he—or she—is willing to work hard enough, even in the face of institutionalized and structural obstacles to success.

The supremacy of the value of individualism led to other interesting contradictions across the questionnaire. For example, in "Section G:

Figure 2.6
Certain Jobs Are for Men and Certain Jobs Are for Women.

by Feminism and Age Groups

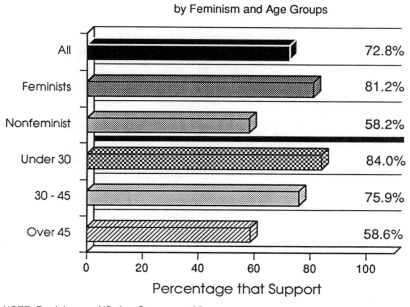

NOTE: Feminism p = NS; Age Groups $p < .05$.

Women and Leadership," participants were asked to rate the statement "I often think I would have more opportunities if I were a man" (Figure 2.10); 59% of feminists and 46% of nonfeminists agreed with that statement, thereby recognizing that a woman's gender affects her opportunities in the workplace. At the same time, as we have seen, almost 83% of the entire sample agreed that a woman will succeed if she works hard. Half of that 83% (or approximately 41% of the entire sample) also believed, however, that men have more opportunities in the workplace than women do.

Similar contradictions can be found in other cross-tabulations within the feminism section of the questionnaire. For example, 53% of those who agreed that a woman's greatest problem is the male-oriented structure of the workplace also agreed that a woman will succeed if she works hard enough. Even direct experience of sexism does not reduce the achieving woman's preference for self-reliance.

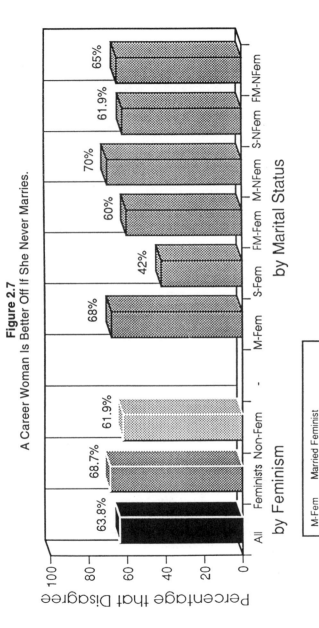

Figure 2.7
A Career Woman Is Better Off If She Never Marries.

NOTE: Feminism p = NS; Marital Status and Feminism p < .001; Marital Status and Nonfeminism p = NS.

M-Fem   Married Feminist
S-Fem   Single Feminist
FM-Fem   Formerly Married Feminist
M-NFem   Married Nonfeminist
S-NFem   Single Nonfeminist
FM-NFem   Formerly Married Nonfeminist

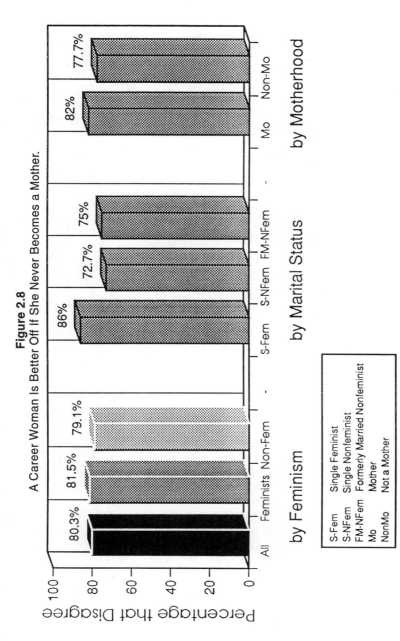

Figure 2.8
A Career Woman Is Better Off If She Never Becomes a Mother.

by Feminism

by Marital Status

by Motherhood

S-Fem	Single Feminist
S-NFem	Single Nonfeminist
FM-NFem	Formerly Married Nonfeminist
Mo	Mother
NonMo	Not a Mother

NOTE: Feminism *p* = NS; Marital Status and Feminism *p* = NS.

39

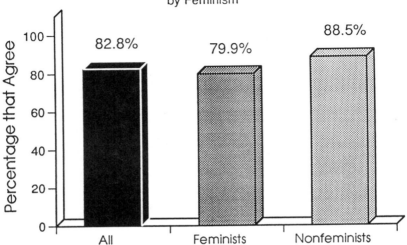

Figure 2.9
A Career Woman Will Succeed in Her Career
If She Works Hard.
by Feminism

NOTE: Feminism *p* < .001.

Work-Family Conflict

Their belief in individual effort reduced the appeal to these participants of social or systemic change as solutions to social problems.
Self-identification as a feminist, however, did have an effect on a belief
in institutional sexism and the recognition of structural barriers to
women's career achievement.

In response to statements about the sexist structures of work and
family and about structural, rather than individual, solutions to the
problems of sexism, feminists were more likely than nonfeminists to
recognize that the structure of work complicates women's responsibilities at home and that the structure of the family interferes with women's
work responsibilities. For example, 48.1% of feminists, compared with
32.7% of nonfeminists, disagreed that "Career women should not expect to shirk their household responsibilities" (Figure 2.11). Disagreement indicates, among other things, a resistance to identifying such
responsibilities only with women. Age was not a significant factor in
respondents' agreement or disagreement with this proposition. In re-

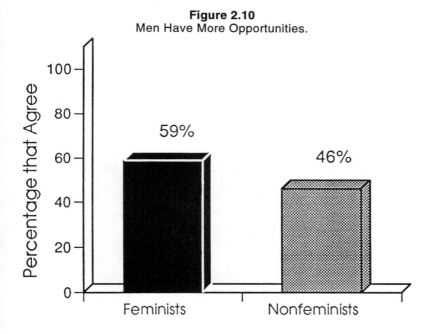

Figure 2.10
Men Have More Opportunities.

sponse to another statement on the same topic, "Women's special duties in the family require them to commit less time and energy to their careers than men do," a higher proportion (63.4%) of feminists than of nonfeminists (48.2%) disagreed, also indicating a resistance to the acceptance of necessary or inevitable (structural) impediments to women in the workplace (Figures 2.12A and 2.12B).

Although not statistically significant, marital status also played a role in this issue for these participants. Single feminists displayed the greatest level of disagreement with the inevitability of gender role definitions (Figure 2.11): 54.4% of them disagreed that married career women should not expect to shirk household responsibilities; 45.3% of married feminists, 29.1% of married nonfeminists, and 33.4% of single nonfeminists also disagreed with that statement. But 55.7% of married nonfeminists, as compared with 42.8% of single nonfeminists, agreed with the statement, demonstrating that experience can modify principle in feminist outlook.

Marital status was also more influential than commitment to feminism among the formerly married. Feminists and nonfeminists who have been widowed or divorced were nearly alike in their views on the

Figure 2.11
Career Women Should Not Expect to Shirk Household Responsibilities.

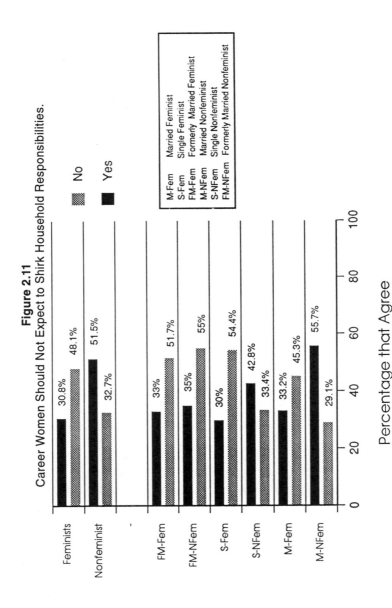

Percentage that Agree

NOTE: Feminism $p < .000$; Marital Status and Feminism p = NS; Marital Status and Nonfeminism p = NS.
*Neutral percentage omitted.

Figure 2.12A
Women's Family Duties Require Reduced Career Commitment.
by Marital Status

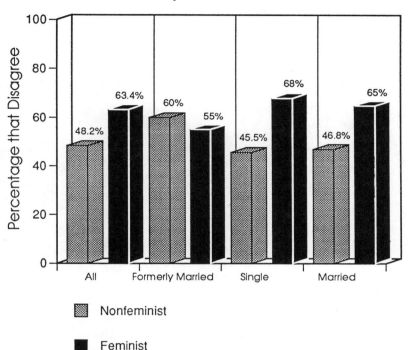

NOTE: Feminism $p < .01$; Marital Status and Feminism $p < .05$; Marital Status and Non-feminism $p =$ NS.
*Neutral percentage omitted.

structural issue of career women's household responsibilities. Formerly married nonfeminists were much less supportive of the necessity for married working women to shoulder household responsibilities than were their single or married counterparts. Only 35% of them agreed, and 55% of them disagreed, that career women should not expect to shirk those responsibilities. Formerly married feminists agreed at a similar rate to their nonfeminist counterparts (33%) and at a rate similar to the level of agreement among single (30%) and married (33%) feminists. They disagreed at a slightly lower rate than single feminists (54%), but at a higher rate than married feminists (45%). Rates of

Figure 2.12B
Women's Family Duties Require Reduced Career Commitment.
by Age Groups

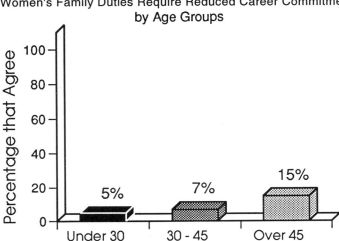

disagreement with the statement among the two groups of formerly married women were also similar: 51.7% among the feminists, and 55% among the nonfeminists (Figure 2.11).

In contrast, marital status had little effect on responses to a statement concerning the reduction of women's career commitment because of household responsibilities (Figure 2.12A). In response to that statement, similar percentages of married and single feminists (65% and 68%, respectively) and of married and single nonfeminists (46.8% and 45.5%, respectively) expressed disagreement with the idea that women's family duties require their reduced career commitment. Formerly married nonfeminists were slightly more opposed (60%) to the statement than were formerly married feminists (55%).

Age played a minor role in the level of agreement with the statement, although all participants, feminists and nonfeminists, over age 45 agreed with the statement at a somewhat higher rate (15%) than did those aged 30 to 45 (7%) and those under age 30 (5%) (Figure 2.12B).

Inconsistencies in the answers to the two similar questions above may be partly the result of their wording. The word *shirk* may have connoted a level of irresponsibility that the married women found particularly unacceptable. The second statement contained no such threatening language.

Despite the higher degree of resistance by feminists than by non-feminists to the structures that create problems for women, feminists displayed relatively low levels of support for structural change. Although significantly higher than the response level of nonfeminists, this relatively low level of feminist response, which pales when compared with feminists' virtually unanimous support for other issues, such as equal pay, indicates a reluctance to acknowledge intransigent conflicts between work and family responsibilities. That reluctance is common among liberal feminists, who fear that any demands predicated on existing gender roles will only reinforce those roles for the future.

The highest level of feminist support for structural change emerged in response to a statement proposing that vast changes must occur in the structure of the family if conditions for career women are to improve (Figure 2.13). The level of feminist support for that statement (69%) resulted from the very high level of support by single and formerly married feminists (74% and 86.5%, respectively). Married feminists were least supportive (62.1%) of such structural family change. Marital status had a similar effect on nonfeminists; only 41% of married non-feminists agreed to the need for changes in family structure, but 47.6% of single nonfeminists and 70% of formerly married nonfeminists agreed to the need for such changes.

Apparently willingness to change traditional family structure—such as the protection of women's responsibilities within that structure—depended, in part, on women's experiences with it. Those who had left or lost the traditional structure—the divorced and widowed—may have seen a greater need for change than those living within it or those who have never experienced that structure for themselves. Still, all feminists were more supportive than nonfeminists of the idea of change in family structure.

The Workplace

All respondents, regardless of self-identification as a feminist, marital status, or any other variable, were less supportive of structural change in the workplace than they were of change in the family. That lack of support may well reflect the superordinate value of individualism noted above.

Although feminists' recognition of sex-based inequities at work was greater than their recognition of sex-based inequities at home and is

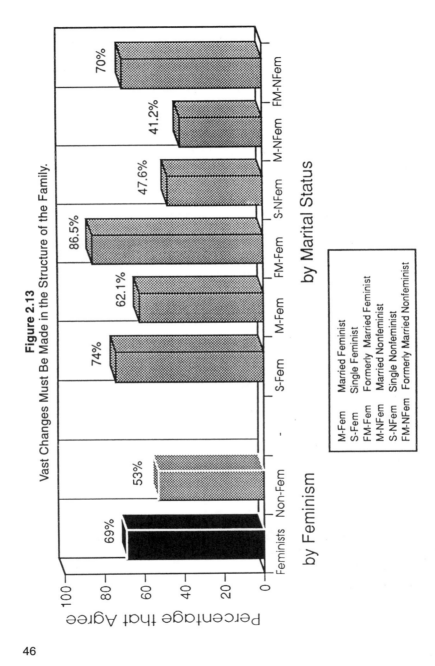

Figure 2.13
Vast Changes Must Be Made in the Structure of the Family.

by Marital Status

by Feminism

M-Fem	Married Feminist
S-Fem	Single Feminist
FM-Fem	Formerly Married Feminist
M-NFem	Married Nonfeminist
S-NFem	Single Nonfeminist
FM-NFem	Formerly Married Nonfeminist

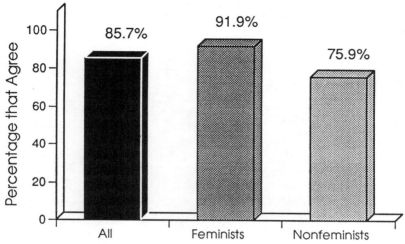

Figure 2.14
The U.S. Workplace Is Male Oriented.

NOTE: Feminism *p* < .001.

arguably more feminist than their response to family questions, feminists are still less demanding of change at work than in the family. For example, 91.9% of feminists, as compared with 75.9% of nonfeminists, agreed that the workplace in the United States is male oriented (Figure 2.14). At the same time, 69.7% of feminists, as compared with 55.1% of nonfeminists, agreed that women's biggest problem is the unsupportive structure of the organizations in which they work (Figure 2.15). Also, 81% of feminists, compared with 58.2% of nonfeminists, disagreed that certain jobs should be reserved for women, while certain jobs are reserved for men (Figure 2.6). Age played a role in answers to this question: Those under 30 were much more opposed to job segregation by sex than were those over 45.

When it came to supporting structural change in the workplace, however, feminists joined nonfeminists in demurring. Only 22.8% of feminists and 11.4% of nonfeminists supported the idea that a woman should make any demands on an employer that would distinguish her from a man (Figure 2.16). Only 56.8% of feminists and 34.1% of nonfeminists supported the idea that corporations and other places of employment have an obligation to offer support services for working

Figure 2.15
Woman's Biggest Problem Is the Structure of the Organization
in Which She Works.

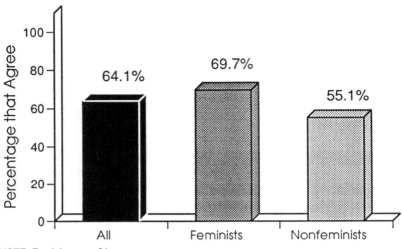

NOTE: Feminism *p* < .01.

Figure 2.16
Women Should Compete on the Same Terms as Men.

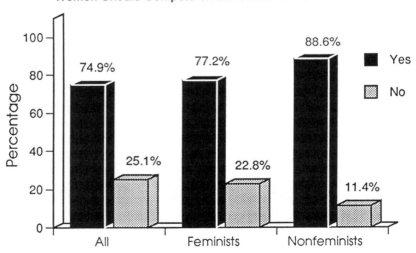

NOTE: Feminism *p* < .05.
*Neutral percentage omitted.

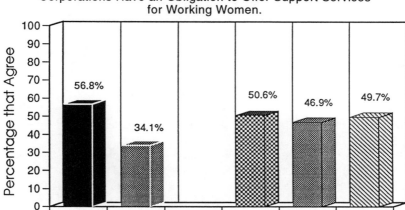

Figure 2.17
Corporations Have an Obligation to Offer Support Services
for Working Women.

NOTE: Feminism *p* < .000; Age Groups *p* < .05.

women (Figure 2.17). Women under age 30 were most supportive of such an obligation. These responses compare with majority support among both feminists and nonfeminists (69% and 53%, respectively) for change in family structure (Figure 2.13).

The differences reflect the sample's liberal views. If participants accepted the workplace as male territory, then the liberal goal of equality with men meant approaching that territory as men do, without displacing men or changing the nature of work to accommodate women's needs. (In contrast, a cultural or radical feminist would regard women's needs and realities as an ameliorative influence on the world of work.) Thus 65% of those respondents who agreed that the workplace is male oriented also agreed that career women must be prepared to compete on the same terms as men. They apparently chose not to claim that any changes resulting from women's equal participation in work could be positive for all.

If the RGWW sample believed that the best career hope for women lies in appearing as much like men as possible, then their views are consistent with national trends. The 1989 *New York Times* poll indicated that 63% of American women (and 70% of American men) believe women must compete at work on the same terms as men.

RGWW study participants' greater support for structural change in the family than in the workplace also can be understood in terms of the liberal feminist value of equality, in conjunction with the American system of prestige, even among nonfeminists. If the home is to be perceived as an "equal opportunity employer," perceptions of sexual difference that, historically, have made it a less prestigious (female) domain must change in order for higher prestige (male) persons to function as full partners there. Thus the structure must change. In the workplace, a more prestigious site than the home, it makes sense for women to change (upward) in order to become equal. Thus the person must change.

The contrast in attitudes toward the work and family domains among the study's participants suggests that husbands and other life partners of women have more to fear (if they find change threatening) than do supervisors and CEOs. In the foreseeable future, new family configurations (although not the abolition of family as an ideal), rather than new organizational patterns or career paths, are likely to emerge.

Collective Identity and Action

Although no questions or statements on the questionnaire asked specifically about the advisability of collective action in seeking solutions to identified problems, some conclusions can be drawn from responses concerning female solidarity and collectivity. For example, that similar percentages of feminists and nonfeminists (67.7% and 60%, respectively) disagreed that homemakers and career women have little in common suggests participants' acceptance of a connection between women in differing occupations and life-styles (Figure 2.18). Despite such a response, other data indicate that the study's participants did not strongly support collective action for the solution of problems women face (Table 2.1). Few were members of feminist groups, such as NOW, National Women's Political Caucus, Women's Equality Coalition (a local group), or even the YWCA. They were most likely to be members of women's groups with a professional focus. Predictably, 93% of those who belong to one or two women's organizations with a somewhat feminist focus identified themselves as feminists, but 72.8% of feminists belonged to no such groups. Only 17.1% ($n = 51$) of feminists belonged to one or two and 10.1% to three or more feminist or quasi-feminist organizations. Surprisingly, 2.4% of nonfeminists belonged to one or two such organi-

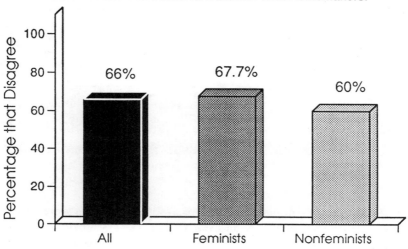

Figure 2.18
Career Women Have Little in Common With Homemakers.

NOTE: Feminism *p* = NS.

zations, and 12.6% belonged to three or more. (Groups such as the YWCA undoubtedly account for this level of membership.)

In contrast, 24% of feminists belonged to one professional organization for women, such as groups for female bankers, business owners, real estate brokers, physicians, and attorneys (Table 2.2). An additional

Table 2.1
Women's Organizations, Feminist or Quasi-Feminist

# of Organizations	None	1 - 2	3 - 5
	%	%	%
Feminists	72.8	17.1	10.1
Nonfeminists	85	2.4	12.6

WOMEN AND CAREERS

Table 2.2
Professional Organizations for Women

# of Organizations	None	1	2
	%	%	%
Feminists	64.4	23.5	12.1
Nonfeminists	49.7	32.9	17.4

12% belong to two or more such groups. Nonfeminists join professional organizations for women at an even greater rate: 33% belong to one, and an additional 17% belong to two or more professional women's organizations; 64% of feminists, but only 50% of nonfeminists, belong to no professional organizations for women.

Such statistics suggest two possibilities. Either collective action on behalf of women's issues is not a high priority for the women in the sample, or women's professional organizations do not have feminist agendas. In either case, it is clear that feminists in the sample do not rally around the concept of collective action.

Feminism

Several of the statements in "Section 4: What Do You Think?" of the questionnaire sought to measure participants' responses to women activists and feminists themselves. Not surprisingly, self-identification as a feminist was relevant to a participant's overt support of feminist groups. For example, 84.9% of feminists, as compared with 58.1% of nonfeminists, agreed that "Women's activist groups have helped to improve things for working women" (Figure 2.19). Age played little role in a participant's overt support of feminist activism. Respondents over age 45 agreed with the above statement at the rate of 73.8%, while 69.3% of those under 30 agreed with it.

In response to a related statement, only 4% of feminists, but 28.8% of nonfeminists, agreed that "working women would be better off if

Figure 2.19
Feminist Activists Have Helped Working Women.

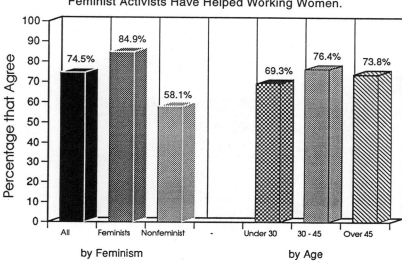

NOTE: Feminism $p < .000$; Age Groups p = NS.

feminist groups would discontinue their efforts to attain greater rights for women" (Figure 2.20). Middle-aged women (30-45) showed the strongest disagreement (69.7%) with this statement of any age group.

Support for feminist groups in the RGWW study seems high when compared with similar national data. In the *New York Times* poll (1989), only 25% of the total sample, and 28% of women employed full-time, agreed that women's organizations had improved their lives. Younger women, aged 18 to 44, were most supportive of the helpfulness of women's organizations (29%), as were the never married (32%), young employed mothers (33%), and women earning over $50,000 per year (38%). Those results compare (confusingly) with 67% who agreed that the United States needs a strong women's movement, a statistic that resembles the earlier *Newsweek* poll's (1986) finding that 71% of all women believed that the women's movement (though not specifically women's organizations) had benefited them.

Although differences between feminists and nonfeminists in the RGWW study are significant on this topic, nonfeminists were not as disparaging of feminist activism as one might expect. The majority of nonfeminists approved of feminist efforts on behalf of working women, and less than a third of nonfeminists thought such activism should stop.

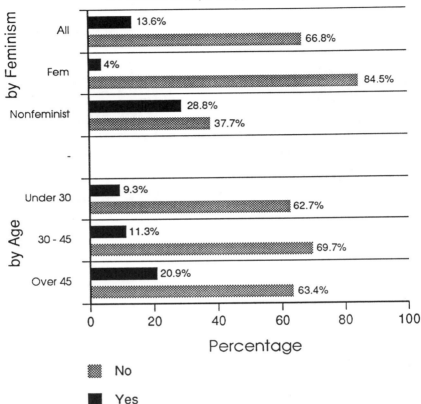

Figure 2.20
Working Women Would Be Better Off
If Feminist Groups Stopped Efforts.

NOTE: Feminism *p* < .000; Age Groups *p* < .05.
*Neutral percentage omitted.

Results: Definitions

The two open-ended questions in "Section 4: What Do You Think?" of the questionnaire provided revealing information about the understanding of *feminism* as a term by both feminist and nonfeminist participants. Ironically some self-identified nonfeminists defined feminism in terms similar to those used by feminists. Both groups included in their definitions of feminism the equality of men and women, the quest for freedom and self-actualization for women, the need for social change, activism on behalf of women and women's rights, and the importance of placing a woman's needs high on her own list of priorities. The two groups simply did not agree on the meaning or significance of those positions for women or for society.

Feminist participants regarded equality between the sexes—a liberal goal—as the primary feminist value. Their concept of equality included social, political, and economic rights, as well as the equality of male and female potential, intelligence, abilities, and worth. "Women are valuable and deserve the same consideration, rights, responsibilities, and tolerance as men," wrote one respondent.

In contrast to their generally liberal views, some respondents showed leanings toward cultural feminism in their definitions by supporting gender differences. They suggested that it is all right to be a woman, even to be "feminine" (though this was not defined), while demanding social equality with men. One respondent explained that she was "proud to be a woman; proud to be feminine . . . realizing we can be both and improve society because of it." Another defined feminism as the "ability to self-actualize without losing femininity."

Content analysis revealed that a rather distant second value of feminism to the feminist group was *activism*—"being willing to make changes" and a "willingness to speak up and act on women's issues." Only half as many feminists referred to activism on behalf of women's rights and dignity as referred to equality, and only a few respondents mentioned collective identity and action—"sticking up for rights . . . of other women."

A third value of feminism to the feminists was the commitment to or belief in the liberal concept of *women's rights*. Self-identified feminists believed that women's rights need protection, advancement, and advocacy and that education about women's issues is important to feminism. Improving choices for women (though reproductive choice is not mentioned), working for change, taking pride in being female, and being pro-woman were other frequently mentioned feminist values in this group.

Although many nonfeminists shared the feminists' basic understanding of the definition of feminism and used the same words to describe it, they did not necessarily share feminists' valuation of its attributes and activities. In fact, nonfeminists tended to consider those attributes and activities as socially or personally destructive. In the nonfeminist definitions, even equality was sometimes seen as negative because it threatens a woman's femininity. In short, nonfeminists took the association of feminism with gender deviance—evident in Dill's study (1990) of feminists—to an extreme.

Examples of that association abound. While admitting that feminism is about equality, one respondent devalued the concept by claiming that "ardent feminists" ruin it. Another said feminism overemphasizes "social and economic equality" of the sexes. One nonfeminist (apparently unaware of either the cultural feminist position or of various levels of feminist commitment) defined a feminist as "a woman who wants to be equal to men but remain feminine," clearly implying that the two are mutually exclusive. Another criticized feminists for "constantly seeking" equality. This group disdained activists as pushy, militant, and hostile and characterized those who join feminist organizations as a threat to the welfare of society.

Other nonfeminists defined feminism in clearly negative terms—like those in Kamen's (1991) study—that were not used by feminists. They described feminists as "abrasive," "anti-male," "antagonistic," "bitter and resentful of their plight in life . . . being a woman," "blaming," "cold," "crude," "reactionary and defensive," "fanatic," "someone like Gloria Steinem," "extremists," "noisy," "radical," and "selfish." One accused feminists of having a "chip on the shoulder"; another claimed that feminism is reverse discrimination. Understandably such characteristics make women "unattractive," uncooperative and unfeminine in traditional terms, the kind of women who would "demand their husbands . . . do household chores," "demand equal rights . . . regardless of qualifications," and "place achievement . . . above family or maternal goals." Some nonfeminist respondents worried that feminists actually exploit their femaleness to exact concessions or favors from men or to gain social power.

Discussion and Implications

The data on attitudes toward feminism and feminist issues among career women in the RGWW study yield both surprising and expected results. A surprising 63% of participants identified themselves as feminists, 7 percentage points higher than the national data would indicate. The high levels of self-identification certainly reflect the sample's relatively high levels of education, but these data also add a new wrinkle to the correlation between educational level and attainment of a feminist viewpoint. They suggest that women in high-prestige, male-associated fields such as medicine and law may be less likely to develop a feminist identity than those in less male-associated fields. Such fields may also discourage feminist identification because they emphasize individual ability versus group identity. Training for law and medicine actually may exaggerate the effect of the liberal feminist position we already have seen; that is, the women who enter the most male-associated occupations may be the least inclined to identify themselves with the category "woman" that historically has been excluded from such occupations. Equality in those fields may require the most extreme male-identification.

In addition, although their numbers are growing, women still comprise less than 20% of all doctors and lawyers.[4] According to some researchers, such proportions constitute low-threat workplaces; that is, the presence of so few women presents no significant threat to male colleagues. Feminist viewpoints (that include collective action) are more likely to develop among women in high-threat workplaces—that is, when they comprise between 27% and 49% of the labor force (Gruber & Bjorn, 1988).

An expected result of the study is the liberal feminist propensity of participants, evidenced by their support for such issues as the political and economic equality of men and women and women's right to equal access in employment and education. Because the term *equality* has different connotations in different settings, however, it can lead to the interesting variations evident in the questionnaire results. Becoming equal in the workplace suggests less structural change than does becoming equal in the family. In addition, respondents may have felt more empowered to make change at home than at work, where efforts by relative newcomers might not only produce little change but also jeopardize still insecure gains.

Comparisons with other parts of the survey suggest more directly the women's resolve to achieve career success without making waves. For example, in response to questions concerning dual-career family issues (see Chap. 6), participants recognized the difficulty of fatigue and role conflict in their lives. Yet they simultaneously accepted the struggle as the price they must pay for a more interesting life. They chose personal struggle over disruptive systemic solutions to problems, even if those problems were induced by the system. Affinity for the American value of individual hard work and effort ultimately superseded any feminist prescriptions for collective action.

National data add another dimension to the issue of individual versus collective, structurally focused action. According to the *New York Times* poll (1989), few women identify the women's movement with the solution to work-family conflicts. Only 7% of poll respondents said that the women's movement should address that juggling act. Instead, 23% believed that job-related problems should be the focus of women's movement efforts and activities.

Questionnaire results also suggest that a woman's marital status has an impact on her assessment of sex inequities in the family. Recognition of such inequities increased among both nonfeminists and feminists in the RGWW study when marriages dissolved. Women who, by choice or chance, had been but were no longer married were more supportive of changes in family structure than either married or single women. They were also less supportive of marriage and motherhood than were single women. This effect is exaggerated in the case of formerly married nonfeminists, who were even less supportive of a reduced career commitment for women because of household duties (and therefore more feminist) than were formerly married feminists.

Interpreting the apparent feminism of such nonfeminists is complicated and requires much speculation and extrapolation from the data. Perhaps Faludi's study (1991) provides some clues. Faludi described the feminist-blaming that accompanied 1980s media analysis of women's problems in juggling home and work. If that blaming had the effect she claims, then working women, inundated with messages that their careers were tainted by selfish ambition instead of driven by economic necessity and human desire for self-realization, were likely to feel guilty and responsible if their marriages ended. They were also more likely than women who had stayed home to romanticize the role that compliance with the family ideal might have played in saving their marriages. If more nonfeminists than feminists in the study were homemakers before their marriages ended, then they might not have felt as personally guilty and responsible as did the feminists who worked while married. The nonfeminists had earned the right, in the backlash 1980s, to feel angry that they played the game and still lost.

Despite the possibility that experience produces feminist consciousness, the results of this study do not support the generalization that feminist consciousness or identification inevitably comes with age and experience. The passage of time produces feminism on some issues, but youthful inexperience produces feminism on others, according to both the RGWW study and other research. For example, although the youngest group of women in the RGWW study were most opposed to the idea of sex roles in the workplace and most supportive of business' obligation to offer support services for working women, they were also the least supportive of all age groups of feminist activism and the least cognizant of sex discrimination. This combination of responses suggests that the younger women may take certain principles and accomplishments of feminism for granted, particularly regarding equality of opportunity and shared parenting and homemaking responsibilities. They may not identify those principles and achievements as related to the feminism and feminist activism that preceded them. Such an ahistorical view has important implications for modern feminism. Even with their support of feminist issues, younger women's failure to support feminist activism may impede further progress toward sexual equality and other feminist values in our society. Complacency may jeopardize the future of the very women who are guilty of it.

The sample in the RGWW survey is much too small to provide definitive conclusions about the impact of race on a woman's support of feminism, but the fact that a higher proportion of African American women than of white women identified as feminist raises some issues. That level of support is consistent with national data and challenges the myth that African American women disdain feminism. Given the absence of women of color from the more visible, white-dominated feminist organizations and causes, however, white feminists should not misinterpret such support for feminism as support for their brand of it. A division among feminists along racial and color lines reflects the tragically intransigent racial divisions of American society. Yet it may still be possible to unite women through a transformed feminism that truly targets the shared interests of women of all races and ethnic groups. Before such unity can occur, however, feminists of diverse backgrounds must accept and understand their differences better than they have in the past.

Despite the relatively high level of participants' self-identification as feminists, the RGWW data contain no clear feminist agenda for change. Marriage, motherhood, and individualism remain strong values to both feminists and nonfeminists in the group. Collective action has minimal support. The clearest mandate for change involves the family structure, but even that change has a fairly low level of support, even among feminists. Furthermore, there is little indication that ordinary feminists will seek legal or public remedies for their problems. Rather, such women believe they can produce most change through individual effort.

In fact, feminism among women such as those in the RGWW study is really a system of adaptation. It is a feminism that allows women to participate more fully in the American social, economic, and political system as it currently exists, rather than demands radical change in that system. The participants perceive flaws only insofar as benefits are not equally available to everyone with appropriate qualifications, and responsibilities are not equally shared. The support for change in the family structure also reflects this value. Participants are asking for the equal responsibility of men and women within the family—a change within, rather than an alternative to, the family system itself.

This form of feminism contradicts media portrayals of feminists as demanding and pushy. Rather, such feminism actually promotes good public and economic citizenship among women and reinforces the American value of individualism. The costs to the social structure from such change are minimal. The cost to the women themselves is another story, however. Although they are not complaining as loudly as they might, women will pay the highest cost, by accommodating themselves to a system that does not acknowledge their burdens and by standing alone as they pursue their goals. A humane society would work to mitigate that cost, whether victims demand such action or not.

Perhaps it is the cost of female achievement in our society that discourages some women from classifying themselves as feminists. The negative definitions of feminism given by some participants may indicate not only a fear of gender deviance but also a fear that the perceived goals of the women's movement confuse the female experience and add to women's burdens. In short, nonfeminists may not see in feminism a satisfying alternative to traditional ways of being a woman.

Other factors no doubt enter into a woman's nonidentification with feminism as well. She may associate femininity with protection by a man and feminism with conflicts between men and women that threaten such protection. If she has learned to place marriage and family relationships ahead of her own development, she may reject an ideology that appears to require dissatisfaction with the life-style she values.

In some ways, however, the conflict between the feminists and the nonfeminists in this study concerns labels. Primarily because of their educational experiences, feminists learn to label as "self-actualization" the development of women's skills and abilities and the valuing of their personal qualities and independence. In contrast, nonfeminists learn to call that same process "selfish." Whereas feminists consider women's competitive impulses and achievement needs as compatible with their identities as females, nonfeminists believe their femininity is threatened by the acquisition of male-associated qualities or behaviors, as one nonfeminist's reference to female strength as "testicular fortitude" suggests. Although some feminist positions and stages of identity emphasize women's traditional personality traits and roles, the fact that few women learn to identify these positions and stages as feminist means that many women reject feminism in its entirety without really knowing what it is.

The most hopeful sign for the future of feminism in the study is its support for the conclusion that feminism is a learned skill or belief. Many differences between feminists and nonfeminists can be eliminated by education—either in college classrooms or in life experiences—unless that education consists of specifically masculinist professional training. Such a conclusion has serious implications for the educational system of our society and for the role of women's studies in that system.

Notes

1. The quotation in the title of this chapter is attributed to Lily Tomlin in *Quotable Women: A Collection of Shared Thoughts* (1989).

2. Although scholarly research does not generally rely on polls reported in the popular press, two factors contribute to the appropriateness of the inclusion of such polls in this chapter. First is the dearth of other relevant research into American women's attitudes toward feminism and feminist issues. Second is the quality and breadth of these particular polls. The 1986 *Newsweek* poll (How women view work, 1986, p. 51) was conducted by the Gallup Organization, which conducted telephone interviews with 1,009 women over the age of 18. The margin of sample error is plus or minus 4 percentage points. The 1989 *New York Times* poll (Women's Lives, 1989) was based on telephone interviews with 1,497 adults in the continental United States. The poll was taken first in June 1989, and then was repeated (with 978 respondents) in July, after the Supreme Court's decision in the Webster case. The survey was random and representative of all regions of the country. Women were sampled at a higher rate than men: 1,025 women and 472 men. Interview results then were weighted to account for population proportion, household size, and other factors. The sampling error for women is plus or minus 3 percentage points in the first survey, and plus or minus 4 percentage points in the second survey. For women aged 18 to 29 in the first survey, the margin of error is plus or minus 6 percentage points.

3. Perhaps individualism is an American value because it has standing in both liberal and conservative positions. Classic *liberalism* emphasizes individual political rights; *conservatism* focuses on individual economic activity and identity.

4. According to recent census data, 19% of the nation's 744,000 lawyers are women (as of 1991) and 19.3% of the nation's physicians are women (as of 1990). Only 0.5% of physicians are African American women (Bureau of the Census, 1992; Ries & Stone, 1992).

References

Agassi, J. B. (1979). *Women on the job: The attitudes of women to their work.* Lexington, MA: Lexington.

Bargad, A., & Hyde, J. S. (1991). Women's studies: A study of feminist identity development in women. *Psychology of Women Quarterly, 15,* 181-201.

Bureau of the Census. (1992). *Statistical abstracts of the United States* (112th ed.). Washington, DC: U.S. Department of Commerce.

Cook, E. A. (1989). Measuring feminist consciousness. *Women and Politics, 9*(3), 71-88.

Dill, K. (1990, January-February). The qualified feminist: A report on a study of feminist identification in undergraduates. *Feminisms, 3,* 9-10.

Downing, N., & Roush, K. (1984). From passive acceptance to active commitment: A model of feminist identity development for women. *The Counseling Psychologist, 13,* 695-709.

Faludi, S. (1991). *Backlash: The undeclared war against American women.* New York: Anchor.

Gruber, J., & Bjorn, L. (1988). Routes to a feminist orientation among women autoworkers. *Gender and Society, 2,* 496-509.

How women view work, motherhood and feminism (poll). (1986, March 31). *Newsweek,* p. 51.

Kamen, P. (1991). *Feminist fatale: Voices from the "twenty something" generation explore the future of the "women's movement."* New York: Donald I. Fine.

Morgan, C. S., & Walker, A. (1983). Predicting sex role attitudes. *Social Psychology Quarterly, 46,* 148-151.

Ransford, H. E., & Miller, J. (1983, February). Race, sex, and feminist outlooks. *American Sociological Review, 48,* 46-59.

Ries, P., & Stone, A. J. (Eds.). (1992). *The American woman, 1992-93: A status report* (Women's Research and Education Institute). New York: Norton.

Thornton, A., & Freedman, D. (1979). Changes in sex-role attitudes of women, 1962-1977. *American Sociological Review, 44,* 831-842.

Walker, A. (1984). *In search of our mother's gardens.* London: The Women's Press.

Wilcox, C. (1990). Black women and feminism. *Women and Politics, 10*(3), 65-83.

William L. Webster v. Reproductive Health Services. (1989). 109 S. Ct. 3040.

Women's lives: A scorecard of change. (1989). *New York Times.*

   Belkin, L. (August 20). Bars to equality of sexes seen as eroding slowly, pp. A1, 26.

   Cowan, A. L. (August 21). Women's gains on the job: Not without a heavy toll, pp. A1, 14.

   Dionne, E. J., Jr. (August 22). Struggle for work and family fueling women's movement, pp. A1, 18

3 Choosing the High Tech Path: Career Women and Technology

If you look into video game arcades anywhere in the country, you inevitably see mostly boys, eyes gleaming and faces reflecting the neon colors of the screens, manipulating the controls. These arcades are the latest manifestation of a long-time truism: Boys' play prepares them better for a technologically sophisticated future than does girls'. A girl in high tech is still regarded as a fluke, if not a freak. Such perceptions are inaccurate, of course, but they still function to prevent some women from achieving the technological skills they need in the workplace.

In exploring women's perceptions of technology in their work, Nancy Brooks's study ventured into a territory that has been nontraditional not only for women but also for managers, who historically have delegated the use of technology to subordinates (often nonmanagerial women). Brooks perceived a change in the role of technology in managers' acquisition of power, however, and she wanted to discover what role women managers and professionals were playing in this change. A few participants' comments reflect her findings: "The more information I have at my fingertips, the more productive I can be," wrote one; "My knowledge of technology gives me an edge over the competitors for promotions/raises," wrote another.

Brooks's discovery that participants were generally enthusiastic about the potential of technology to improve their lives as managers and professionals debunks stereotypes about technologically backward women, although it does not erase lingering organizational barriers to women's access to the technology that will help fulfill that potential. Her work also raises some interesting questions about the relationship of technology to power. Might technology be a means by which managers who are unaware of its potential actually lose power, as middle-class occupations are de-skilled by sophisticated software into easily automated jobs? Might women be disproportionately ghettoized into the positions most vulnerable to such a change? Or will the power of technology to facilitate communication and to promote alternative forms of organizational interaction help promote the kind of flexible and sensitive management style women both need and favor? What forces will prevail—those with Orwellian overtones of control, or those with humane objectives, such as giving workers greater access to career mobility and flexibility? What role will women play in determining that outcome?

NANCY A. BROOKS

T hrough my readings and observations, I saw that more women were entering professions and that advanced technology was becoming part of our lives. I became curious about the combined impact of those two events. In my own career, I was doing quite a bit to acquire computer skills, and I observed women in my family who had advanced their careers through technology. My entrepreneurial niece, through computer skills, has been able to establish her own business in financial consulting and is doing very well on a national level by networking with people all over the country (she advises firms doing financial counseling). My readings of Lewis Mumford stimulated me to consider women and technology. He offered some provocative questions (in fact, his questions are almost like Freud's: "what do women want?") in that they ask how in the world are women managing with technology when they get so little support? I began to wonder how women do manage and how their careers will be affected.

We can be certain that the future world of work will be one of sophisticated technologies and that women's careers will be affected by their use of technology. I asked career women who are now using high technology in their work what role they foresee for high technology in their career development and how they associate high technology with their professional values.

Sex Roles and Technology

Learning about women's current circumstances, we become better prepared to consider future choices. Questions surrounding technology touch not only the role of career women but also broader social concerns. Common wisdom maintains two assumptions that predict little involvement with technology by career women. First, women generally are assumed to be inept with all sorts of technology and loath to use it. Second, managers and professionals are perceived as aloof from high technology because they delegate work to others. Yet high technology is certainly evident in the career woman's professional development. Office computers, programmable telephones, electronic mail, and a host of other sophisticated devices are changing the way people accomplish their daily tasks. We may be missing some fundamental evidence about women's careers if we overlook the implications of high technology for women's careers.

A *professional* is a specialist who practices a complex set of skills to accomplish self-defined tasks (Lunsbury, 1978). Being a professional means having a high degree of autonomy in work, having the preparation and judgment to make important decisions independently. Thus, according to this definition, most of the career women in this study are also professionals. Professionals often are able to choose or avoid technology according to how they define a task. The proportion of women in professions is increasing rapidly (Parrish, 1986). Because professionals are often free either to avoid or to use technology, an increasing number of women such as those in this study will have a choice in enhancing career mobility with technological literacy.

The increased representation of women in careers and the acceleration of technological advancement may create a double impact. This impact may occur in the reformulation of policies and social systems of organizations. If managers and professionals relate differently to high technology than do other workers, and if women in those roles also bring new values and experiences to organizational functions, the structure and processes of entire systems may be altered. But before such a combined effect can occur, women professionals actually must use technology and be willing to include technological literacy in their own career development. It was the purpose of this study to determine the nature and extent of career women's professional involvement with high technology.

Women's Experience
in Technology-Based Careers

A number of social changes now contribute to the development of childhood attitudes conducive to women's technological careers. Recent surveys have found that attitudes toward technology are more positive among boys than girls, but not strikingly so (Wilder, Cooper, & Cooper, 1985). It is possible that the more negative attitudes of girls may not be associated so much with mechanical implements themselves as with gender-restricted activities that are often associated with mechanical objects. Video game centers, for example, are usually youthful male preserves.

Although it may be realistic to acknowledge that American gender role expectations still favor more male involvement with all forms of technology, women and girls are rapidly joining traditional male technological occupations and professions. This trend challenges the commonly held assumption that women are fearful of and inept with technology. In particular, the highly technological careers of science and engineering are attracting more women (Malcolm, 1985; Zimmerman, 1983).

The decisive characteristics of women in such atypical professions appear to arise from stimulating family backgrounds that did not restrict career choices by gender (Lemkau, 1983). The pursuit of "masculine" activities and the development of confidence in being able to succeed in "male" arenas may be more important to women in technological careers than the acquisition of technological aptitude. If the ideology of computer culture privileges structured, hierarchical strategies based on abstract, formal reasoning, as Turkle and Papert (1990) suggested, women whose "ways of knowing" are contextual and associational may benefit from the development of a future computer culture more supportive of pluralistic epistemology.

A study of the careers of MIT women engineering graduates of the 1950s found that their lower professional achievement (as contrasted with that of men) was associated with family and social arrangements, rather than with technological demands of their profession (Bailyn, 1980). Now, almost 40 years after those women graduated, circumstances for women in engineering have changed. Women now constitute 25% of engineering undergraduates and enter the labor force successfully. Still the profession requires changes that will support the full professional achievement of these women, such as recognition that the early childbearing years of women may not always be compatible with professional demands for early career development (Dresselhaus, 1985, p. 195).

As women overcome disciplinary barriers, they are represented increasingly in science and other highly technological fields. In addition to confronting disciplinary stereotypes, women in this technological arena often find child-rearing strains, professional restrictions against nontraditional career lines, and exclusion from informal networks as impediments to advancement. Organizational obstacles, rather than lack of technological accomplishment, are responsible for inhibiting women's advancement (Schiebinger, 1987, p. 299). Although women increasingly are entering professions that employ technology, structural and social problems may limit women's applications of technology in those professions.

Technologically Assisted Management

Addressing the second relevant point of common wisdom, that most professionals at the management level are not using much high technology, requires investigation of recent management studies. In an empirical investigation of male and female managers' attitudes toward computers, Gutek and Bikson (1985) found that both males and females are moderately comfortable with computers in the work environment. Males in this study had more computer skills and higher organizational positions, which allowed them to make more computer-related decisions. However, women managers were somewhat more enthusiastic than men about computers and reported having access to resources for training and computer applications. Managers indeed were using computers, probably the most visible symbol of high technology in today's work world.

This application of technology is recent, however. Managers have been slow to accept and apply computers to their work. Until recently, they often were not the direct users, but rather delegated others to operate the machines (Eason, Damordan, & Stewart, 1975). Whether this pattern of little direct use resulted from "technophobia" or lack of appropriate functions designed for management tasks is unclear, but managers have reported that finding appropriate computer applications has been difficult. Even with more computer power and flexibility, managers have found that computers often presented problems and that their use did not always suit the needs of managing work.

Other studies have found that managers use computers selectively and that their activities with computers affect the flow of information within entire organizations. Rockart and Treacy (1982) found that managers use computers to solve organizational problems through access to complete and current computerized data and analyze those data to solve problems and to make decisions (Stewart, 1981). Rockart and Treacy proposed that this shift in management use is occurring both because executives are now better informed about applying technological capability and because increasingly volatile and competitive business conditions are spurring them to develop new skills (Rockart & Treacy, 1982, p. 83).

Gutek and Bikson (1985) proposed that women organize around the potential of high technology and thereby strengthen their place within organizations. Women will learn that computers in management can be used for complex tasks, that managers are likely to get personalized training, and that the system is likely to be user-friendly. Managers have many opportunities to apply computers in more comprehensive ways than in staff workers' use.

Women managers, an important cohort of career women, are no doubt aware that the computer and other forms of high technology are current symbols of a manager's success (Forcht & Pearson, 1987). The power of computer and advanced communication systems to gather and analyze information provides great advantages to managers skilled in the use of these tools. "Those with a knowledge of current real-time information typically find themselves in a power position" (Forcht & Pearson, 1987, p. 10). Given these enticements, the new manager is likely to have a complex work station designed just for management tasks and will use the communication and computer systems to diagnose problems and to plan, communicate, and make decisions for organizing and supervising projects. Although managers also will need standard personal relations and organizational skills, professional advancement probably will require technological expertise and sophistication. This survey of career women's responses to high technology will provide a baseline from which to observe changes for women, the professions, and technology.

Technology and RGWW Women

Respondents to the current study reported extensive and varied use of technology (see Figure 3.1). Career women in this sample were more likely to report using computers than other office-related technological devices, but substantial proportions also are using word processors, programmable telephones, and "smart typewriters." In addition to using these

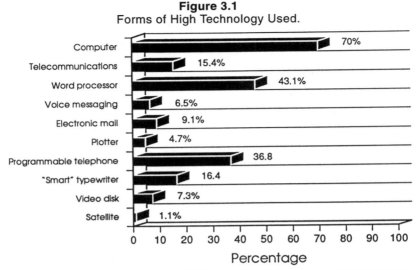

Figure 3.1
Forms of High Technology Used.

NOTE: Percentages total greater than 100% because respondents gave multiple responses.

standard forms of work-related high technology, some respondents do use such newer systems as voice messaging, plotters (e.g., for calculating and producing precise graphic material needed in engineering), and video disks (computerized visual communications that interact with the user). When asked to give the total number of high technology devices they use, 67% replied they used two to four devices, which was the modal category.

Respondents not only use a substantial number of high technology devices, but they also use them for many purposes. Although data storage tasks were the most frequent application, numerous other activities were reported (see Figure 3.2). Such diversity indicates the range of occupations in the sample, as well as participants' comfort with various high technology uses.

Using these devices has required respondents to acquire training: 61% (the mode) reported they had received from 1 to 6 months of training, a period neither negligible nor extensive. A combination of training methods was used most frequently; 37.2%, the sample mode, indicated they had used combinations of on-the-job training, self-instruction, and formal education in combination to acquire their high technology skills. The second most frequent response to the query on training source was the

Figure 3.2
Tasks Employing High Technology.

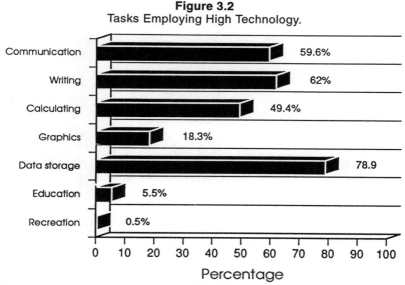

NOTE: Percentages total greater than 100% because respondents gave multiple responses.

sole use of on-the-job training (27.3%). Because many forms of high technology only recently have become generally available, training apparently has been a multifaceted process, managed at the same time that workers also are performing other functions.

Participants frequently had experience with and exposure to a variety of technological devices, as well as other kinds of office equipment, which may predispose them to use newer, more complex equipment. In fact, 33.8% reported having worked with standard forms of office machinery, such as typewriters, copy machines, banking equipment, or telephone switching systems. In addition, 41.9% of the respondents reported they have used machinery that is less standard to offices, such as stereo amplification systems and remote television communications, and 30.4% said they had used non-office equipment, such as farm machinery and scientific instruments. According to these findings, technology is not new to these women.

Against this background of technological use and preparation, the participants' positive attitudes toward high technology are understandable. When asked how high technology had influenced their work effectiveness, a large proportion of respondents (70.9%, the mode) said its effect was positive. A majority of respondents described their feelings about high technology as enthusiastic (63.9%, the mode), although 23.4% of participants reported cautious feelings about high technology.

Despite these positive interpretations, the exigencies of working circumstances may not support participants' optimism. Having access to technology is crucial to seeing its actual benefits, yet the modal response to the query about access to high technology indicates that only 40% have total access. The second most frequent response indicates that 32.4% have only moderate access. When the sample was asked how much effect high technology has on their incomes, the most frequent response (41.5%) was that it was not applicable; 20% reported that its effect was moderate. On the basis of the current power of high technology to boost effective professional practices, these findings suggest that positive attitudes may not be perceived as being directly related to work outcomes and remuneration.

The survey next asked how high technology was seen in relation to respondents' goals for their career paths. The questions on this section of the survey required written replies, a requirement that may have reduced substantially the number of responses to this section. The nearly 300 participants responding saw high technology as having varied effects, with no one effect drawing a majority of responses (see Figure 3.3). Some 28% indicated that high technology affects one's career path by boosting efficiency, but other replies were scattered. The 13.1% who agreed that high technology was not applicable to their career paths will receive further study in the analysis below because their collective experience frequently and consistently differed from that of the total sample.

Next the survey asked respondents to consider the overall effect of high technology on their career paths. The career women in this sample did not foresee a substantial effect. Although 26.8% saw high technology as integral to their work (the modal response), that proportion is smaller than expected. Furthermore, 21.7% reported that high technology had little effect on their achieved career paths, which is not surprising, considering that many participants in our study had established career patterns before the technology explosion.

Cross-tabulations were conducted to determine whether associations existed between technological effect and career experience. Variables influencing this measure include (a) user's demographic characteristics, (b) type of user's technological applications, and (c) user's feminist orientation.

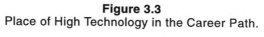

Figure 3.3
Place of High Technology in the Career Path.

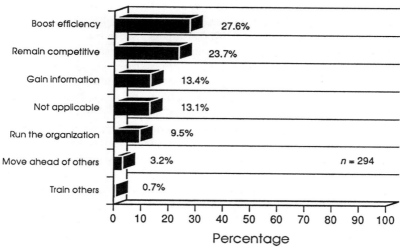

Age was considered to be a probable influence on users' attitudes toward and activities with high technology. In this research, that assumption was confirmed, as several differences were found between the 20 to 34 age group, as compared with the group 35 years of age and older. Younger women were more likely to be enthusiastic in their attitudes toward high technology (Cramer's $V = .17$, $N = 470$) and to say that the use of high technology would help them remain competitive (Cramer's $V = .16$, $N = 283$). They also were more likely to see high technology as having a strong effect on their income (Cramer's $V = .17$, $N = 283$) and as being an integral part of their job (Cramer's $V = .13$, $N = 200$). Although these associations are small, they show a trend that is consistent with my observations of people learning to use high technology.

Responses to work-related high technology also were affected by the respondents' occupation or job type. The occupations compared in cross-tabulations were business owner, administrator, manager, self-labeled professional, sales representative, and other.

A majority (64%) of the self-labeled professionals showed enthusiasm for high technology. Administrators showed the least enthusiasm and the most caution (Cramer's $V = .26$, $N = 461$). The self-labeled professionals had the most positive feelings about the effectiveness of high technology at work, while administrators and managers saw less effectiveness (Cramer's $V = .27$, $N = 437$). Two other trends showed positive reactions but did not produce notable associations. Many respondents (37.2%) perceived that high technology allows them to be efficient and productive, and, across job categories, respondents tended to perceive moderate/restricted access to work through knowledge of technology (modal response = 45.65%, $N = 435$). Respondents acknowledged little effect of high technology use on their income, with business owners and self-labeled professionals as those least likely to see a positive effect of technological use on work income.

In sum, persons in all work settings tended to express acceptance of high technology and to acknowledge its contribution to work effectiveness. Those who labeled themselves professionals tended to express more positive feelings, in contrast with administrators and managers, who were somewhat more negative. Respondents in all groups foresaw little effect on income, although they acknowledged that technology could affect career success if it contributed to work outcomes.

The user's application of high technology to her work is related to her attitudes toward technology. The number of devices used is related to the user's perceptions of the relationship of technology to career development; using four or more high technology devices correlates with assuming that technology aids career advancement, while those who applied one or none assumed that technology aids work productivity (Cramer's $V = .17$, $N = 251$). Those making the first assumption appear to see career development as venturesome enough to be linked with unusual work style (more technology); those making the second assumption appear to favor clear work outcomes (productivity) that can be accomplished by a more standard work style (less technology). Using four or more devices also was related to seeing high technology as having a positive effect on work (Cramer's $V = .16$, $N = 413$) and being enthusiastic about high technology (Cramer's $V = .14$, $N = 420$).

One subgrouping within the sample became clear as the analysis of responses to high technology proceeded. This subgroup of 13.1% ($N = 37$) of the total sample reported quite different reactions to high technology at work and perceived a different effect for their careers. This subgroup was analyzed separately from the total to determine what characterized this distinct response. Examining a "deviant case" can outline the typical pattern more clearly.

Whereas 63.9% of the total reported enthusiastic feelings about high technology, the subgroup reported a smaller mode (41.5%) as enthusiastic. The subgroup also was less likely to see the effectiveness of high technology for their work (70.9% total mode, 40% subgroup mode). The subgroup thought that high technology would have less effect on their income than did the total; 64.7% of the subgroup, compared with 41.5% of the total thought that high technology was not relevant to their incomes. The most substantial difference lies in the different perceptions of career effects: 73% of the subgroup thought that the effect of high technology on their careers was not clear, while 26.8% (mode) of the total sample reported high technology as integral to their work. Despite these more negative responses to high technology, the subgroup did report having slightly greater access to it. The mode of the subgroup was 41.2% having total access, while the mode of the total sample having total access was 40%.

The characteristics of the subgroup shed some light on the differing patterns just described. Participants in the subgroup were somewhat older than the total sample. Their modal age of 44 compared with a modal age of 35.6 for the total sample. However, the subgroup described their age as "young." In education and income characteristics, the subgroup did not differ from the total sample, but in type of work, the subgroup did tend to hold more autonomous positions than the sample as a whole. In the subgroup, 71.4% termed their work as "professional," as compared with 48.6% of the total, and a much smaller proportion of the subgroup (6.6%, compared with 22.7% of the total group) held administrative positions.

The combined effects of age and more independent work roles may have led this subgroup to different experiences with high technology, and thus to produce distinct responses. Alternatively the subgroup may have made a realistic analysis of their particular forms of work, which may be independent of technology, or they simply may have delegated technological tasks to other workers. The inclusive nature of this sample of career women makes certainty on these points impossible. The findings given in this section also report small but consistent observations of relationships between responses to high technology and feminist values. All five of the selected indicators of feminist values have associations with the ways women professionals expect high technology to influence career outcomes.

Women who identified themselves as feminists were more likely to see high technology as integral to their work, while others saw the effects of high technology as inapplicable or unclear (Cramer's $V = .10$, $N = 285$). Women who agreed with the feminist principle of equal pay for equal work were also more likely to see high technology as integral to the job; those who held nonfeminist values on comparable pay were more likely to say that high technology had no or little effect on their jobs (Cramer's $V = .13, N = 284$).

Women in this study who opposed the concept of separate jobs for men and women (a feminist position) were more likely to see high technology as advancing their careers, whereas women who did not hold that position tended to see high technology as enhancing their productivity (Cramer's $V = .10, N = 269$). A similar difference was discussed earlier: Some women did see high technology as a means to individual advancement, while others saw it as a tool for filling job requirements.

Taking the position that all workers should compete like men is opposed to the feminist principle of restructuring the workplace to accommodate the needs of both women and men workers. Women who held the feminist view were more likely to perceive high technology as having less effect on their incomes than did respondents who did not take the feminist view (Cramer's $V = .11, N = 271$). Women with this feminist value also had greater access to high technology (Cramer's $V = .10, N = 285$). Feminist values here may be associated with feeling less dependent on technology while also having access to it. Finally feminist subjects who disagreed with the traditional view that hard work brings success were more likely to see that high technology is integral to their job (Cramer's $V = .10, N = 282$).

Women with a feminist orientation were more likely than others to see high technology as a means of career advancement. A feminist orientation appears to include the valuation of technology as an important career asset, particularly where women see technology as integral to their work in an independent, rather than a required, way.

These findings refute popular wisdom by showing that women professionals are employing high technology and see it as a feature of their career paths. Although there are variations in the degree and kind of support according to age and occupational subgroup, the overall trend is optimistic. Older respondents and those holding the most autonomous jobs perceive high technology with less favor and have less application for it. Perhaps the career track already is established for these women, or they may hold such specialized positions that they do not require the linkages and analytical assistance of high technology.

Women who expressed feminist values tended to hold more forward-looking attitudes toward high technology and its effect on their careers. Such a venturesome attitude is well suited to these transitional times in which high technology and women professionals both are beginning to have substantial impacts on organizations and society.

Implications

The combined effects of high technology and the greater proportion of career women in the work world have the potential to produce new patterns of organizational processes. Women managers may find that advanced technologies can change the organization itself, because there are unintended social effects from computer use. If these changes occur, they may have particular benefits for career women in managerial and professional roles within the formal system.

Technology affects the way we use our time and, eventually, our thought habits as well (Kiesler, 1986). Kiesler observed that computer applications in large organizations have had a tendency to break down hierarchies because they override the old norms and structures of communication. Using electronic mail, accessing data directly instead of reading others' reports about the data, and having the opportunity to simulate possible project outcomes all tend to change old information channels and power arrangements. When such a shift in communication and data distribution occurs, new styles of work, organization, and management emerge.

One possible negative shift in policy that may occur with increased technological systems throughout the organization is the trend to "proletarianize" formerly middle-class occupations. Such a shift can occur as positions experience the "de-skilling" that technology often brings and can result in loss of power, whether or not the people involved are aware of these changes. When managers are part of this proletarianization, they may believe they are increasing management control over work, but they may, in fact, lose control if they are not aware of the potential of technology. Another negative aspect that becomes increasingly troubling as we consider ourselves to be partici-pants in a global community pertains to awareness of our complicity in the international division of labor that exploits women in the electronics industries, where women are underpaid and fall prey to disorders related to repetitive motion operations (Spivak, 1989).

Now that management, decision-making, and highly specialized soft-ware are available, middle management and professional positions may be automated as easily as other job levels. Although these technological power shifts may be seen as threats to those centered on "control," they also may be seen as a trend toward the empowerment of greater numbers within the organization that experiences this flattening of the hierarchy.

If technology is used to increase communication and alternative interactions within an organization, it may facilitate the new forms of management that are advocated for future productivity and personal growth of all workers, professionals and staff alike. Kanter (1983) observed that contemporary managers must see across organizational boundaries, focus on the task rather than on maintaining the existing formal system, and see people more than bureaucracy. Increased access to high technology would benefit such a management style.

Maccoby and Brooks (1986) foresee a management style in which managers facilitate teams, rather than channel directives. They see a management future that grows from negotiation toward evolving goals, a management process in which workers increase their knowledge and discretion in accordance with general objectives. These workers will have a "technoservice" orientation; drawing from their technical skills and backgrounds, they will provide service as an organizational outcome and as organizational style. Such an ideal organization also would apply high technology within its system to facilitate communication and flexible decision making.

Women who work in technological settings, perhaps at management and other professional functions, will find that organizations will be required to devise new plans for linking management, technology, and the expertise of specialists and professionals. From her research on women engineers, some of whom developed management careers, Bailyn (1987) predicted that role conflict and overall professional ambivalence about career development experienced by women technical professionals will be reduced when organizations restructure their expectations about women, technology, and organizational policies by encouraging flexibility and diversity.

Whatever model shapes future organizations, this research shows that career women appear to have a good start in using technology and considering it as a feature of their careers. Now is the time to confront personal and organizational restrictions against women's use of technology and also to question structures and processes that have worked against women and the values they would choose to apply with technology. The very definitions of women that have been justified by masculine science challenge women scientists and engineers to use their training for a critique and modification of technological fields (Schiebinger, 1987). Because women obviously are creating a place for themselves in areas that depend on skill with highly advanced technologies, the old arguments proclaiming women incapable of technological capability dissolve.

Advanced technology and the presence of feminists within organizations can contribute to the development of more humane outcomes through technological applications. Acquisition of technological literacy can give women greater access to career mobility and can empower them to make significant contributions to the organizations in which they serve. But the humane outcomes must be the product of active choices made by women, for technology also facilitates "command and control" organizational practices. Career women may discover that technological enthusiasm and skills may lead unexpectedly to the development of organizational options.

References

Bailyn, L. (1980). *Living with technology: Issues at mid-career.* Cambridge: MIT Press.

Bailyn, L. (1987). Experiencing technical work: A comparison of male and female engineers. *Human Relations, 40,* 299-312.

Dresselhaus, M. (1985). Reflections on women graduate students in engineering. *IEEE Transactions in Education, 4,* 196-203.

Eason, K. D., Damordan, L., & Stewart, T. F. M. (1975). Interface problems in man-computer interaction. In E. Mumford & H. Seekman (Eds.), *Human choice and computers* (pp. 91-105). Amsterdam: North-Holland.

Forcht, K. A., & Pearson, J. K. (1984). Women, science, and technology. *American Psychologists, 39,* 1183-1186.

Forcht, K. A., & Pearson, J. K. (1987). The personal computer: A management status symbol. *Data Management, 25,* 10-71.

Gutek, B., & Bikson, T. K. (1985). Differential experience of men and women in computerized office. *Sex Roles, 13,* 123-135.

Kanter, R. M. (1983). Women managers: Moving up in high tech society. In J. Farley (Ed.), *The woman in management: Career and family issues* (pp. 21-36). New York: Cornell University Press.

Kiesler, S. (1986). Thinking ahead: The hidden messages in computer networks. *Harvard Business Review, 64,* 46-60.

Lemkau, J. (1983). Women in male-dominated professions: Distinguishing personality and background characteristics. *Psychology of Women Quarterly, 8,* 144-165.

Lunsbury, R. D. (1978). *A study of behavior in organizations.* St. Lucia: University of Queensland Press.

Maccoby, M., & Brooks, H. (1986). Why management style has to change. *Research Management, 29,* 44-45.

Malcolm, S. M. (1985). Women in science and engineering: An overview. *IEEE Transactions in Education, E-28,* 190-195.

Parrish, J. B. (1986). Are women taking over the professions? *Challenge, 28,* 54-58.

Rockart, J., & Treacy, M. E. (1982). The CEO goes on line. *Harvard Business Review, 60,* 62-88.

Schiebinger, L. (1987). The history and philosophy of women in science: A review essay. *Signs: Journal of Women in Culture and Society, 12,* 305-332.

Spivak, G. (1989). The political economy of women as seen by a literary critic. In E. Weed (Ed.), *Coming to terms: Feminism, theory, politics* (pp. 218-229). New York: Routledge.

Stewart, T. F. M. (1981). The specialist user. In B. Shackel (Ed.), *Man-computer interaction: Human factor aspects of computers and people* (pp. 457-483). Rockville, MD: Sijthoff & Noordhoff.

Turkle, S., & Papert, S. (1990). Epistemological pluralism: Styles and voices within the computer culture. *Signs: Journal of Women in Culture and Society, 16*(1), 128-157.

Wilder, G., Cooper, D. M., & Cooper, J. (1985). Gender and computers: Two surveys of computer-related attitudes. *Sex Roles, 13,* 215-228.

Zimmerman, J. (1983). *The technological woman: Interfacing with tomorrow.* New York: Praeger.

4 Mentor: Career Women and Supervision

A participant in the RGWW study described the review process by which her supervisor evaluates her: "We have an annual conference in which my supervisor reviews my performance in relation to the role description for my job. It is a very formal occasion, and I always get good ratings, but because it is the only time he ever acknowledges that I make a contribution, I never feel good about it. I wish he appreciated my work." Another woman noted: "I get good evaluations and I am evaluated by explicit criteria. Still, I like to exceed the job expectations. That's how I know I'm a professional." Although both women place importance on their supervisor's evaluation, neither conveys the impression that the supervisor is as motivating as she might wish. Both comments create the impression of a strained supervisory relationship. On the other hand, the participant who said, "My supervisor and I set my performance goals and we frequently assess my progress in meeting and changing them to meet new challenges," conveys respect for her supervisor and enthusiasm for her work.

Popular career literature abounds with advice to women concerning the importance of networking, mentoring, and sponsorship in their career advancement. In their personal testimonials, women often relate career success to the encouragement they received from supervisors and administrators. Many women and minorities have entered administrations with the specific goal of increasing opportunities for the women and minorities who follow them into organizational culture. Some of the companies most committed to the nurturance of diversity in the workplace and to the advancement of women have established training programs to encourage supervisors to pay special attention to the career development of women and minorities and to redefine advancement paths to increase access to the opportunity structure.

Knowing how important supervisory relationships can be in shaping careers, Brooke Collison set out to determine how the career women in this study viewed their supervisory relationships. He wanted to discover how much influence participants thought their supervisors exercised on their performance and advancement and how satisfied or rewarded they were in those relationships. He also wanted to know whether perceptions of supervisory relationships differed according to the gender and age composition of the supervisor-supervisee partnership. Collison's findings are equally provocative for supervisors and for supervisees, suggesting ways in which we can both provide and receive more intentional assistance with career advancement and with the creation of a gender-positive organizational climate.

BROOKE B. COLLISON

Several years ago, a good friend in middle management in a large professional firm told me of his concern about dilemmas facing male supervisors with increasing numbers of new young professional women entering the mostly male firm. His dilemma: How did one supervise a new female professional?

The existing supervision model had been in operation for years—recruit new professionals carefully, train them intensively, evaluate them severely, give them increasingly responsible tasks, and the few who remained after several years would succeed in the firm. The others, who could not take the competition, the severe evaluation, or the other job strains incumbent in the firm's success rituals, would have made a good decision to leave.

My friend was not pleased with the system that existed for males, but it had worked over the years and had resulted in a group of survivors in the firm who were achievement oriented and tough minded. The inhumaneness of the system was moderated by its obvious success, as measured by the typical productivity standards.

The new group of females presented a different situation. In particular, the "project evaluation" component bothered him. Typically a junior person was assigned a project, instructed, and left alone. At the completion of the project, it and the junior professional were subject to an intense, scathing review filled with criticism and threat, but also filled with instruction and praise. Even though the junior person might have made errors, even lost money (or made less than could have been expected), there was a sense in the evaluation that mistakes were forgiven in view of a "next time." The end project evaluation might contain personal ridicule (e.g., "I don't see how any stupid college graduate could make such a ridiculous error"), but always there was the implication that the junior professional would move on to a more responsible project armed with a new, painful learning that had come from the evaluation experience.

The problem was that no one was willing to do the same thing with the new female professionals. Their evaluation sessions tended to be kind, supportive, much less intrusive, forgiving, certainly not profane, and much less specific. As a result, my friend observed that new males in the firm were advancing with additional knowledge, while new females were maintaining an entry level knowledge. More seriously, when placed in positions of increased responsibility, new female professionals were more vulnerable because of the lack of "hard" instruction that the males were gaining through their baptisms of fire. Women's failures were occurring at higher levels of operation, where it was more costly to the company and themselves. The diagnosis was that they had missed some essential learning that accrued to the males through their fiery crucible evaluations.

In the absence of a different model of evaluation and review, my friend confessed that, although painful, it had worked; but the same could not be done with females. It would tear them up. "I couldn't handle it if they would feel bad, and I know that most of the partners would feel the same way."

Thus my interest in supervision was born. The questions are simple: Is there a best model of supervision? Is any one model more appropriate for any of the four supervisor and subordinate gender combinations? What are the accurate and the erroneous assumptions made about supervisor-subordinate behaviors based on gender? How can the workplace be enhanced through supervisor relationships?

History

Progress certainly has been made since Donald and Eleanor Laird (1942) wrote *The Psychology of Supervising the Working Woman*. The only reason to look at the book today is to have a marker point from which to measure progress. Chapter titles such as "Adjusting Work to Woman's Brain Power" make one want to open the cover cautiously. The volume does contain points of historical significance, however, including the efforts of General Frances E. Spinner, who petitioned President Abraham Lincoln in 1862 to use women workers, even though

Spinner's rationale was that they could do certain work (using large shears to cut the new paper money issued by the government) better than men and that, furthermore, they could be employed for the same job as men at half the wage.

Various war efforts, with their subsequent increases in women's work force participation, have resulted in the clear demonstration of women's abilities in the workplace. Their skills as supervisors and as subordinates are now unquestioned.

The Situation

Many aspects of supervision are similar to other dimensions of social interaction. To that extent, the stereotypes and assumptions that people make about men or women in general permeate work and supervision situations. Some of those assumptions may improve supervisor-subordinate relationships; others may impede effectiveness or satisfaction.

Studies of supervision have focused on differences in the way men and women evaluate others, how they evaluate themselves, how much influence they are seen to have in the workplace, the way they reward or punish worker behaviors, the degree that workplace support may influence health conditions and life satisfaction, and to what they attribute success or failure.

Supervision studies are fraught with the difficulties of laboratory versus workplace research. Although workplace studies may have more relevance, the control of variables is difficult, at best, and often is such that generalizations cannot be made. Osborn and Vicars (1976) concluded that where leaders and subordinates are involved in long-term, ongoing, real-life situations, there is a consistent absence of differences between male and female leaders. Recently attention has been given to research emphases and methods for the study of women in management (Doyle, 1990) and gender-based differential supervision in education (Shakeshaft, Nowell, & Perry, 1992), and it is common to see articles describing how to attract and retain women in the business environment (Thornburg, 1991). More of the supervision studies in current literature reflect concerns about sexual harassment than about differential styles of supervision that might be gender based.

Attribution

Studies by Deaux and Emswiller (1974) have shown that men frequently attribute their success to ability, while women attribute their success to hard work, good luck, or ease of the task. Failure, however, often is attributed to lack of ability for women, while for men it may be attributed to bad luck, task difficulty, or lack of effort. In the work setting, if a supervisor makes typical sex-typed assumptions about male and female workers, he or she may respond to workers in very different ways for the same worker behaviors.

Evaluation

Supervision always implies some worker evaluation. Supervisors tend to evaluate subordinates lower than subordinates rate themselves (Shore & Bleicken, 1991), and women supervisors tend to have a more accurate view of how their subordinates would evaluate them than do male supervisors (London & Wohlers, 1991). Studies have indicated that men generally are evaluated more favorably than women in many situations (Nieva & Gutek, 1980). Other studies have pointed out that men distribute rewards to workers based on a norm of equity and that the size of the reward is correlated with the degree to which individuals contribute to group performance. Women leaders typically distribute rewards based on a norm of equality, with the size of the reward independent of the degree to which individuals contribute to group performance. Dobbins (1985) conducted laboratory studies to point out that male leaders were equally supportive of men and women subordinates, while female leaders were more supportive of women than men subordinates. His studies also support the conclusion that male supervisors respond to poor performance with equity, while women use a norm of equality; that is, they are as likely to punish or train subordinates who perform poorly because of lack of effort or lack of ability. Dobbins speculated that women supervisors, operating from their typically socialized posture of wanting harmony, use the equality response to minimize status differences in the workplace. Men, however, may prefer equity response because they are taught to value achievement, performance, and contributions to team accomplishment. Rubner (1991) cited results of Gallup surveys to indicate that both men and women prefer male supervisors. He further stated that a rise continues in the number of women who are supervisors and speculated that older, less educated workers will be uneasy with that condition.

Support

It is logical to believe that social support is a necessary requisite to a healthy life. Various researchers have suggested that health and well-being are influenced positively by adequate social support. Further, it has been assumed that males benefit mainly from work-based sources of support, whereas females rely on family and nonwork sources. Furilier, Ganster, and Mayes (1986) studied workers in three job settings—a police department, an electrical contracting firm, and a construction firm—and concluded that social support does have beneficial effects on health outcomes. More women than men reported receiving social support from supervisors. Women and men were equal in support received from co-workers or from family and friends. The data indicated that support from supervisors had the strongest positive effect on job satisfaction but less effect on life satisfaction. For men, nonwork sources of support were associated with increased life satisfaction and decreased depression, whereas work-based sources of support appeared to be more helpful for women with regard to anxiety.

Influence

A supervisor who is seen as having power and influence is judged to be a better supervisor than one who appears to lack either power or influence. The socialization processes for men and women have implications for the acquisition of power, the use of power, and the perception of power or influence (or the lack of it) by others merely because of their gender. Ragius and Sundstrom (1990) found that subordinates rated male and female managers similarly on power dimensions of reward, legitimate, expert, and referent power. Female managers were rated higher than male managers on expert power, and female subordinates rated male managers lower on expert power. Self-confidence and social influence were studied in a simulation by Instone, Major, and Bunker (1983), who observed that men and women supervise others similarly when they have equal access to power resources. They pointed out that there is a general lack of empirical evidence for gender differences in social influence behavior but that, in general, highly self-confident individuals are more likely to exercise influence, become personally involved, and use persuasive strategies in leadership or supervision situations. Women in their studies reported less self-confidence in their ability to effectively supervise their workers than did men and, subsequently, tended to make fewer influence attempts and to use a more limited range of influence strategies than did their male counterparts.

When workers see that their manager has influence (e.g., the ability to do something for the workers), they tend to be more satisfied with their jobs, regardless of manager gender (Trempe, Rigny, & Haccoun, 1985). Because manager gender may be associated falsely with degree of influence, gender has been identified by Trempe et al. as a proxy variable.

A related influence study was conducted by Sherman, Ezell, and Odewahn (1987), who obtained data from 187 subjects in three different industrial settings. Supervisor-supervisee pairs reflected all possible gender combinations, with the results indicating that female employees perceived that they were delegated less authority or influence in decisions affecting their work than were men. Females also perceived that their supervisors, either male or female, had greater influence in decisions regarding their work than was indicated by male subordinates. To complicate this finding, females saw that they had less influence over their jobs but felt more responsible than males for the mistakes they made.

Shore and Bleicken (1991) and Shore and Thornton (1986) pointed out that the literature generally indicates that subordinates' self-ratings are higher than those of their supervisors. Their own studies indicated that those differences are not gender specific when the tasks are familiar tasks in a real work setting in which performance feedback is available. When performance criteria are ambiguous, however, women tend to be more likely than men to underestimate their performance.

Age

An additional protected class are older workers. To the surprise of O'Brien, Robinson, and Taylor (1986), female supervisors were found to be more unfavorable in their evaluation of older employees than were male supervisors. Other studies have shown that supervisors, as a group, demonstrate less favorable attitudes toward older employees, regardless of the supervisor's age, than do rank-and-file workers, even though older workers may outperform young workers and be more reliable in terms of attendance, punctuality, and the like. The unfavorable attitude about older workers has not changed over time, as indicated by a 30-year replication study of Bird and Fisher (1986). In a study with supervisors from the public and private sector (O'Brien et al., 1986), the public sector supervisors were more objective in their evaluation of older workers, even though the gender differences that were noted (female supervisors had less favorable attitudes toward older workers) were counter to much of the literature in the field. The authors speculated that female supervisors, having overcome obstacles and prejudices to gain their positions, may set higher standards for all of their employees, not just the older ones.

Job Socialization

How a new worker "learns the ropes" in a new job is an important process in becoming an "experienced" worker. Job socialization has been discussed by some persons who have written about mentoring. Posner and Powell (1985) found that the gender of the individual supervisor did not appear to have a difference in either the perceived availability or helpfulness of various socialization opportunities. In fact, an unexpected result of studying 84 women and 134 men after 8 to 10 months into new jobs was that women reported more mentor or sponsor relationships than did men. A second difference in the subjects was that men reported more business travel in the same period. The mentor results were somewhat different from those reported in work by Deaux (1976), in which male first-level supervisors reported experiencing better relationships and receiving more task approval from their male managers than their female counterparts.

Trust

An ideal supervisor-supervisee relationship would involve a good deal of trust. Obviously supervisors need to trust those they supervise, and trusted supervisors would be viewed as more powerful and helpful persons by those supervised. Scott (1983) examined supervisor trust through a study of a large number of county extension workers in the Midwest. He found that respondents reporting to someone of the same gender had significantly higher trust in their superior than did men or women reporting to someone of the opposite sex. An additional finding was that people assign more challenging tasks to same-sex persons, believing there will be less conflict with someone of their own sex. This finding certainly has implication for equitable assignment of work in a large group. Rubner (1991) used Gallup data to show that most workers see their supervisors as fair and honest.

The Current Study

Participants in the RGWW study responded to five specific questions about supervision. A total of 387 women responded to questions asking them whether they were supervised by a male or a female, how many males and females they themselves supervised, whether they were treated fairly by their supervisor, whether they learned job skills from their supervisor, and whether their supervisor helped them advance professionally.

Responses to the supervision questions were analyzed by using Chi-square contingency tables. Variables used in analysis were gender of supervisor, number of males or females supervised, age of respondent, reported income, educational level, and type of job. Where significant differences ($p < .05$) were observed, additional three-way analyses were performed to help understand the results.

Most of the respondents were supervised by males. A total of 282 (73.4%) had male supervisors; 102 (26.6%) reported having female supervisors, slightly lower than numbers reported by Rubner (1991) for a national sample.

Most respondents indicated that their supervisors treated them fairly. Further, no significant differences were found in the fairness responses when analyzed by gender of supervisor; however, age of the respondent did make a difference in the fairness question, with older respondents seeing supervisors as slightly less fair than did younger respondents. No differences in the fairness question were observed when analyzed by number of persons supervised, income, education, or type of job of the respondent.

Although 72% of the participants agreed that their supervisor treated them fairly, only 65% of participants aged 40 to 49 agreed that they were treated fairly, whereas 85% of those aged 20 to 29 agreed. Of participants over age 40, 16% disagreed with the statement (see Table 4.1).

An assumed part of a supervisor's role would be to assist workers with advancement. Of the 384 respondents who marked this item, 62% of those supervised by a female agreed that they would be assisted in professional advancement (see Table 4.2). Only 47% of those super-

Table 4.1

Supervisor Fairness Analyzed by Age of Subject

Age	Agree 1	2	3	4	Disagree 5	TOTAL	(%)
20-29	34	22	6	2	2	66	[17.1]
30-39	65	41	22	10	11	149	[38.5]
40-49	50	15	17	16	2	100	[25.8]
50-60+	32	19	11	6	4	72	[18.6]
TOTAL	181	97	56	34	19	387	
(%)	[46.8]	[25.1]	[14.5]	[8.8]	[4.9]	[100]	

NOTE: Chi-square (12, N = 387) = 22.268, p = .03.

vised by a male agreed that their supervisor would assist them with professional advancement.

In view of the age differences observed in the analysis of the first question on fairness, additional analyses were performed on the item "My supervisor will help me advance professionally," examining response by age and by gender of supervisor (see Table 4.3).

The younger the respondent supervised by a male, the more likely she was to see her supervisor as assisting her with professional advancement. The percentage agreeing dropped from 71% among the 20-29-year-old group to 43% among those over 50.

Table 4.2

Supervisor Helps With Advancement

Supervisor	Agree 1	2	3	4	Disagree 5	TOTAL
Male (73.4%)	81	53	68	40	40	282
Female (26.6%)	31	33	17	10	11	102
TOTAL (100%)	112	86	85	50	51	384
(%)	[29.2]	[22.4]	[22.1]	[13.0]	[13.1]	[100]

NOTE: Chi-square (12, N = 387) = 22.268, p = .03.

Table 4.3
Supervisor (Male) Helps With Advancement

Age	Agree 1	2	3	4	Disagree 5	TOTAL	(%)
20-29	22	13	6	3	5	49	[17.4]
30-39	26	22	35	15	13	111	[39.4]
40-49	18	11	12	15	15	71	[25.2]
50-60+	15	7	15	7	7	51	[18.1]
TOTAL	81	53	68	40	40	282	[100]
(%)	[28.7]	[18.8]	[24.1]	[14.2]	[14.2]	[100]	

NOTE: Chi-square (12, N = 282) = 24.2363, p = .02.

When the responses were analyzed by age of respondent, it was found that respondents saw supervisors in a very different light in terms of the degree to which they learned skills from them (see Table 4.4).

A generalization would be that only young women indicated they were learning job skills from their supervisors. The 40-49-year-old age group indicated the lowest agreement with the question (18%), compared with the 20-29-year-old age group, where 46% agreed that they learned job skills from their supervisor. Supervisor gender made a

Table 4.4
I Learn Skills From My Supervisor

Age	Agree 1	2	3	4	Disagree 5	TOTAL	(%)
20-29	13	17	14	12	9	65	[17.1]
30-39	19	19	38	28	44	148	[38.8]
40-49	11	7	22	28	33	101	[26.5]
50-60+	7	9	10	10	31	67	[17.6]
TOTAL	50	52	84	78	117	381	[100]
(%)	[13.1]	[13.6]	[22.0]	[20.5]	[30.7]	[100]	

NOTE: Chi-square (12, N = 381) = 31.7747, p = .001.

Table 4.5
Skills Learned, Analyzed by Supervisor (Male) and by Age

Age	Agree 1	2	3	4	Disagree 5	TOTAL	(%)
20-29	10	13	13	7	6	49	[17.5]
30-39	12	13	29	22	35	111	[39.6]
40-49	9	3	13	21	25	71	[25.4]
50-60+	7	6	6	7	23	49	[17.5]
TOTAL	38	35	61	57	89	280	[100]
(%)	[13.6]	[12.5]	[21.8]	[20.4]	[31.8]	[100]	

NOTE: Chi-square (12, N = 280) = 32.3881, p = .001.

difference in their analysis, with nonsignificant differences observed for female supervisors (see Table 4.5).

Discussion

It is not surprising that the majority of women respondents were supervised by males. Because of the cross-sectional nature of the data, it is not possible to indicate whether the numbers represent a change from previous data. Nor is it possible to indicate whether the tendency to have a male or a female supervisor is changing even though current statistical data indicate an increase nationally in the female supervisor pool (Rubner, 1991; Thornburg, 1991).

It is somewhat reassuring to note that a majority of the women who responded indicated that their supervisors treated them "fairly"; however, nearly 14% of the respondents disagreed with the fair treatment question. The older the respondent, the more likely she was to perceive unfair treatment from her supervisor, regardless of supervisor gender, perhaps accurately reflecting the differential view that supervisors have of older workers (Bird & Fisher, 1986; Rubner, 1991).

Only 18% of those participants in the 40-49-year-old age group thought they were treated fairly. Additional study and analysis are needed to identify the treatment that is labeled as "unfair." In view of other literature cited in this chapter, it would be interesting to know whether women who saw their supervisors as unfair also saw them as having little influence and as providing little job feedback or evaluation.

Participants saw women supervisors as more likely than men supervisors to assist with job advancement. This finding is in keeping with literature indicating that greater trust is placed in same-sex supervisor pairs. Trust is a logical component of a mentoring relationship in which job advancement would be a part. At the same time, it is somewhat discouraging to note that 26% of the respondents did not agree that their supervisor would assist them with advancement. This finding places the woman respondent in a somewhat isolated situation in terms of her own career development.

The age-related outcome of the responses concerning supervisors as a source of job skill acquisition is not surprising. One would expect younger workers to be in a learning mode. Older workers might be more likely to be in established positions where job skills have already been acquired. What is surprising is the striking finding that the respondents who saw their supervisors as sources of skill training were young women with male supervisors. Perhaps women supervisors are more gender fair and age fair in some respects than are men.

Recommendations

Supervisors should know that workers, especially women, need to understand job expectations and need specific feedback on performance. It should not surprise supervisors that workers place more trust in same-sex supervisors, but they should not assume that different-sex supervisor-supervisee relationships are dysfunctional. In fact, the most critical element in the relationship may be the assumed power or influence that workers see in their supervisor. To see that women are recruited and retained in the work force, companies need to address the issues that are both subtle and obvious barriers (Rosen, Miguel, & Pierce, 1989; Thornburg, 1991).

Supervisors should examine their own behavior in learning what they do to indicate their willingness to assist their employees in the acquisition of new skills or preparation for advancement. In addition, supervisor behavior can be significant for workers in terms of their own perception of job performance (satisfaction) and their own sense of health and well-being. Support for both job and personal well-being is critical for workers. Supervisors can provide degrees of support in both situations.

References

Bird, C. P., & Fisher, T. D. (1986). Thirty years later: Attitudes toward the employment of older workers. *Journal of Applied Psychology, 71,* 515-517.

Deaux, K. (1976). *The behavior of women and men.* Monterey: Brooks/Cole.

Deaux, K., & Emswiller, T. (1974). Explanation of successful performance on sex-linked tasks: What is skill for the male is luck for the female. *Journal of Personality and Social Psychology, 29,* 80-85.

Dobbins, G. H. (1985). Effects of gender on leaders' responses to poor performers: An attributional interpretation. *Academy of Management Journal, 28,* 587-596.

Doyle, W. (Ed.). (1990). Women in management [Special issues]. *Journal of Business Ethics, 4 & 5.*

Furilier, M. R., Ganster, D. C., & Mayes, B. T. (1986). The social support and health relationship: Is there a gender difference? *Journal of Occupational Psychology, 59,* 145-153.

Instone, D., Major, B., & Bunker, B. B. (1983). Gender, self-confidence, and social influence strategies: An organizational simulation. *Journal of Personality and Social Psychology, 44,* 322-333.

Laird, D. A., & Laird, E. C. (1942). *The psychology of supervising the working woman.* New York: McGraw-Hill.

London, M., & Wohlers, A. J. (1991). Agreement between subordinate and self-ratings in upward feedback. *Personnel Psychology, 44,* 375-390.

Nieva, V. F., & Gutek, B. A. (1980). Sex effects on evaluation. *Academy of Management Review, 5,* 267-276.

O'Brien, F. P., Robinson, J. F., & Taylor, G. S. (1986). The effects of supervisor sex and work environment on attitude toward older employees. *Public Personnel Management, 15,* 119-130.

Osborn, R. N., & Vicars, W. M. (1976). Sex stereotypes: An artifact in leader behavior and subordinate satisfaction analysis? *Academy of Management Journal, 19,* 439-449.

Posner, B. Z., & Powell, G. N. (1985). Female and male socialization experiences: An initial investigation. *Journal of Occupational Psychology, 58,* 891-895.

Ragius, B. R., & Sundstrom, E. (1990). Gender and perceived power in manager-subordinate relations. *Journal of Occupational Psychology, 63,* 273-287.

Rosen, B., Miguel, M., & Pierce, E. (1989). Stemming the exodus of women managers. *Human Resource Management, 28,* 475-491.

Rubner, M. B. (1991). More workers prefer a man in charge. *American Demographics, 3,* 11.

Scott, D. (1983). Trust differences between men and women in superior-subordinate relationships. *Group and Organizational Studies, 8,* 319-336.

Shakeshaft, C., Nowell, I., & Perry, A. (1992). Gender and supervision in school personnel. *Education Digest, 57*(6), 14-17.

Sherman, J. D., Ezell, H. F., & Odewahn, C. A. (1987). Centralization of decision making and accountability based on gender. *Group and Organizational Studies, 12,* 454-463.

Shore, L. M., & Bleicken, L. M. (1991). Effects of supervisor age and subordinate age on rating congruence. *Human Relations, 44,* 1093-1105.

Shore, L. M., & Thornton III, G. C. (1986). Effects of gender on self- and supervisory ratings. *Academy of Management Journal, 29,* 115-120.

Thornburg, L. (1991). Working toward change. *HR Magazine, 36*(6), 52-55.
Trempe, J., Rigny, A. J., & Haccoun, R. R. (1985.) Subordinate satisfaction with male and
    female managers: Role of perceived supervisory influence. *Journal of Applied
    Psychology, 70,* 44-47.

5 Perceptions of Equity: Career Women and Discrimination

The root of all evil, the key to happiness, the primary motivator of human behavior? Much of what we know about money is from the perspective of the men who, mythology notwithstanding, have controlled it throughout history. Flo Hamrick decided to study women's relationship to money, specifically their satisfaction with their salaries in relation both to their own skills and experiences and to the salaries of men in similar positions.

Her results are interesting. A comment written in a margin of the questionnaire summarizes an attitude that pervades participants' responses to her questions: "When I'm ready to look for a new job, more money won't keep me here. In the meantime, I don't think I'm too dreadfully underpaid as non-profit executives go. I make enough to live reasonably well, and I like what I do." Although better paid than most of the study's participants, this woman's attitude toward money is shared by many who were less well paid but appear to agree that salary is not their primary career motivator. Another woman wrote, "I'm not just working for money, but for personal growth and achievement." The participants recognize the intangible rewards of their work, even as they seek appropriate tangible rewards and pursue economic equity in the workplace. Some also recognize that being well paid is not the same as being an equal player in the work force. "Although I have equal pay," wrote one participant, "I do not have equal decision-making roles. Since I am the only female on the professional staff, I am permitted to supervise programs, but not people." Apparently, power, rather than money, is the last bastion of male privilege.

Hamrick's findings also underscore the importance of pay scale to the development of women's attitudes toward traditional values, work satisfaction, feminism, and social change, as well as to women's perceptions about their own experience of sex discrimination; that is, women who are relatively well paid and are paid commensurately with their male peers are less cognizant of sex discrimination and less interested in activism on behalf of women than are those who are under- and incommensurately paid. Yet, because money does provide some freedom, well paid women are also less cautious about exercising woman-identified options, such as flex time and leave policies, than are less well compensated women.

Hamrick's study raises important questions about the role of financial comfort in women's levels of social conformity and interest in feminist activism. Although American society has a history of underpaying women—at its best so far, in 1990, the rate of women's pay as compared with men's was only 65 cents on the dollar—it may be that such a strategy not only ensures women's (and children's) poverty but also fuels the women's movement.

Her study also highlights the costs to women's lifetime earnings of interrupting careers for childbearing and child rearing. As women fulfill the social mandate to reproduce, they disadvantage themselves and threaten their own independence. This effect is exaggerated for the growing number of women who are required to rear their children alone.

FLO HAMRICK

Throughout my youth and years of education, I was aware of gender-based salary inequities because they were detailed in research reports, news broadcasts, and articles in popular magazines. As I began my first full-time job, I was nonetheless taken aback when I discovered that a male colleague with the same job title, education level, and experience level was paid more than I. The reason given for the disparity was a common one: his responsibility for his family's financial support. As my career evolved to include many years of counseling college graduates about career choice and placement issues, evidence of inequities surfaced both in numerical compilations of salary offers on a national scale and in the stories of male and female students with whom I worked. Through constant exposure to this apparently enduring social reality, I became interested in exploring not only women's salary levels and perceptions but also their work-related experiences. Participation in the Research Group on Women and Work afforded me a chance to explore these issues, and that exploration is the substance of this chapter.

Numerous studies have documented the inadequacy of women's pay as compared with men's pay. The Bureau of the Census reported that in 1986, women earned 62 cents for each dollar earned by men (Bureau of the Census, 1989), up slightly from the 59-cent figure made famous in the early days of the current women's movement. Figures for 1990 indicate a current level of 65 cents (Bureau of the Census, 1992). Issues of women's pay adequacy and comparability to men's pay are critical because remuneration typically is related to levels of responsibilities within an organization or industry. Issues directly related to wage disparity include the "glass ceiling" phenomenon, which exists when women are present in entry to middle levels but not within the highest ranks of an organization (Morrison, White, & Van Velsor, 1987). According to a recent Market Opinion Research Company survey, women account for about 50% of entry-level managers, about 25% of middle managers, and only a small percentage of upper management ("You've come a long way," 1984). Although slight progress has been documented recently, examples of industries in which women typically have not achieved the highest organizational positions include accounting (Pillsbury, Capozzoli, & Ciampa, 1989), telecommunications (Wexler, 1988), investment banking (McGoldrich & Miller, 1985), advertising (Hill, 1987), finance (Quinn, 1987), science (Sharma, 1987), and general management (Devanna, 1987; Gallese, 1989; Loden, 1987). Given this national pattern of disparate pay and underrepresentation of women in positions of responsibility, it was critical to study salary, work satisfactions, and discrimination experiences of women participating in this study.

For the purposes of this study, *salary perceptions* is defined as a respondent's view of her salary's relationship to her own skills and experiences, as well as its relationship to salaries of men in similar positions. These responses correlate to participants' reported life experiences and philosophies, including the interruption of career for childbearing, a perceived struggle for promotions or respect, and a belief that more opportunities might be available for males. Grouped salary responses also correlate with responses to items measuring attitudes toward supervisory experiences and feminism.

Because rank and salary alone may not account for the primary sources of work satisfaction, respondents were presented with generative questions regarding other types of work satisfaction to provide additional insight into women's perception of career rewards. The discussion of discrimination focuses on both the incidence and contexts of the participants' work-related discrimination experiences. Response percentages to the various items (rounded to the nearest whole number) are presented with selected correlations. Statistical significance noted throughout is reported at the .05 or higher level. Statistically significant results in this chapter, determined through the use of Pearson's r, were judged by using an alpha level of .05.

Commensurate Salary Perceptions

When asked whether their current salaries were commensurate with their skills and experiences, the majority of participants reported an

Figure 5.1
Salary Perceptions.

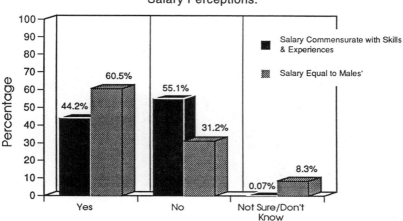

inverse relationship of their pay to their abilities: 44.2% of all respondents indicated that their salaries were commensurate, 55.1% believed that their salaries were not commensurate; and less than 1% were unsure (see Figure 5.1). Younger women were significantly more likely to indicate commensurate salaries than were older women (see Figure 5.2). A majority (51.4%) of women aged 30 to 39 believed that their salaries were commensurate, as did 49.3% of women aged 20 to 29. However, much smaller percentages of women older than 40 shared this perception. Three quarters of women over 60 were paid salaries that they believed inadequately rewarded their skills and experience.

The higher the individual income of respondents, the more likely they were to report a commensurate salary: 48% of those reporting commensurate salaries earned $30,000 or more, while 83% of those reporting inadequate salaries earned less than $30,000. Respondents' perceptions of salaries also were influenced by achieved educational level and type of education. Women with some college course work, an associate or bachelor's degree, or a graduate professional degree in law or medicine reported commensurate salaries more often than did those with a high school diploma or less, or those with a master's degree or a PhD (see Figure 5.4).

Survey participants were more or less dissatisfied with their salary adequacy according to their job type. Participants reporting higher

Figure 5.2
Salary Perceptions by Age of Respondent.

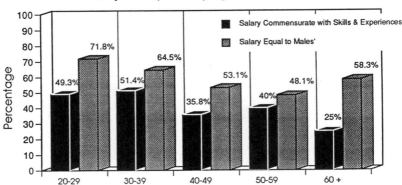

percentages of satisfaction than the 44% average for all participants included administrators (47.2%), clerical workers (50%), and business owners (68.4%). Survey participants indicating noncommensurate salaries at percentages higher than the 55% overall rate were professionals (56%), managers (62%), salespersons (62%), production workers (67%), and "other" (64%) (see Figure 5.5).

Participants' length of tenure did not seem to influence whether salaries were perceived as commensurate (see Figure 5.6A and Figure 5.6B). No difference was found between salary perception of the 44% of the sample who had been at current levels of work for 3 or more years and the 24% who had been in their current job for 1 year or less. These women had not "grown into" adequate salary levels. Additionally job change by itself did not seem to provide a more commensurate salary. Women who had changed jobs recently were no more likely than those with long tenure to report commensurate salaries.

Women with greater numbers of female peers at work were more likely to report inadequate salaries than those with fewer female peers ($p < .05$); 51% of women with no female peers at work reported inadequate salary levels; 62.5% with 20 or more female peers reported inadequate salaries (see Figure 5.7). As experienced by these survey participants, a workplace with many women at the same levels of work significantly correlates with noncommensurate salary levels.

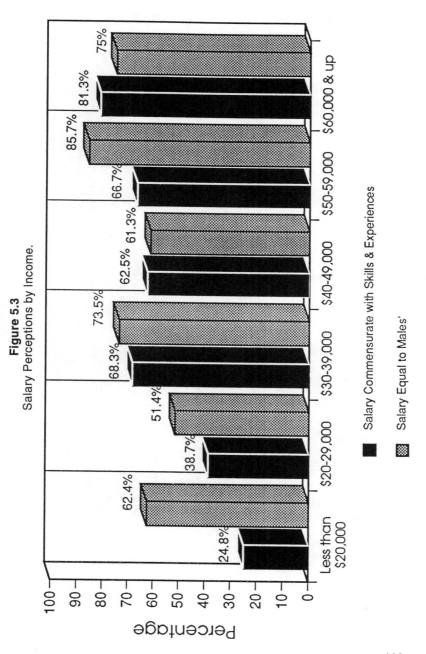

Figure 5.3
Salary Perceptions by Income.

■ Salary Commensurate with Skills & Experiences

▒ Salary Equal to Males'

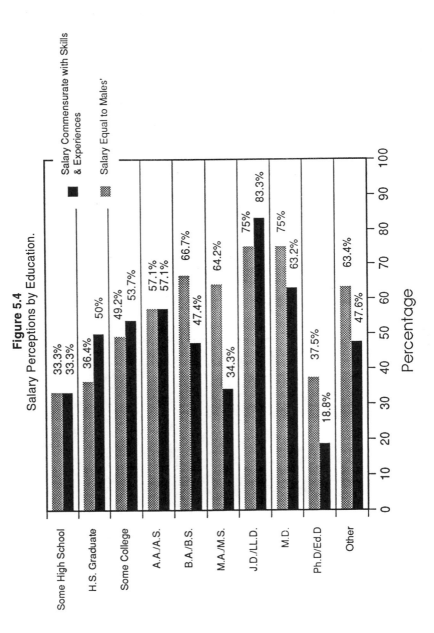

Figure 5.4
Salary Perceptions by Education.

Salary Commensurate with Skills
& Experiences

Salary Equal to Males'

Percentage

Some High School
H.S. Graduate
Some College
A.A./A.S.
B.A./B.S.
M.A./M.S.
J.D./LL.D.
M.D.
Ph.D/Ed.D
Other

33.3%
33.3%
36.4%
50%
49.2%
53.7%
57.1%
57.1%
66.7%
47.4%
64.2%
34.3%
75%
83.3%
75%
63.2%
37.5%
18.8%
63.4%
47.6%

Figure 5.5
Salary Perceptions by Job Type.

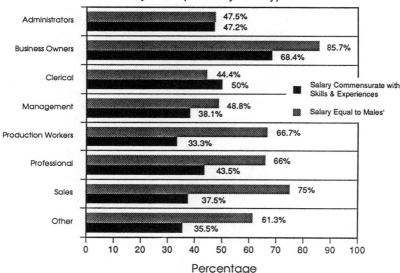

Participants in the study also were asked questions concerning their perception of career interruption related to child rearing, questions concerning their struggle for respect and promotions, and questions concerning their perceptions of job opportunities as a function of their gender. Respondents who had interrupted their careers for children were significantly more likely than those who had not to report noncommensurate salaries. Among persons who interrupted work to accommodate children's needs, 40% reported commensurate salaries, contrasted with the 49% of participants who did not experience this career interruption ($p < .05$). Whereas 53% of participants with commensurate salaries reported a past or current struggle for promotion, 72% of respondents with noncommensurate salaries reported this struggle ($p < .001$). Respondents who perceived themselves to be inadequately paid also perceived advantages for males in the current work force: 43% of respondents with commensurate salaries, as contrasted with 64% of those without commensurate salaries, agreed that more opportunities would be available if they were male ($p < .0001$).

Figure 5.6A
Salary Perceptions by Tenure at Present Job Level.

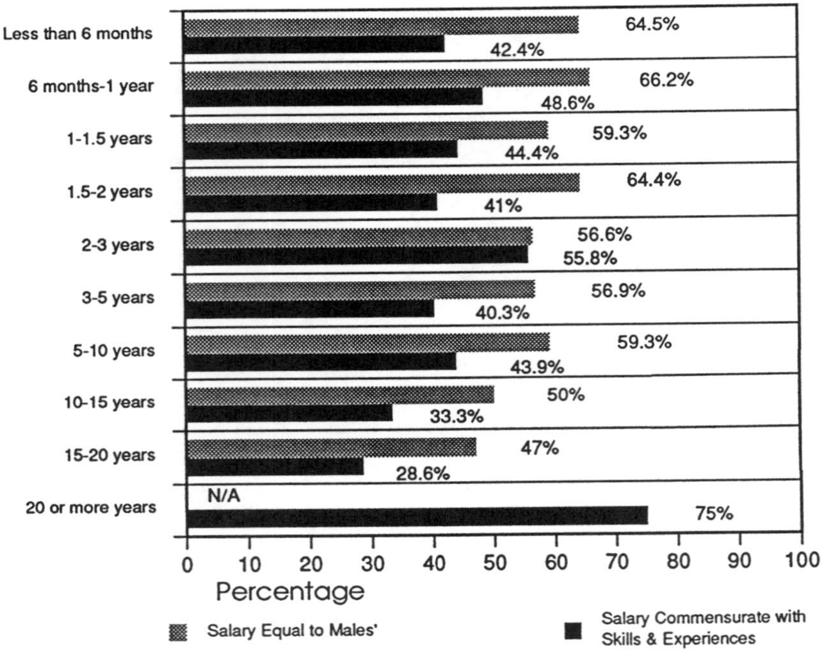

Less than 6 months	64.5%	42.4%
6 months-1 year	66.2%	48.6%
1-1.5 years	59.3%	44.4%
1.5-2 years	64.4%	41%
2-3 years	56.6%	55.8%
3-5 years	56.9%	40.3%
5-10 years	59.3%	43.9%
10-15 years	50%	33.3%
15-20 years	47%	28.6%
20 or more years	N/A	75%

Percentage

░ Salary Equal to Males'   ■ Salary Commensurate with Skills & Experiences

Equal Salary Perceptions

Several studies have indicated incomparable pay between male and female workers as a problem in various industries, including credit unions (Fredrickson & Condon, 1986), public relations (Lukovitz, 1989), and corporate marketing (Jung, 1988). When participants in this study were asked whether their current salaries were equal to those of males in the same occupation doing the same or equivalent work, 60.5% of survey respondents reported that their salaries were equal to men's salaries, 31.2% reported that their salaries were not equal to their male peers' wages, and 8.3% were not sure how their salaries compared (see Figure 5.1).

As was true in the case of commensurate salaries, more younger than older respondents perceived their salaries as equal to those of males (see Figure 5.2): 71.8% of respondents younger than age 30, but only 51%

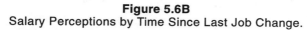

Figure 5.6B
Salary Perceptions by Time Since Last Job Change.

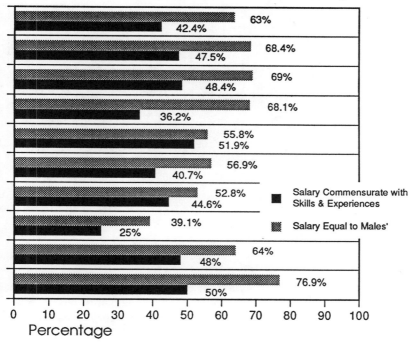

aged 50 and above, perceived their salaries to be equal to those of male counterparts ($p < .01$). Older subjects also tended to be less sure of the comparability of their salaries with those of men: 13% aged 50 and above were not sure whether their salaries were equal; only 4% of subjects younger than 30 were unsure. Given these figures, we perhaps could assume more idealism on the part of younger women regarding the adequacy and equity of their salaries. We also could interpret these data to mean that a gender gap in salaries increases with age or promotion. The existence of a salary gap is supported by studies of men and women in science careers (Smith, LaPlante, Angiolillo, & Cantrell, 1989) and in the packaging industry (Ashton, 1988). Although we also could view these data as indicating evidence of growing equity of

Table 5.7

Salary Perceptions by Number of Female Work Peers.

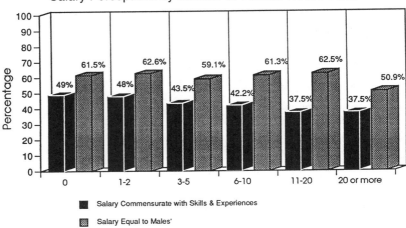

■ Salary Commensurate with Skills & Experiences

▨ Salary Equal to Males'

salaries beginning with today's younger workers, comparative census data from 1970 to 1990 do not support such a conclusion. The percentage change in median income during those years did not approach parity between women and men workers (Bureau of the Census, 1992).

Respondents with both the highest and the lowest individual incomes agreed strongly that they were paid equally to males in similar jobs (see Figure 5.3). Respondents earning $50,000 to $59,000 agreed most strongly (85.7%) that parity existed; but 62.4% of the group earning less than $20,000 believed that their salaries were equal to those of men in their occupations. Respondents with salaries in the middle range of $20,000 to $29,000 perceived a salary gap at a rate higher than the overall 61% equal-salary response. Only 51.4% of respondents earning $20,000 to $29,000 indicated that their salaries were comparable to those of males.

In this population, education level correlates with salary equity only up to a point. The majority of degreed respondents, with the exception of those holding doctoral degrees, were more likely to report equal salaries (see Figure 5.4), whereas respondents at the high and low ends of the education range were more likely to report unequal salaries. Unequal salaries were reported by women with some high school or a high school diploma, some college course work, or a PhD/EdD. Although women and men in the same or similar occupations are now more likely to have the same median level of education, salary levels in business are still not equal (VonGlinow & Mercer, 1988).

Participants' perceptions of salary equity with male counterparts did not seem to be affected greatly by type of job. Women representing different job types tended to reflect the overall majority response of general salary equity with male peers (see Figure 5.5). Business owners showed the highest percentage (85.7%) of affirmative response. Clerical workers were most unsure (33%) of salary comparability with male peers, which is not surprising, considering the underrepresentation of men in clerical work.

Although the difference is not statistically significant, respondents with shorter tenure at their present job levels were slightly more likely to report salaries comparable to men's (see Figure 5.6). Among respondents who had been at their current level 2 years, between 59% and 66% reported receiving comparable salaries. Among respondents with much longer tenure (10 through 20 years), only between 47% and 50% reported comparable salaries. Respondents who changed jobs more recently were also slightly more likely to indicate receipt of salaries equal to those of male counterparts. Respondents with salaries comparable to men's generally had experienced shorter tenure at jobs with different work settings. In these women's experiences, longevity at one level had not resulted in equitable pay.

Participants in this study in work settings with fewer than 20 female co-worker peers were slightly more likely to earn salaries comparable to men's, although the difference is not statistically significant (see Figure 5.7). Between 59.1% and 62.6% of participants in work settings with fewer than 30 female peers reported receiving equal salaries, whereas only 50.9% of those with more than 20 female peers reported comparable salaries.

Respondents reporting salaries comparable to men's were significantly less likely to have interrupted their careers for childbearing and child rearing (see Figure 5.8): 66.3% of women who did not experience this interruption reported equal salaries, but only 50.5% of the women who interrupted their careers for children reported equal salaries ($p < .05$).

Also, 44.1% of women with equal wages perceived that they did not have to struggle for respect or promotions in their occupations, whereas 77.6% of women with unequal salaries reported experiencing this struggle ($p < .0001$) (see Figure 5.9). A majority of respondents with per-

Figure 5.8
Career Interruption for Children by Salary Perceptions.

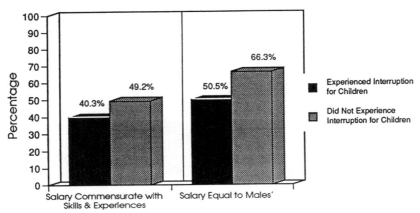

ceived unequal salaries acknowledged the advantage of being male in today's work force. In fact, 71.2% of respondents with unequal salaries believed they would have more opportunities if they were male. Among respondents with salaries equal to those of males, 44.4% believed they would have more opportunities if they were male.

Dissatisfaction with current salary is an obvious motivation for considering a job change. Respondents were asked whether they would stay in their current position or seek other work if their current salaries were raised. In response, 62% of the overall sample indicated they would stay, whereas 37% indicated they would seek another position. Additionally 21 respondents (4%) indicated in comments that they were looking continually for other opportunities. Respondents' perceptions of their salaries correlate significantly with the hypothetical stay-or-seek decision (see Figure 5.10). Specifically 60% of the respondents with commensurate salaries and 62.4% with noncommensurate salaries reported they would stay if their salaries were raised; 57.3% of those who earned salaries equal to men's and 66.7% with unequal salaries would stay if their salaries were raised ($p < .05$). Regardless of current salary perceptions, most respondents would stay in their current positions if their salaries were raised. However, because a pay raise may not

Figure 5.9
Salary Perceptions by Selected Success Attitudes.

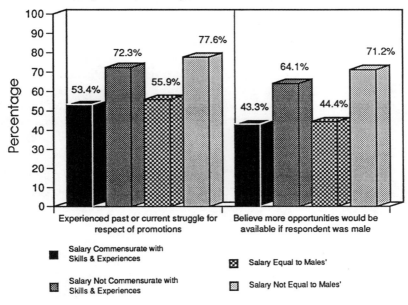

Figure 5.10
Salary Perceptions by Remain in Current Job If Salary Raised.

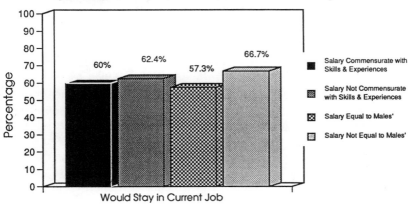

be a sole factor to be considered in this decision, other factors influencing work satisfaction were sought.

Nonremunerative Work Satisfactions

Satisfaction with one's salary can be a primary indicator of work
satisfaction, but other factors also may play a role. Women respondents
who were dissatisfied with their salaries were asked to specify other
factors that are attractive about their current jobs (see Table 5.11). Half
of all survey participants responded with one or more of the following
factors or strategies.

More than 41% of these respondents cited the nature of their current
work as a positive consideration, suggesting that they like what they do
and consider it to be important. Also, 18.8% indicated that although
current conditions may not have been satisfactory, they anticipated
promotions or raises in the long run and planned to stay in their present
settings to reap these eventual rewards. Just 10% pointed out the
short-term nature of their current work level, indicating that they were
waiting and preparing for better opportunities; 15.7% provided responses assigned to the "my job is better than nothing" category,
responses that indicate not only dissatisfaction with work but also
personal issues such as burn-out or low self-confidence.

Just over 4% cited current supervision as a reason for staying, and
6% cited other positive work relationships with co-workers, customers,
and others. Nearly 25% of these respondents cited generally unspecified
internal or personal reasons for remaining in their current jobs. Geo-
graphic location was a factor for 6% of the respondents. These last two
factors may suggest issues that influence work decisions, such as
accommodation to a dual-career relationship or other family situations.
Around 2% reported feelings of obligation to the company or work site
as contributing to the decision to continue in the current position.

Perceptions of Supervisors

At least one work relationship—the supervisor-supervisee relationship—may correlate with perceptions not only of work satisfaction but
also of fair treatment with regard to salary. Respondents' perceptions of
their supervisors were generally positive and are reported in more detail

Figure 5.11
Nonremunerative Work Satisfactions.

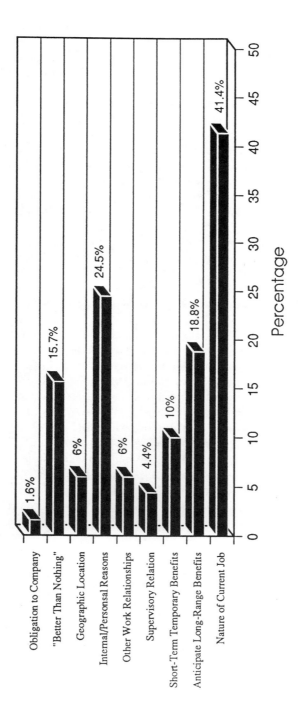

in another chapter (see Chap. 4). However, respondent perceptions of supervisors also significantly correlate with perceptions of their own salaries (see Figure 5.12).

Persons with commensurate salaries were significantly more likely to agree that their supervisor treats them fairly and assists with their professional advancement. Almost 82% of respondents with commensurate salaries believed they were treated fairly ($p < .0001$), and 62% agreed their supervisor would help them advance professionally ($p < .0001$). Persons with salaries equal to those of males also expressed these impressions of their supervisors: 80.1% with equal salaries believed they received fair treatment from their supervisors ($p < .0001$), and 57.5% anticipated supervisory assistance with advancement ($p < .001$).

When respondents were asked whether they learned job skills from their supervisors, they generally gave negative or neutral responses. Significantly, the most disagreement came from those respondents who were paid neither equally nor commensurately: 60% with inadequate salaries and 61% with unequal salaries indicated they did not learn skills from their supervisor.

The gender of the respondent's supervisor had little direct correlation with respondents' perceptions of the equity of their salaries (see Figure 5.13). Among respondents supervised by males, 59.6% reported an equal salary and 32% reported an unequal salary, while 59.2% of those respondents reporting to females believed they were paid equally and 32% did not. These figures closely parallel the overall rate of respondents with equal pay (61%) and those without (31%).

Women in this study who were supervised by females were slightly less likely than women supervised by males to believe that their salaries were commensurate with their skills and experiences. Among all respondents, 44% believed that their salaries were commensurate, and only 45.8% of respondents with male supervisors believed that their salaries were commensurate, whereas 33.7% of respondents with female supervisors believed that their salaries were commensurate.

Discrimination

Literature in this field suggests that discrimination based on gender affects women's access to specific types of jobs and work settings, as well as their achievement of subsequent promotions and salary gains (Dubno, 1985). To test these propositions,[1] respondents in this study

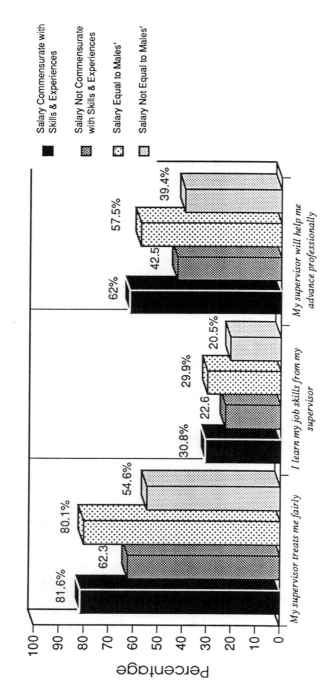

Figure 5.12

Salary Perceptions by Attitudes Toward Supervisor.

115

116

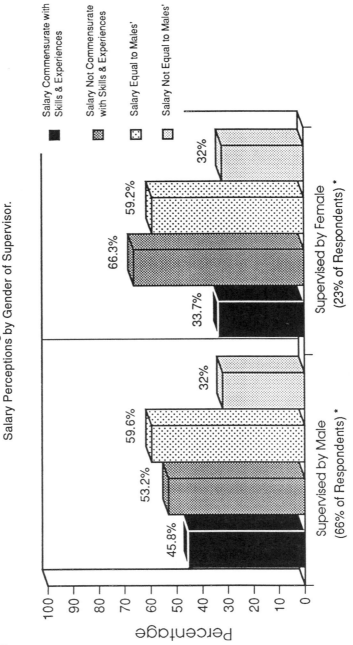

Figure 5.13
Salary Perceptions by Gender of Supervisor.

NOTE: *11% of respondents did not report to a supervisor.

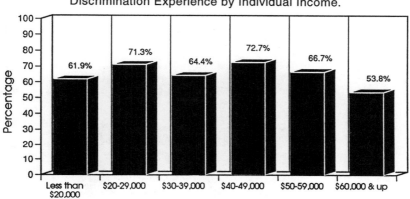

Figure 5.14
Discrimination Experience by Individual Income.

were asked whether they had experienced gender discrimination and, if so, to specify the context of the discrimination and any action they took in response.

Two thirds (66%) of the sample indicated they had experienced gender discrimination, and the general experience of discrimination appears throughout all demographic categories. Women in the highest income group ($60,000 and above) experienced discrimination less often than women earning less income. However, between 61.9% and 72.7% of women in the remaining income categories also had experienced discrimination (see Figure 5.14).

Respondents with college degrees reported experiencing discrimination at a higher rate than women without college degrees, but the difference is not statistically significant (see Figure 5.15). Respondents with bachelor's, master's, law, and doctoral degrees were more likely to report experiencing discrimination than were respondents with education below and through the associate degree level, and, interestingly, with medical degrees. In this study, associate degree graduates reported the fewest discrimination experiences (28.6% of AA/AS graduates), and law degree graduates reported the most discrimination experiences (78.6% of degree holders). Marital status was not a factor: 66% of unmarried respondents and 66% of married respondents reported having experienced discrimination.

Perhaps surprisingly, job type does not seem to correlate strongly with discrimination experiences (see Figure 5.16): 84.1% of the managerial

Figure 5.15
Discrimination Experience by Education.

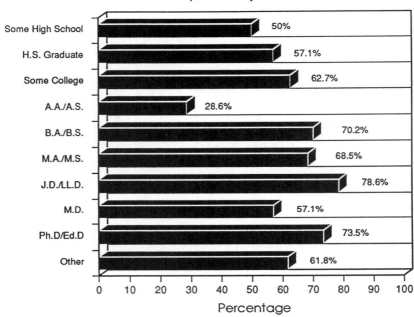

women in the sample had experienced discrimination, as had 80% of clerical and sales workers. Even among women in the job category with the least occurrence of discrimination—business owners—the majority of respondents (57.5%) had experienced discrimination.

Respondents who had experienced discrimination were asked to indicate the context or contexts of discrimination experiences, and one or several could be noted by each respondent (see Figure 5.17): 36% of the respondents noted discrimination in salary level, which compares relatively closely to the overall 31% of respondents who thought their salaries were not equal to those of male counterparts.

Respondents cited achievement of promotions and assignment to challenging work as problem areas, however. Indeed 22% reported they did not receive equitable and challenging tasks, and 21% reported discrimination in promotions. These last two figures may relate closely because a person's visibility in carrying out responsibilities often directly relates to supervisory notice and opportunities for promotion

Figure 5.16
Discrimination Experience by Job Type.

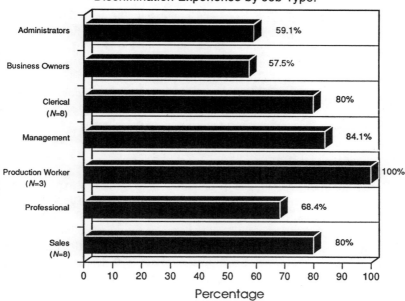

Figure 5.17
Contexts of Discrimination Experiences.

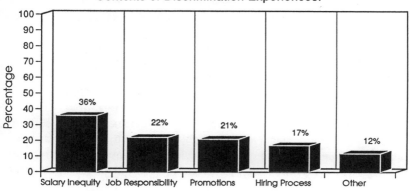

NOTE: More than one response could be checked.

(Mai-Dalton & Sullivan, 1981). Gender discrimination, therefore, can play a role in creating or maintaining the "glass ceiling" found by many women workers. Other studies have noted that the practice of using creative job titles for women avoids line promotions and that the persistent perception of women as secondary earners helps mask essentially discriminatory practices (Stephan, 1987).

Only 17% of participants in this study indicated that selection processes leading to hiring had entailed discriminatory episodes. In contrast to findings in other studies, access to a work setting or entry into a position did not seem to present a problem to these participants. Other experiences, including lack of cooperation, feeling left out, blatant harassment, and propositioning were cited by 12% of respondents (Loudermilk, 1987).

Given the high percentages of personal discrimination experiences, as well as the general discussion of discrimination as an issue, it is clear that sex discrimination is a pattern among the women in this study. As stated above, 66% of the total sample had experienced one or more episodes of sex discrimination. However, 76% of the overall sample had discussed the issue of sex discrimination only with friends or family. Respondents apparently see the issue as relevant and timely, with friends and family members providing the most common forum for discussion. Only 30% of the respondents had discussed sex discrimination (either as an issue or as a specific incident) with their employers, and only 7% had held discussions with a government agency or representative regarding their discrimination experiences.

A coping mechanism found by other researchers is the decision by women to "play by the rules" and ignore or live with discrimination (Williams, 1988). Loudermilk (1987) found that research participants, when asked to give advice to female college students preparing to enter the work force, advised them to "expect it," and/or to "ignore it (you can't fight it)." Some respondents in Loudermilk's study reported that, through displays of competence, they avoided sex discrimination. The hypothetical college students also were advised to pick up hints through selection and hiring processes, to examine the organizational climate, to seek support and solidarity with other women in the work setting, and to familiarize themselves with legal recourse (including documentation of incidents, confrontation, and channels of appeal). The overall message was to face the reality of discrimination, but not always to fight it (Loudermilk, 1987).

Discrimination and Salary Levels

Although the majority of respondents had experienced discrimination, persons who perceived themselves as earning noncommensurate or unequal salaries were significantly more likely to report having experienced discrimination than were those with commensurate or equal salaries (see Figure 5.18). Just over 56% of respondents with commensurate salaries reported having experienced discrimination, as did 76.1% of respondents with inadequate salaries ($p < .0001$). Among respondents with salaries equal to those of men, 58.1% had experienced discrimination, while 84.3% of respondents with unequal salaries had experienced discrimination ($p < .0001$).

Some of the various contexts of discrimination also correlate with salary perceptions (see Figure 5.19). Respondents with perceived inadequate salaries encountered discrimination much more frequently than respondents with perceived commensurate salaries. Salary discrimination was the major problem reported by inadequately salaried women (44% of all respondents): 45.2% of inadequately salaried respondents believed they had been subject to salary discrimination, while 28.9% of all adequately paid respondents considered themselves to have been affected by salary discrimination ($p < .001$).

Promotions and job responsibilities provided the next most frequent contexts of discrimination for inadequately paid respondents. Just over 26% of these respondents believed they had been given inappropriate job responsibilities, compared with 18.9% of women with commensurate salaries. And 28% of respondents with inadequate salaries thought they had not received fair promotions, while 14.7% of respondents with commensurate salaries indicated discrimination in this area ($p < .001$). Discrimination through the selection and hiring process was experienced by 20.5% of women with inadequate salaries and by 15% with adequate salaries. "Other" additional contexts of discrimination (described above) were experienced by 12.6% with inadequate salaries and by 12.1% with commensurate salaries.

Among women with unequal salaries, 21.2% reported selection and hiring discrimination. Inequitable delegation of responsibility was reported by 25.8% of women with unequal salaries ($p < .05$). The two most prevalent problem areas in discrimination for unequally paid women were in promotions and, predictably, compensation: 35.6% of unequally paid women encountered promotion discrimination, while 14.2% of equally paid women experienced that problem ($p < .0001$). The greatest

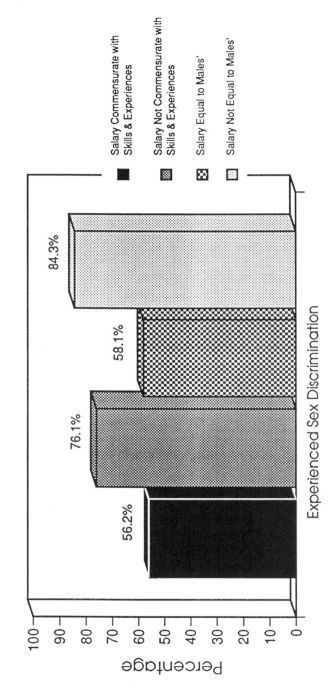

Figure 5.18
Salary Perceptions by Discrimination Experience.

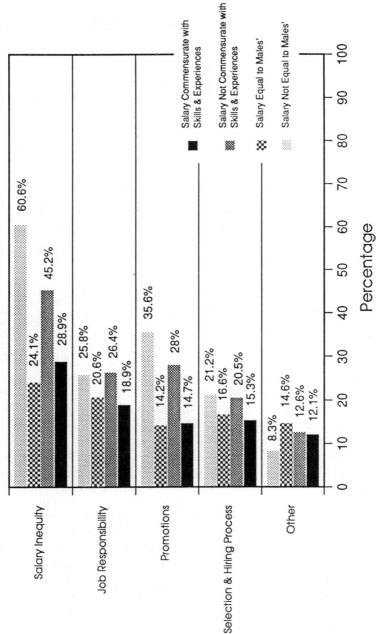

Figure 5.19
Salary Perceptions by Context of Discrimination.

123

difference between the groups of unequally and equally salaried women lies in their experience of salary discrimination: 60.6% of those unequally paid experienced, and attributed the wage inequality to, salary discrimination. Although 31% of the entire sample believed they were not paid on a par with men in the same or similar jobs, 24.1% of that group reported having experienced salary discrimination ($p < .0001$).

Women in the study who received unequal compensation were the most frequent recipients of the types of sex discrimination discussed above, but there are "other" types of sex discrimination that participants with equal salaries are subjected to more often than their unequally salaried counterparts. Respondents were given the opportunity to provide "other" contexts of discrimination, and examples generated were typically extreme, as in extremely subtle (lack of cooperation) or extremely flagrant (blatant harassment). Indeed 15% of respondents with equal salaries cited one or more experiences of these "other" types of discrimination, and 8% of unequally paid women cited such experiences ($p < .05$).

Attitudes Toward Feminism

Because issues of pay adequacy for women and equal compensation for both genders typically are identified as goals of feminism and the women's movement, salary perceptions were also correlated with items dealing with feminist identification and attitudes (see Chap. 2). Women with salaries commensurate with their skills and experiences were significantly less likely to identify themselves as feminists and more likely to define feminism negatively. In fact, 69.9% of respondents reporting noncommensurate salaries, but only 55.4% reporting commensurate salaries identified themselves as feminists ($p < .01$). About 75% of inadequately paid women provided positive definitions of feminism, but only 66.2% of adequately paid women supplied positive definitions of feminism ($p < .05$) (see Figure 5.20).

The equality of a woman's salary to a man's salary does not, however, correlate strongly with respondents' identification as feminists: 65.2% of respondents with equal salaries and 62.8% of respondents with unequal salaries identified themselves as feminists. Additionally the vast majority of both groups identified feminism positively. Over 87% of respondents with equal salaries and 92.2% of those with unequal salaries gave positive descriptions of feminism.

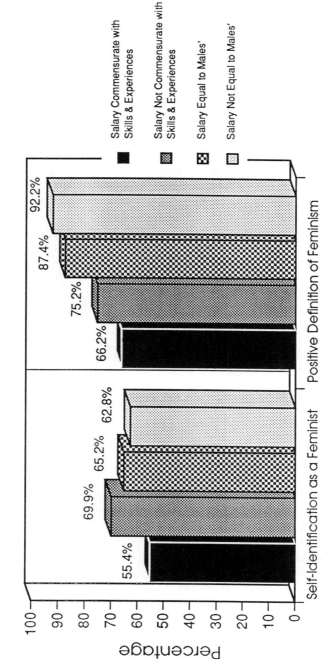

Figure 5.20
Salary Perceptions by Feminist Identification and Evaluation.

125

Commensurate Pay and Feminist Attitudes

Although respondents with commensurate salaries did not strongly identify with feminism directly, women with inadequate salaries took the lead in expressing feminist principles dealing with the inequities of work and family (see Table 5.1). In response to 20 items designed to gauge their views on feminist issues, these participants were more likely than those with commensurate salaries to question traditional family values and were less optimistic about an individual woman's ability to succeed through her individual effort. For the sake of clarity, I group responses into simple "agree" and "disagree" categories in the text discussion. Full dimensionality of the 5-point Likert scale responses, however, is presented in the tables corresponding to this section. The reported statistical significance was established by using the full range of responses and not through the use of the collapsed agree and disagree categories.

General attitudes of inadequately paid respondents concerning pay equity, as gauged by the items cited in Kitch's (Chap. 2) survey of feminist attitudes dealing with equal pay for equal work and comparable pay for comparable work, were primarily feminist in response. Perhaps due to their personal experience of being underpaid, however, inadequately paid women believed most strongly in equal pay for equal work (99.2%) and comparable pay for comparable work (96.7%, $p < .0001$). Although 98.4% of commensurately paid women agreed with the equal pay for equal work item, only 86.1% extended their agreement to include comparable work.

As discussed earlier, women with inadequate salaries were significantly more likely to have experienced sex discrimination than were women with commensurate salaries. Those women were also significantly more likely than their better paid peers to agree that all women have been subjected to sex discrimination in their lives (93.5%). A smaller majority of women with commensurate salaries (85.5%) agreed that all women have been subjected to sex discrimination ($p < .0001$). The vast majority of all respondents overwhelmingly supported the right of women to have access to all types of education and jobs. Within this majority, women with insufficient salaries were even more likely than women with sufficient salaries to support the right of access ($p < .01$).

Women with insufficient salaries were more likely than women with sufficient salaries to dispute traditional values associated with marriage and children, although the majority of respondents supported these

text continued on page 130

Table 5.1
Commensurate Salary by Feminist Attitudes
(With Original 5-Point Likert Scale Data)

	Commensurate Salary		Insufficient Salary	
	Agree	**Disagree**	**Agree**	**Disagree**

1. Men and women should receive equal pay for equal work.

Agree	**Disagree**	**Agree**	**Disagree**
98.4%	1.5%	99.2%	0.8%

Commensurate Salary	Insufficient Salary
93.8% Completely Agree	96.3% Completely Agree
4.6% Partially Agree	2.9% Partially Agree
0.0% Neutral	0.0% Neutral
1.0% Partially Disagree	0.0% Partially Disagree
0.5% Completely Disagree	0.8% Completely Disagree

2. All workers should receive comparable pay for work of comparable worth. ($p < .0001$)

Agree	**Disagree**	**Agree**	**Disagree**
86.1%	18.7%	96.7%	2.0%

Commensurate Salary	Insufficient Salary
72.2% Completely Agree	85.2% Completely Agree
13.9% Partially Agree	11.5% Partially Agree
5.2% Neutral	1.2% Neutral
7.2% Partially Disagree	1.6% Partially Disagree
1.5% Completely Disagree	0.4% Completely Disagree

3. Most women have been subjected to sex discrimination at some time in their lives, whether they know it or not. [$p < .0001$]

Agree	**Disagree**	**Agree**	**Disagree**
85.5%	8.2%	93.5%	3.2%

Commensurate Salary	Insufficient Salary
58.2% Completely Agree	75.1% Completely Agree
27.3% Partially Agree	18.4% Partially Agree
6.2% Neutral	3.3% Neutral
6.7% Partially Disagree	2.4% Partially Disagree
1.5% Completely Disagree	0.8% Completely Disagree

4. Certain jobs should be reserved for women, just as certain jobs should be reserved for men.

Agree	**Disagree**	**Agree**	**Disagree**
19.7%	73.1%	18.0%	75.1%

Commensurate Salary	Insufficient Salary
9.3% Completely Agree	7.8% Completely Agree
10.4% Partially Agree	10.2% Partially Agree
7.3% Neutral	6.9% Neutral
16.1% Partially Disagree	15.9% Partially Disagree
57.0% Completely Disagree	59.2% Completely Disagree

5. Women's special duties in the family require them to commit less time and energy to their careers than men do.

Agree	**Disagree**	**Agree**	**Disagree**
35.0%	59.3%	37.1%	54.3%

Commensurate Salary	Insufficient Salary
7.2% Completely Agree	9.9% Completely Agree
27.8% Partially Agree	27.2% Partially Agree
5.7% Neutral	8.6% Neutral
18.6% Partially Disagree	19.3% Partially Disagree
40.7% Completely Disagree	35.0% Completely Disagree

6. Women's activist groups have helped to improve things for working women.

Agree	**Disagree**	**Agree**	**Disagree**
72.3%	8.8%	75.1%	11.1%

Commensurate Salary	Insufficient Salary
28.2% Completely Agree	32.7% Completely Agree
44.1% Partially Agree	42.4% Partially Agree
19.0% Neutral	13.9% Neutral
6.2% Partially Disagree	7.8% Partially Disagree
2.6% Completely Disagree	3.3% Completely Disagree

Table 5.1
Continued

	Commensurate Salary		Insufficient Salary	
	Agree	Disagree	Agree	Disagree
7. Working women would be better off if feminist groups would discontinue their efforts to attain greater rights for women. [p < .01]	17.4%	60.0%	11.9%	72.2%
	3.6% Completely Agree 13.8% Partially Agree 22.6% Neutral 22.6% Partially Disagree 37.4% Completely Disagree		2.9% Completely Agree 9.0% Partially Agree 15.9% Neutral 24.9% Partially Disagree 47.3% Completely Disagree	
	Agree	Disagree	Agree	Disagree
8. Women should be able to obtain education in any field and to enter any field in the work world. [p < .01]	97.4%	1.5%	99.1%	0.4%
	84.1% Completely Agree 13.3% Partially Agree 1.0% Neutral 0.5% Partially Disagree 1.0% Completely Disagree		93.0% Completely Agree 6.1% Partially Agree 0.4% Neutral 0.0% Partially Disagree 0.4% Completely Disagree	
	Agree	Disagree	Agree	Disagree
9. In order to improve conditions for women with careers, vast changes will have to be made in the structure of the family.	58.7%	24.8%	68.1%	18.8%
	17.5% Completely Agree 41.2% Partially Agree 16.5% Neutral 18.6% Partially Disagree 6.2% Completely Disagree		22.0% Completely Agree 46.1% Partially Agree 13.1% Neutral 12.7% Partially Disagree 6.1% Completely Disagree	
	Agree	Disagree	Agree	Disagree
10. A career woman's best friend is her house-keeper or babysitter.	46.4%	29.3%	37.2%	3.2%
	14.4% Completely Agree 32.0% Partially Agree 24.2% Neutral 14.9% Partially Disagree 14.4% Completely Disagree		12.0% Completely Agree 25.2% Partially Agree 30.6% Neutral 13.2% Partially Disagree 19.0% Completely Disagree	
	Agree	Disagree	Agree	Disagree
11. A career woman's best friend is her non-sexist husband.	89.6%	3.2%	88.1%	4.0%
	60.6% Completely Agree 29.0% Partially Agree 7.3% Neutral 1.6% Partially Disagree 1.6% Completely Disagree		68.0% Completely Agree 20.1% Partially Agree 7.8% Neutral 2.0% Partially Disagree 2.0% Completely Disagree	
	Agree	Disagree	Agree	Disagree
12. A career woman is better off if she never marries. [p < .05]	15.0%	69.0%	16.0%	60.9%
	3.1% Completely Agree 11.9% Partially Agree 16.0% Neutral 24.2% Partially Disagree 44.8% Completely Disagree		4.9% Completely Agree 11.1% Partially Agree 23.0% Neutral 22.6% Partially Disagree 38.3% Completely Disagree	
	Agree	Disagree	Agree	Disagree
13. Career women should not expect to shirk their household responsibilities. [p < .01]	45.6%	37.7%	33.8%	44.8%
	12.6% Completely Agree 33.0% Partially Agree 16.8% Neutral 25.7% Partially Disagree 12.0% Completely Disagree		9.9% Completely Agree 23.9% Partially Agree 21.4% Neutral 26.7% Partially Disagree 18.1% Completely Disagree	

continued

Table 5.1
Continued

	Commensurate Salary		Insufficient Salary	
	Agree	**Disagree**	**Agree**	**Disagree**
14. Career women have very little in common with full-time homemakers.	26.7%	62.1%	22.0%	66.9%

7.2% Completely Agree	6.1% Completely Agree
19.5% Partially Agree	15.9% Partially Agree
11.3% Neutral	11.0% Neutral
40.0% Partially Disagree	42.4% Partially Disagree
22.1% Completely Disagree	24.5% Completely Disagree

	Agree	**Disagree**	**Agree**	**Disagree**
15. The biggest problem a career woman faces is the structure of the organization in which she works; most firms, companies, or institutions in today's society are not supportive of career women's needs. [$p < .01$]	59.8%	23.7%	71.6%	18.9%

13.4% Completely Agree	25.1% Completely Agree
46.4% Partially Agree	46.5% Partially Agree
16.5% Neutral	9.5% Neutral
20.6% Partially Disagree	16.0% Partially Disagree
3.1% Completely Disagree	2.9% Completely Disagree

	Agree	**Disagree**	**Agree**	**Disagree**
16. Any woman who wants to succeed in her career had better be able to compete on the same terms as a man; asking for special consideration or support services because she is a woman is a big mistake.	74.2%	18.6%	73.9%	20.0%

33.5% Completely Agree	37.6% Completely Agree
40.7% Partially Agree	36.3% Partially Agree
7.2% Neutral	6.1% Neutral
16.0% Partially Disagree	15.5% Partially Disagree
2.6% Completely Disagree	4.5% Completely Disagree

	Agree	**Disagree**	**Agree**	**Disagree**
17. Corporations, firms, and other institutions are under no obligation to offer support services for working women.	37.5%	44.8%	36.1%	51.7%

12.0% Completely Agree	15.6% Completely Agree
25.5% Partially Agree	20.5% Partially Agree
17.7% Neutral	12.3% Neutral
33.9% Partially Disagree	32.0% Partially Disagree
10.9% Completely Disagree	19.7% Completely Disagree

	Agree	**Disagree**	**Agree**	**Disagree**
18. A woman who wants a career should choose not to become a mother. [$p < .05$]	5.6%	82.0%	10.6%	78.8%

1.0% Completely Agree	3.7% Completely Agree
4.6% Partially Agree	6.9% Partially Agree
12.3% Neutral	10.6% Neutral
20.5% Partially Disagree	20.0% Partially Disagree
61.5% Completely Disagree	58.8% Completely Disagree

	Agree	**Disagree**	**Agree**	**Disagree**
19. The very structure of work in modern American society is male-oriented; even women without families face obstacles as they pursue their careers. [$p < .0001$]	79.9%	12.8%	91.8%	4.1%

30.4% Completely Agree	49.2% Completely Agree
49.5% Partially Agree	42.6% Partially Agree
7.2% Neutral	4.1% Neutral
8.2% Partially Disagree	2.5% Partially Disagree
4.6% Completely Disagree	1.6% Completely Disagree

	Agree	**Disagree**	**Agree**	**Disagree**
20. When all is said and done, a woman will succeed in her career if she is willing to work hard for that success. [$p < .01$]	88.7%	5.2%	79.8%	13.6%

47.2% Completely Agree	39.1% Completely Agree
41.5% Partially Agree	40.7% Partially Agree
6.2% Neutral	6.6% Neutral
4.7% Partially Disagree	10.7% Partially Disagree
0.5% Completely Disagree	2.9% Completely Disagree

traditional institutions. Almost 61% of women with insufficient salaries disputed the proposition that career women would be better off staying single, compared with 69% of women with commensurate salaries ($p <$ .05). Participants expressed even stronger disagreement with the proposition that career women should not have children: 78.8% of inadequately paid women favored motherhood, or the freedom to choose motherhood, for career women, and 82% of commensurately paid women supported that choice ($p < .05$).

Although generally supportive of traditional values, women with inadequate salaries seemed also to acknowledge the potentially negative effects of combining work and family roles. In addition, inadequately paid women were also more likely than adequately paid women to relax their expectations for career women's household responsibilities ($p < .01$).

Underpaid women also seemed more aware than adequately paid women of the problems inherent in family and work structures: 68.1% of underpaid women would support changes in the family structure, but 59% of the commensurately paid women would support these changes. Significant differences between these two groups were found in the perceptions of work structures. Among inadequately paid women, 71.6% agreed that corporate or organizational structure was a problem because these structures are generally not supportive of career women's needs. Only 60% of commensurately paid respondents agreed that organizational nonsupport posed a major problem ($p < .01$). A greater percentage of inadequately paid women (91.8%) agreed that work structures were male oriented, thus introducing obstacles for working women. A smaller proportion (79.9%) of commensurately paid women agreed, and more than 1 in 10 (13%) disagreed, with this perception ($p < .0001$).

Perhaps partly due to their willingness to acknowledge external causes or components to the problems of working, inadequately paid women were also less likely to agree that women will succeed if they are willing to work hard. Although only 5% of adequately paid women disagreed with this "bootstrap" approach, almost three times as many (13.6%) of the inadequately paid women disagreed ($p < .01$). These insufficiently paid women seem slightly less likely to internalize responsibility for obstacles, many of which they see as external.

Although three quarters of each group of commensurately and inadequately paid respondents agreed that women's groups have helped improve conditions for working women, there is more debate about whether feminist groups' sustained efforts will continue to benefit working women. Commensurately paid women voiced less support for continued activism: 60% of respondents with commensurate salaries supported further activist efforts, and 72.2% of respondents with inadequate salaries agreed that further activism is needed ($p < .01$).

Equal Pay and Feminist Attitudes

Because advocating equal pay for women workers has long been a central issue of organized feminism, it is important to examine how these and other feminist issues are regarded by women who receive equal pay and by those who do not (see Table 5.2). As indicated in the previous discussion, of the feminist attitudes of adequately and inadequately paid respondents, the underpaid group generally took the lead in espousing feminist values. Support of fair remuneration of workers and acknowledgment of structural inequities inherent in work were the most striking examples of this support, yet there was slightly less support for feminist organizations among women paid disproportionately to men than among women paid commensurately. Espousal of traditional cultural values, however, did not seem to be affected by earning equal or unequal pay. Again I group responses to the feminism items into agree and disagree categories in the text discussion, but full dimensionality of the responses is presented in Table 5.2.

Fully 97% of respondents with unequal salaries agreed that comparable work should be rewarded with comparable pay, while a smaller majority of respondents with equal salaries agreed (88.8%, $p < .05$). The presence of sex discrimination in women's lives was denied by only 3% of women with equal salaries. More than twice that proportion of respondents with unequal salaries (6.6%) disputed this generalized experience in women's lives ($p < .01$).

Just under 63% of women earning equal salaries and 70.1% of women earning unequal salaries ($p < .05$) acknowledged lack of organizational support for women's needs. Participants were even more willing to acknowledge the male-oriented work structure than to acknowledge lack of organizational support for women's needs. All but 11.5% of participants with equal salaries and all but 1% of those with unequal salaries ($p < .01$) agreed that work structures are male oriented.

Women with unequal salaries were more likely to acknowledge structural obstacles in the workplace than to acknowledge organized feminism as a source of support. Although the majority of all respondents

text continued on page 135

Table 5.2
Equal Salary by Feminist Attitudes
(With Original 5-Point Likert Scale Data)

	Salary Equal to Males		Salary Not Equal to Males	
	Agree	Disagree	Agree	Disagree

1. Men and women should receive equal pay for equal work.

Agree	Disagree	Agree	Disagree
98.4%	1.6%	99.3%	0.7%

94.6% Completely Agree
3.8% Partially Agree
0.0% Neutral
0.8% Partially Disagree
0.8% Completely Disagree

95.6% Completely Agree
3.7% Partially Agree
0.0% Neutral
0.0% Partially Disagree
0.7% Completely Disagree

2. All workers should receive comparable pay for work of comparable worth. ($p < .0001$]

Agree	Disagree	Agree	Disagree
88.8%	7.3%	97.0%	0.8%

76.9% Completely Agree
11.9% Partially Agree
3.8% Neutral
6.5% Partially Disagree
0.8% Completely Disagree

83.5% Completely Agree
13.5% Partially Agree
2.3% Neutral
0.0% Partially Disagree
0.8% Completely Disagree

3. Most women have been subjected to sex discrimination at some time in their lives, whether they know it or not. [$p < .0001$]

Agree	Disagree	Agree	Disagree
87.7%	6.6%	95.6%	3.0%

61.2% Completely Agree
26.5% Partially Agree
5.8% Neutral
5.4% Partially Disagree
1.2% Completely Disagree

79.3% Completely Agree
16.3% Partially Agree
1.5% Neutral
1.5% Partially Disagree
1.5% Completely Disagree

4. Certain jobs should be reserved for women, just as certain jobs should be reserved for men.

Agree	Disagree	Agree	Disagree
17.0%	76.8%	21.5%	69.7%

7.3% Completely Agree
9.7% Partially Agree
6.2% Neutral
16.2% Partially Disagree
60.6% Completely Disagree

12.6% Completely Agree
8.9% Partially Agree
8.9% Neutral
15.6% Partially Disagree
54.1% Completely Disagree

5. Women's special duties in the family require them to commit less time and energy to their careers than men do.

Agree	Disagree	Agree	Disagree
35.8%	55.8%	41.8%	53.0%

7.3% Completely Agree
28.5% Partially Agree
8.5% Neutral
20.0% Partially Disagree
35.8% Completely Disagree

12.7% Completely Agree
29.1% Partially Agree
5.2% Neutral
12.7% Partially Disagree
40.3% Completely Disagree

6. Women's activist groups have helped to improve things for working women.

Agree	Disagree	Agree	Disagree
78.1%	7.3%	68.1%	14.1%

35.0% Completely Agree
43.1% Partially Agree
14.6% Neutral
5.0% Partially Disagree
2.3% Completely Disagree

25.9% Completely Agree
42.2% Partially Agree
17.8% Neutral
11.1% Partially Disagree
3.0% Completely Disagree

continued

Table 5.2
Continued

	Salary Equal to Males		Salary Not Equal to Males	
	Agree	**Disagree**	**Agree**	**Disagree**

7. Working women would be better off if feminist groups would discontinue their efforts to attain greater rights for women. [*p* < .01]

	Agree	**Disagree**	**Agree**	**Disagree**
	13.5%	68.4%	15.6%	67.4%

3.5% Completely Agree   3.7% Completely Agree
10.0% Partially Agree   11.9% Partially Agree
18.1% Neutral   17.0% Neutral
24.6% Partially Disagree   25.2% Partially Disagree
43.8% Completely Disagree   42.2% Completely Disagree

8. Women should be able to obtain education in any field and to enter any field in the work world. [*p* < .01]

	Agree	**Disagree**	**Agree**	**Disagree**
	98.1%	0.8%	99.2%	0.7%

89.6% Completely Agree   88.1% Completely Agree
8.5% Partially Agree   11.1% Partially Agree
1.2% Neutral   0.0% Neutral
0.0% Partially Disagree   0.0% Partially Disagree
0.8% Completely Disagree   0.7% Completely Disagree

9. In order to improve conditions for women with careers, vast changes will have to be made in the structure of the family.

	Agree	**Disagree**	**Agree**	**Disagree**
	61.0%	22.4%	65.2%	23.0%

17.8% Completely Agree   22.2% Completely Agree
43.2% Partially Agree   43.0% Partially Agree
16.6% Neutral   11.9% Neutral
16.2% Partially Disagree   16.3% Partially Disagree
6.2% Completely Disagree   6.7% Completely Disagree

10. A career woman's best friend is her house-keeper or babysitter.

	Agree	**Disagree**	**Agree**	**Disagree**
	41.7%	32.0%	41.8%	28.3%

11.3% Completely Agree   14.9% Completely Agree
30.4% Partially Agree   26.9% Partially Agree
26.5% Neutral   29.9% Neutral
16.0% Partially Disagree   8.2% Partially Disagree
16.0% Completely Disagree   20.1% Completely Disagree

11. A career woman's best friend is her non-sexist husband.

	Agree	**Disagree**	**Agree**	**Disagree**
	91.1%	3.2%	84.3%	6.0%

65.5% Completely Agree   64.9% Completely Agree
25.6% Partially Agree   19.4% Partially Agree
5.8% Neutral   9.7% Neutral
1.6% Partially Disagree   3.0% Partially Disagree
1.6% Completely Disagree   3.0% Completely Disagree

12. A career woman is better off if she never marries. [*p* < .05]

	Agree	**Disagree**	**Agree**	**Disagree**
	13.2%	66.5%	20.9%	61.2%

3.1% Completely Agree   6.7% Completely Agree
10.1% Partially Agree   14.2% Partially Agree
20.2% Neutral   17.9% Neutral
23.3% Partially Disagree   24.6% Partially Disagree
43.2% Completely Disagree   36.6% Completely Disagree

13. Career women should not expect to shirk their household responsibilities. [*p* < .01]

	Agree	**Disagree**	**Agree**	**Disagree**
	38.6%	42.2%	44.0%	35.8%

11.0% Completely Agree   14.9% Completely Agree
27.6% Partially Agree   29.1% Partially Agree
19.3% Neutral   20.1% Neutral
26.8% Partially Disagree   25.4% Partially Disagree
15.4% Completely Disagree   10.4% Completely Disagree

continued

Table 5.2
Continued

	Salary Equal to Males		Salary Not Equal to Males	
	Agree	**Disagree**	**Agree**	**Disagree**
14. Career women have very little in common with full-time homemakers.	24.2%	65.4%	26.7%	63.0%
	6.9% Completely Agree 17.3% Partially Agree 10.4% Neutral 42.3% Partially Disagree 23.1% Completely Disagree		6.7% Completely Agree 20.0% Partially Agree 10.4% Neutral 39.3% Partially Disagree 23.7% Completely Disagree	
	Agree	**Disagree**	**Agree**	**Disagree**
15. The biggest problem a career woman faces is the structure of the organization in which she works; most firms, companies, or institutions in today's society are not supportive of career women's needs. [$p < .01$]	62.9%	22.4%	70.1%	20.8%
	17.0% Completely Agree 45.9% Partially Agree 14.7% Neutral 17.4% Partially Disagree 5.0% Completely Disagree		26.1% Completely Agree 44.0% Partially Agree 9.0% Neutral 20.1% Partially Disagree 0.7% Completely Disagree	
	Agree	**Disagree**	**Agree**	**Disagree**
16. Any woman who wants to succeed in her career had better be able to compete on the same terms as a man; asking for special consideration or support services because she is a woman is a big mistake.	71.8%	20.1%	81.5%	13.4%
	34.7% Completely Agree 37.1% Partially Agree 8.1% Neutral 16.6% Partially Disagree 3.5% Completely Disagree		41.5% Completely Agree 40.0% Partially Agree 5.2% Neutral 11.9% Partially Disagree 1.5% Completely Disagree	
	Agree	**Disagree**	**Agree**	**Disagree**
17. Corporations, firms, and other institutions are under no obligation to offer support services for working women.	36.9%	49.0%	40.3%	46.3%
	13.2% Completely Agree 23.7% Partially Agree 14.0% Neutral 35.0% Partially Disagree 14.0% Completely Disagree		17.9% Completely Agree 22.4% Partially Agree 13.4% Neutral 28.4% Partially Disagree 17.9% Completely Disagree	
	Agree	**Disagree**	**Agree**	**Disagree**
18. A woman who wants a career should choose not to become a mother. [$p < .05$]	7.7%	82.3%	10.4%	78.5%
	3.1% Completely Agree 4.6% Partially Agree 10.0% Neutral 20.8% Partially Disagree 61.5% Completely Disagree		3.0% Completely Agree 7.4% Partially Agree 11.1% Neutral 20.7% Partially Disagree 57.8% Completely Disagree	
	Agree	**Disagree**	**Agree**	**Disagree**
19. The very structure of work in modern American society is male-oriented; even women without families face obstacles as they pursue their careers. [$p < .0001$]	83.4%	11.5%	91.8%	0.7%
	36.7% Completely Agree 46.7% Partially Agree 5.0% Neutral 7.3% Partially Disagree 4.2% Completely Disagree		49.3% Completely Agree 42.5% Partially Agree 7.5% Neutral 0.0% Partially Disagree 0.7% Completely Disagree	
	Agree	**Disagree**	**Agree**	**Disagree**
20. When all is said and done, a woman will succeed in her career if she is willing to work hard for that success. [$p < .01$]	88.7%	4.7%	78.4%	14.9%
	45.7% Completely Agree 43.0% Partially Agree 6.6% Neutral 4.3% Partially Disagree 0.4% Completely Disagree		38.1% Completely Agree 40.3% Partially Agree 6.7% Neutral 11.2% Partially Disagree 3.7% Completely Disagree	

were supportive of the history of activism by women's groups, 7.3% of women with equal salaries disagreed that women's activism had helped improve conditions. Twice that proportion (14.1%) of women with unequal salaries were not supportive of this past activism ($p < .01$). Respondents in this study with unequal salaries were also slightly more likely to agree that working women would be better off without continuation of feminist group efforts, but the difference is not significant, and those who did not support feminist efforts were in the minority (15.6% to 13.5%). On the basis of the popular identification of equal pay for equal work with the organized feminist movement, the level of nonsupport of feminist efforts among current recipients of unequal pay is a bit surprising.

The equity of a woman's salary did not significantly determine her attitudes toward family and home values, although equally salaried women were slightly more likely to support traditional values. Changes in family structure were advocated by 61% of equally paid women and 65.3% of unequally paid women. Support for motherhood and marriage were generally comparable in both groups, with 66.5% of equally paid women and 61.2% of unequally paid women advocating the choice of marriage for career women, and 82.3% of equally paid women and 78.5% of unequally paid women agreeing that motherhood should be a viable choice for career women.

The majority of participants agreed that hard work will ensure success. In fact, 14.9% of unequally paid women and only 4.7% of equally paid women disagreed with this concept ($p < .01$). Respondents with unequal salaries were less likely than those with equal salaries to accept the belief that hard work is sufficient to ensure success.

Summary

Participants in this study can be said to have a bootstrap response to salary inequity and inadequacy, which places individual effort above structural change. This conclusion seems most clearly represented by the respondents who are the financial "haves" in these data, the respondents who are paid at a level commensurate with their skills and experiences, and/or the respondents who believed that their salaries are commensurate with those of their male counterparts at the same or similar jobs. These women were less likely to have experienced sex discrimination and were more likely to advocate a "superwoman" approach in dealing with work and family roles. Although a majority of the respondents either identified as feminists or espoused many feminist attitudes, the respondents more satisfied with their salaries were more likely to reject a feminist, collective approach toward changing society. These respondents were more likely to espouse the bootstrap approach to success, to accept the problems and present circumstances, and to plan success through individual accommodation within the present structures of work and family.

On the other hand, the strong feminists in this research were the financial "have nots," those who have experienced salary inadequacy or inequality, as well as gender discrimination. These women were also more likely to believe a change should be made in the structure of society so that women as a group can contribute more effectively. Within this sample, feminist attitudes and identification are correlated with economic class, as well as gender.

Although a clear majority of all respondents supported options within the traditional family roles of marriage and motherhood for working women, again the "have nots" expressed significantly more caution about working women exercising these options. Although career interruption for childbearing and child rearing had affected adversely respondents' perceptions of their salary parity and adequacy, and although various constraints and barriers were acknowledged, most respondents supported traditional family options for working women without advocating family or workplace changes to support nontraditional family arrangements. A self-contingent approach to success, or at least coping, is implicit in this view of the world.

Note

1. Discrimination data first analyzed by Kim Loudermilk and presented in her paper to the Fourth Annual Women and Work Conference in Arlington, Texas, 1987.

References

Ashton, R. (1988). 1988 salary survey focuses on packaging functions. *Packaging, 33,* 56-59.
Bureau of the Census. (1989). *Statistical abstract of the United States 1989* (109th ed.). Washington, DC: U.S. Department of Commerce.

Bureau of the Census. (1992). *Statistical abstract of the United States 1992* (112th ed.). Washington, DC: U.S. Department of Commerce.

Devanna, M. A. (1987). Women in management: Progress and promise. *Human Resource Management, 26,* 469-481.

Dubno, P. (1985). Attitudes toward women executives: A longitudinal approach. *Academy of Management Journal, 28,* 235-239.

Fredrickson, C., & Condon, M. (1986). CEO salaries rise 12% in two years. *Credit Union Magazine, 52*(1), 46-57.

Gallese, L. R. (1989). Corporate women on the move: Here are the women to watch in corporate America. *Business Month, 133,* 30-56.

Hill, J. S. (1987). Women find equality is foreign. *Advertising Age, 58,* 62-63.

Jung, M. (1988). Marketing's gender gap: Men are paid more than women at almost every level. How salary gap affected the lives of two women. *Marketing News, 22,* 1-5.

Loden, M. (1987). Recognizing women's potential: No longer business as usual. *Management Review, 76,* 44-46.

Loudermilk, K. (1987, May). *Sex discrimination in the workplace as reported by Wichita, Kansas, area professional women.* Paper presented at the Fourth Annual Women and Work Conference, Arlington, TX.

Lukovitz, K. (1989). Women practitioners: How far, how fast? *Public Relations Journal, 45,* 15-22, 34.

Mai-Dalton, R., & Sullivan, J. J. (1981). The effects of manager's sex on the assignment to a challenging or dull task and reasons for the choice. *Academy of Management Journal, 24,* 603-612.

McGoldrich, B., & Miller, G. (1985). Wall Street women: You've come a short way, baby. *Institutional Investor, 19,* 85-96.

Morrison, A. M., White, R. P., & Van Velsor, E. (1987). *Breaking the glass ceiling: Can women reach the top of America's largest corporations?* Reading, MA: Addison-Wesley.

Pillsbury, C. M., Capozzoli, L., & Ciampa, A. (1989). A synthesis of research studies regarding the upward mobility of women in public accounting. *Accounting Horizons, 3,* 63-70.

Quinn, L. R. (1987). Breaking the glass ceiling: Can it be done? *Executive Financial Woman, 2,* 13-20.

Sharma, S. (1987). Women in scientific professions: The emerging trends. *Equal Opportunities International, 6,* 1-6.

Smith, E. T., LaPlante, A., Angiolillo, P., & Cantrell, C. L. (1989, August 28). The women who are scaling high tech's heights. *Business Week,* pp. 86-89.

Stephan, P. (1987). The career prospects of female MBAs. *Business, 37,* 37-41.

VonGlinow, M. A., & Mercer, A. K. (1988). Women in corporate America: A caste of thousands. *New Management, 6,* 36-42.

Wexler, J. (1988). Are women's telecom careers measuring up? *Telecommunications Products and Technology, 6,* 20-26.

Williams, M. J. (1988). Women beat the corporate game. *Fortune, 118,* 128-138.

You've come a long way, baby—but not as far as you thought. (1984, October 1). *Business Week,* pp. 126-131.

6 Sharing Home Responsibilities: Women in Dual-Career Marriages

Although it recently has acquired a "scientific" name—*the dual-career couple*—Wayne Carlisle's study suggests that the phenomenon of two-earner households has not yet settled into a wholly satisfactory family pattern. Its synonym is still *struggle,* and its realities entail "the balancing act." Participants agreed that life in a dual-career couple can produce role conflict, work overload, and reduced time for relationships. Women also acknowledged that they assume primary responsibility for multiple functional tasks. Only 26% of participants reported that their partners shared household responsibilities equally. Yet, by far, most believed that advantages outweigh disadvantages. They expressed a willingness to hire help, reduce stress, and change their own behavior—or their spouse's—in order to ease the burden somewhat, but as in so many aspects of their lives in the study, very few identified collective action as a preferred means of improving conditions for working couples.

   Despite participants' generally positive response to the benefits of dual-career relationships and their belief that life in such relationships is preferable to the alternatives, however, certain strains surfaced that cause concern. For example, one participant commented:

> My biggest problems as a professional woman are those that deal with burn-out, wear out, managing motherhood and my job and plain and simple: fatigue and depression. . . . I doubt that I will live to my targeted retirement age (50) because I will just wear out. I feel used, overused, unappreciated, underpaid and overworked and no one really cares.

Such heart-rending remarks reveal the high price women pay for seeking what men generally consider to be their due: an opportunity to use their educations, to pursue individual goals, to make a social contribution, and to achieve self-esteem, a decent income, and respect from their partners. Despite their willingness to bear the burdens of a double day of work, to sacrifice friendships and leisure time activities, and to function on inadequate levels of rest or exercise, perhaps our society should reexamine the ethics of allowing women to do so.

WAYNE CARLISLE

$\mathbf{M}$y interest in dual-career issues springs from my role as a career placement professional and as a partner in a dual-career marriage. Like many other career placement professionals, I have sought information to better assist career aspirants in preparing for the "balancing act" that seems to complicate women's and men's careers and relationships, as well as to apply this understanding to my professional and personal roles. Although issues relating to dual-career/two-income couples have been examined and discussed in the academic and popular press for at least the past two decades (Price-Bonham & Murphy, 1980; Sekaran, 1986), I was eager to see whether I could gain new insights by studying dual-career relationships from the perspective of business and professional women considering dual-career issues in the context of their lives, rather than in the context of organizational or professional expectations. The 70% of participants in this study who described themselves as part of dual-career relationships provided interesting insights into the advantages and challenges of such relationships.

Pleck (1987) noted that women in career positions view their work much differently from those who have "jobs." Although the distinction between a career and a job is blurred and is probably best self-defined, participants in this study can be regarded as career oriented, particularly on the basis of their preference for individualistic resolution of problems and their determination to forge a successful life through hard work. Participants' responses to dual-career issues expressed their commitment to extraordinary individual effort, their satisfaction with overcoming obstacles, and their rejection of the need for structural changes to accommodate their needs. Although they acknowledged societal and personal problems involved in dual-career relationships, they fully endorsed the advantages they experience in dual-career relationships.

Dual-Career Advantages

Participants involved in dual-career relationships had very positive responses to what they saw as six potential advantages to dual careers. These six advantages were provided as options because they have been noted in previous research (Cramer & Herr, 1984; Hall & Hall, 1979; Voydanoff, 1984; Walls & Krieshok, 1987). Although these items have been listed before, they have not been compared with each other or with other possible advantages. About 10% of the respondents added unsolicited comments to the prepared advantages section of the questionnaire. These added comments do not suggest another category, but do support the view that the advantages make the dual-career relationship a positive experience. Whereas most previous research has shown primarily strains and disadvantages of dual-career relationships, especially for the woman in the relationship (Hunt & Hunt, 1982; Rapoport & Rapoport, 1977), results of this study confirm the view of Pendleton, Poloma, and Garland (1982) that the dual-career relationship basically is rewarding and that the net gain in satisfaction is worth the costs (see Figure 6.1).

More than 91% of the RGWW participants acknowledged larger income as the biggest advantage. Also 58% responded positively to items suggesting greater respect from the partner and greater cohesion due to shared experience, confirming the possibility that relationships are enhanced by dual careers. And 48% responded positively to items suggesting increased balance of power and increased autonomy as advantages.

A consideration of demographic variables contributes further insight into participants' perceived advantages in dual-career relationships. Business owners (73%) were more likely than women in all other career categories combined (55%) to see relational cohesion as a positive attribute.

Respondents with high incomes were more likely than those with low incomes to cite relational cohesion as an advantage, although equal power, autonomy, and self-esteem were not cited more frequently by this group than by those with lower incomes. When total income for the couple was considered, the lowest income groups were less likely to view greater respect from their partner as an advantage.

Although age was not a factor in self-esteem, respect, or income, age did influence some perceptions: 58% of women over age 40 saw autonomy as an advantage, while only 42% of those under 40 did so, indicating that autonomy may be valued more with the advancement of age.

Figure 6.1
Advantages of a Dual-Career Relationship.

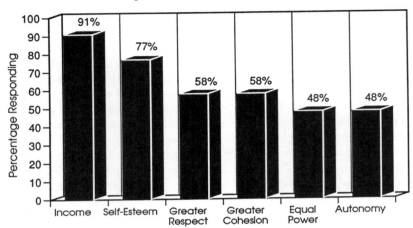

Cohesion within the relationship due to shared experience was valued more for women aged 30 to 39 than by women aged 40 to 49. These findings contribute to interesting speculation about the movement from valuing cohesion to valuing autonomy as stages of adult development. It is also possible that cohesion is more available than autonomy during the earlier life stage.

Dual-Career Disadvantages

The disadvantages of dual-career relationships have been classified as everything from significant to insurmountable in most popular press articles and in some research (Nadelson & Nadelson, 1980). Rapoport and Rapoport (1977) listed five disadvantages—role conflict, work overload, slowed or leveled career progress, societal pressure/attitude, and little time for relationships—as potentially significant problems. Their results acknowledge disadvantages, but respondents' responses to disadvantages were much lower than their responses to advantages. In fact, only two of the five issues were rated at levels predicted from previous research. Respondents seemed to see advantages outweighing disadvantages while still acknowledging the presence of disadvantages.

In the RGWW study, 82% of the participants saw overload as a disadvantage; 63% cited little time for relationships as a disadvantage. These responses show the clear problem of time availability to women respondents. Although it is important to exercise caution in making inferences from the data, these responses may suggest that women assume primary responsibility for multiple functional tasks. Although the definition of time for relationships does not specify the type of relationships, respondents may refer to relationships beyond the family. If less time is available for friendships, quality of life may be diminished.

Whereas some previous research has cited role conflict as a major dilemma for women, only 28% of this sample cited role conflict as a disadvantage for dual-career relationships. Although respondents saw role overload (too much to be done) as a disadvantage, they did not necessarily see a conflict between roles. This result supports Konek's finding (Chap. 10) of integrative leadership strategies among respondents. Only one respondent saw role conflict as a disadvantage.

A further surprising indication that the dual-career relationship presents few strong disadvantages is the fact that only 21% of the women thought their career progress had been slowed or leveled. The finding that a dual-career relationship required the woman to accept career leveling (Hunt & Hunt, 1982) is not supported by these data. The common assumption that the partner's career and the woman's multiple roles will take priority over the woman's career seems unfounded for this group. Finally only 14% noted societal pressure as a disadvantage. Perhaps pressure for women to give primary focus to partner, home, and/or family is much less now than it was previously, or perhaps women in this sample were unusual in their ability to ignore or cope with pressure (see Figure 6.2). There is also a possibility that these responses reflect the participants' reliance on rugged individualism to overcome adversity, whether presented as work demands or social pressure.

There were few variations on the disadvantages of dual-career relationships when demographic variables were cross-tabulated. Few business owners saw their careers slowed or plateaued. More women in professional roles rated less time for relationships as a disadvantage than cited slowed or plateaued careers as a disadvantage. A consideration of this issue in relation to couple income level shows that the higher

Figure 6.2
Disadvantages of a Dual-Career Relationship.

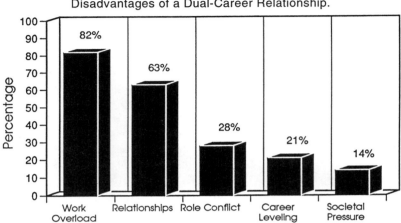

the income, the less the time for relationships. This finding may have more to do with time commitment at work than with the income level itself. Although participants, in general, did not cite role conflict as a major disadvantage, 44% of the youngest group (aged 20 to 29) rated role conflict as a disadvantage. This finding may indicate an adult development stage of trying out and learning various roles, or it may show a frustration with the discrepancy between expectation and reality.

Women with BA/BS, MA/MS, or PhD degrees were more likely than those with associate or law or medical degrees to cite slowed or leveled career progress as a dual-career disadvantage.

Coping Strategies

When participants were asked about their most effective coping strategies, many indicated that simply learning to live with the disadvantages was the best choice, especially in light of the advantages. There are some clear indications of coping strategies: 65% suggested encouraging partners to share the workload, while 44% suggested hiring household help as a coping strategy. More individualistic coping strate-

Figure 6.3
Most Effective Ways of Coping.

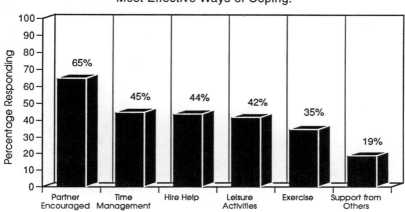

gies included improvement of time management skills (45%), giving higher priority to leisure and relaxing activities (42%), and exercise (35%) (Figure 6.3).

By far the least used coping strategy cited (19%) was locating support from others in a similar situation. Although participants acknowledged lack of time for relationships as a disadvantage, it seems that social support and shared experiences either were not available or were not viewed as viable by these women. It is possible that the focus on the partner relationship itself may provide support. The complexity of coping emotionally was noted by Wilcox-Matthew and Minor (1989), Gilbert and Rachlin (1987), and Voydanoff (1984). The strain of worrying about ways to cope may be as difficult as actual overload for women who viewed the possibility of seeking support beyond that of the partner as either unavailable or ineffective (see Figure 6.3).

Women in law and medicine were less likely to encourage their partners to share responsibilities and more likely to hire help than were women in other careers. Also, hiring help was an increasingly popular coping strategy as individual or joint income increased. Younger women were more likely to report encouraging their partners to share work and using leisure and exercise as coping strategies than were older women.

Voydanoff (1984) and Sekaran (1986) noted in two of the very few research studies of coping strategies that the responsibility for finding ways for the family or couple to cope is often assumed by the woman. This finding is consistent with the finding that, even in relationships in which partners share the workload, planning for the completion of tasks often is done by the woman. Comments made by participants in the RGWW study support the perception that arrangements for home and/or child care are the woman's responsibility. This study supports the general consensus that coping with dual-career issues is possible but is basically an individualized response. Participants made few suggestions that could be generalized to most relationships. The comments of many participants stressed the acceptance of disadvantages, rather than the expectation that coping strategies will be very effective.

Women in this study indicated that the pressure of role overload and less time for relationships are disadvantages in dual-career relationships, but they also placed a higher value on the advantages than on the disadvantages of the dual-career relationship. They evidently found that benefits outweigh sacrifices. Time for relationships cannot be delegated, purchased, hired, or accomplished by the partner. The other disadvantages presented in the research can be seen as individual responses to external pressures. The loss of time for relationships may deprive women of enjoyment and a coping strategy for handling other disadvantages. This limitation also may contribute to preferring individualistic, rather than structural, strategies for perceived inequities noted in other chapters. Women may be individualistic if relationally deprived or disconnected.

Partner's Contribution

More than one in four of the respondents in this study indicated that their partner shares equally in all areas of responsibility. Another 56% said their partner shares significantly, and only 13% said their partner provides insignificant or no support. The level of partners' actual contribution to child rearing, housework, and the woman's career reported by these participants was greater than that reported in previous research (Hall & Hall, 1979; Rapoport & Rapoport, 1977). This sample reported a much higher rate of contribution than was reported by working married women in general. It is impossible to know how much of this difference is related to the woman's expectations and negotiated sharing and how much is related to partners' willingness to contribute. It

Figure 6.4
Partner's Contribution.

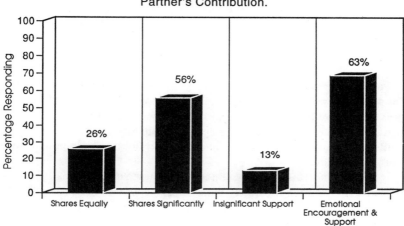

is possible that the women and perhaps the couples in this study differ from the general population. The high level of partner contribution may be related to the general positive response to the advantages of dual-career relationships. It must be noted, however, that a woman still may be expected to plan housework and child care while her partner is "helping" with what are perceived to be *her* responsibilities. The difference between "helping" and actually "sharing responsibilities" is not clearly defined.

Another question in this section raises the deeper concern of sexist beliefs and behaviors on the part of some partners. Only 63% of participants saw their partner as giving emotional support and encouragement. That percentage should be higher, considering the level of perceived partner contribution. Some partners are evidently more willing to contribute to tasks than they are to give emotional support (see Figure 6.4).

The level of a partner's contribution could not be distinguished by women's career categories, although income level did contribute to such a distinction, with women earning incomes in the $40,000 to $50,000 range reporting more equal sharing of responsibility than did women earning less. As might be expected, women over age 50 reported less equality of sharing than did younger women. Women with AA, BA/BS, and law degrees noted less contribution from partners than did women with MA/MS, PhD, or medical degrees. Emotional support was consistent across all variables.

Effective Preparation

Participants were asked how women might more effectively prepare for and cope with disadvantages of dual-career relationships. The one area of preparation that was suggested by over half of the participants was reading, an individual form of preparation. Most of the participants evidently believed that preparation is impossible or is the responsibility of the individual.

In their comments, a large number of women suggested early negotiation with partners regarding dual-career issues: 55% of the women recommended reading advice, 39% recommended taking courses, 36% recommended advising in school settings, and 38% of respondents endorsed employer-provided advice and flexibility. It seems clear that just over a third of respondents saw an educational approach to addressing disadvantages as effective. Respondents seem to have seen individual preparation and responsibility as more effective than structured or organizational solutions. Comments provided by 32% of the sample reinforces this impression. Comments were primarily of two types: (a) Participants suggested that there is no good preparation for dual-career relationships and that the advantages, disadvantages, and coping strategies are learned only in process; and (b) participants saw dual-career experiences as so individualized on the basis of human differences, expectations, demographics, family circumstances, and so forth that "packaged advice is probably not very effective" (see Figure 6.5).

Demographic cross-tabulations with effective preparation variables provided little noteworthy information, although women managers and women with less education were more likely to see courses and advice as effective than were others.

Career Interruption for Child Rearing

In this study 37% of the women interrupted their careers for childbearing or child rearing. Others in the sample may yet make a similar decision, so this percentage reflects the timing of the study, rather than the life cycle of the women included in it. Those who did interrupt their

Figure 6.5
Effective Preparation.

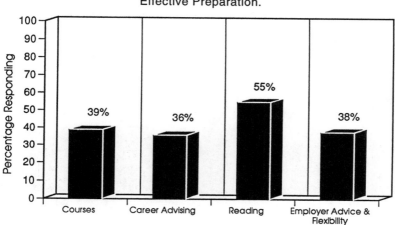

careers were asked what effect the time away had on their careers: 26% returned to the position they had left, 22% found that they had lost responsibility and had to rebuild their reputation, 38% made a career change on reentry, and 36% sought additional education. It is obvious that the career interruption associated with childbearing or child rearing had a major effect on the careers of these women, but in many cases women used this experience as an opportunity for change and education, suggesting that they created career advantages for themselves. This finding may provide an additional indication of the way respondents perceived the advantages of choices and minimized disadvantages (see Figure 6.6).

Women in couples with a combined income over $40,000 were much more likely to return to education after the interruption than those with incomes of less than $40,000 (44%, compared with 6%). The small sample size and the inappropriateness of age and education variables make other cross-tabulations meaningless.

Single Women

In this study 30% of the women included were single. This group was asked two questions: (a) Are the issues faced in a dual-career relationship

Figure 6.6
Career Interruption.

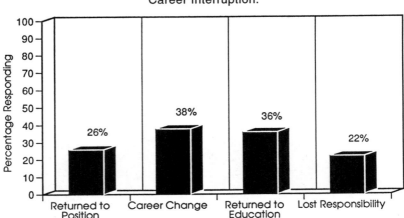

a concern for you if you consider marriage? (76% responded positively) and (b) If divorced, were dual-career issues a contributing factor in the divorce? (61% responded positively). Dual-career issues were seen as an important part of a marriage relationship by the single respondents. Because those in relationships saw few avenues for effective preparation, the gap between concern and ability to prepare is a problem. Perhaps awareness of the issues involved will be enough to encourage individuals and couples at least to discuss potential problems prior to the crisis management approach often referred to in the literature (Gilbert & Rachlin, 1987; Sekaran, 1986).

Conclusions

Women in this study provided a collective view of the dual-career relationship as a positive experience. Advantages include more income, increased self-esteem, and greater respect from and cohesion with partners. They identified as disadvantages work overload and little time for relationships. Fewer women than expected noted role conflict, career leveling, and societal pressure as disadvantages.

Participants offered few encouraging coping strategies. Rather, the general response seemed to be "Learn to live with the disadvantages." According to the group, the advantages compensate for the problems, and the disadvantages will not change. Respondents recommended extra work and self-management as a way of designing the life-work structure they desire. Although participants might prefer a more equitable personal and work environment, they found their current situations preferable to alternatives, and perhaps as equitable as they could expect. Their coping behaviors included encouraging partners to share the workload, improving their own time management skills, and hiring housework help. Surprisingly, seeking support from others was not frequently noted as an effective strategy.

Participants in this study reported a more balanced contribution from partners for child rearing, housework, and support of their careers than expected from previous studies: 26% of those surveyed reported equal sharing of responsibility with their partner, while 56% reported significant, but not equal, sharing from their partner.

Also 37% of the participants had interrupted careers for childbearing or child rearing. Although a mere 27% of these women returned to the same position, only 20% thought they had "lost ground." Frequently the women returned to education and/or changed careers after the interruption.

The only preparation for dual-career relationships that was suggested by this group of women was to read literature and advice on dual-career issues. Their comments and advice for other women urged them to expect problems but to enjoy the many advantages of dual-career relationships. They did not see structured courses in academic or employment settings as very effective in contributing to their coping strategies.

The career women viewed dual-career relationships as positive but expressed resigned acceptance of the problems involved. They apparently rely on the dual-career relationship or on themselves for effective coping strategies. These findings contribute to an emergent view of participants in this study as self-reliant, seeking individualistic solutions to career challenges.

References

Cramer, S. H., & Herr, E. L. (1984). *Career guidance and counseling through the lifespan* (2nd ed.). Boston: Little, Brown.

Gilbert, L. A., & Rachlin, V. (1987). Mental health and psychological functioning in dual-career families. *Counseling Psychologists, 15,* 7-49.

Hall, F. S., & Hall, D. T. (1979). *The two-career couple.* Reading, MA: Addison-Wesley.

Hunt, J. G., & Hunt, L. L. (1982). Dual career families: Vanguard of the future or residue of the past? In J. Aldous (Ed.), *Two pay checks: Life in dual-earner families* (pp. 41-59). Beverly Hills, CA: Sage.

Nadelson, C., & Nadelson, T. (1980). Dual-career marriages: Benefits and costs. In F. Pepitone-Rockwell (Ed.), *Dual-career couples* (pp. 91-109). Beverly Hills, CA: Sage.

Pendleton, B. F., Poloma, M. M., & Garland, T. N. (1982). An approach to quantifying the needs of dual-career families. *Human Relations, 35,* 69-82.

Pleck, J. H. (1987). Dual-career families: A comment. *Counseling Psychologists, 15,* 131-133.

Price-Bonham, S., & Murphy, D. (1980, April). Dual-career marriage: Implications for the clinician. *Journal of Marital and Family Therapy,* 181-187.

Rapoport, R., & Rapoport, R. N. (1977). *Dual-career families reexamined.* New York: Colophone.

Sekaran, U. (1986). *Dual-career families: Contemporary organizational and counseling issues.* San Francisco: Jossey-Bass.

Voydanoff, P. (1984). *Work and family: Changing roles of men and women.* Palo Alto, CA: Mayfield.

Walls, C., & Krieshok, T. (1987, March). *The rise of the dual-career family: Stresses, strains, and gains.* Paper presented to the American College Personnel Association, Chicago, IL.

Wilcox-Matthew, L., & Minor, C. (1989, November/December). The dual career couple: Concerns, benefits, and counseling implications. *Journal of Counseling and Development, 68,* 194-198.

7 Career Women and Motherhood: Child Care Dilemmas and Choices

Whereas Wayne Carlisle's study (Chap. 6) raises the issues of the cost to women of their careers, Nancy McCarthy Snyder's study of child care explores a deep-seated root cause for the burdens many career women bear. "The 'propensity to mother' is present and strong, and puts women at a disadvantage," quotes Snyder. Although she does not explore that propensity, there is evidence all around us of the pressure that women feel to become mothers, often at the sacrifice of their own development. For example, one participant noted that if she had it to do over again, "I would have graduated from college. I would have waited a couple more years to marry so I would have had my education."

The real disadvantage of motherhood is created by a society that has failed to provide adequate child care services despite the fact that more than 58% of American mothers with children under age 6 are in the labor force. It is created also by the reluctance of men to participate in the daily care of their children and by the control of the work force by those very same men.

As Kitch's study (Chap. 2) reveals, motherhood is sacred among the participants in this study, and those who fulfill that role take it very seriously. Snyder discovered that participants demand good quality child care of varying types and are willing to pay for it. The costs of motherhood extend beyond money, however. As Carlisle's chapter (Chap. 6) suggests, these women maintain primary responsibility for the most burdensome aspects of child rearing, including the planning and organizing of children's care and activities. They also sacrifice career advancement and productivity. "The fact of having children and arranging care has limited what I expect from myself right now," said one participant. "Having children definitely affects my productivity and ability to work overtime," said another.

As with dual-career relationships, participants are willing to make the career sacrifices required by having a family, even to abandon their careers altogether if their child care arrangements become unsatisfactory. Once again, the willingness of these women to assume the burdens and pay the costs required of them by a society insufficiently attuned to their needs is impressive. Their appreciation for even the minimal participation of their husbands in child care is touching. They credit luck, rather than justice, for a father's assumption of any child care responsibility.

Snyder points out that one key to change in women's assumption of the burden of child care is the attitudes and behaviors of employers. Participants reported some success in this area already. Although they noted that employers grumble about lost work time for children's illnesses and appointments and convey messages that a preoccupation with children is not respected, most participants reported positive employer attitudes toward their child care arrangements. Much employer satisfaction, however, can be attributed to the employee's ability to keep her child care needs from interfering with work.

Snyder's and others' studies of child care needs of working women raise questions about social values. To what extent should the rearing of children be regarded as a private, rather than a social, responsibility? Its perception as a private matter historically kept women confined to the home and disadvantaged in the work force. If working women accept the idea that they alone are responsible for child care, are they not perpetuating the source of their own disadvantage? If, on the other hand, child rearing is at least partly a social responsibility, how should its social costs be borne? Should quality of care be a function of a parent's ability to pay? Can employers legitimately be regarded as beneficiaries of good quality day care for their employees' children? Should they pay for the benefit they derive from an employee freed of worry about his or her children's well-being?

NANCY McCARTHY SNYDER

One of the major issues that has emerged as women have entered the labor force during the past 25 years is the question of balance between work and family, particularly the question of responsibility for child rearing. My personal interest in this topic arises from my own experience. I had our first child 2 months before I defended my dissertation and began my first academic job. Despite a strong marriage and a partner who willingly bears half of the household responsibilities, the years of rearing three young children were difficult ones. The challenge of finding dependable child care piqued my interest in the child care market, particularly in family day care, the costs of care, and the regulation of care.

I was not an original member of the Research Group on Women and Work and did not participate in the first survey. When I shared a copy of a paper I had written on family policy with one of the members, I was asked to write an article for *Working Papers,* the RGWW newsletter, and was invited to join the group. At that time, there was interest in expanding the scope of the study to include questions of work-family conflict.

Sex Roles and Child Rearing

Although women have made great strides in labor market equality, they continue to be socialized to be the primary parent.

> Historically, women have been disadvantaged in many ways—by law, by religion, by custom and by prejudice. These handicaps are gradually being eliminated. In contemporary America, the greatest barrier to economic equality is children. Most women want to bear children and are concerned about their well-being once they are born . . . the "propensity to mother" is present and strong, and puts women at a disadvantage. (Fuchs, 1989, pp. 39-40)

Although it is also true that most men want to be fathers, the demands of the parental role for most fathers continue to be significantly lighter than they are for most mothers. "It has been far easier to convince husbands to share economic responsibilities with their wives than to assume domestic and child care responsibilities" (Furstenburg, 1988, p. 209). Studies of children's daily activities show that young girls still learn domestic skills at an earlier age and do more household chores than do young boys (Zill & Rogers, 1988).

This socialization process, which has failed to adjust to changing gender roles, puts great pressure on women in the labor force.

> Today, in the developed world, the only role still uniquely gender related is childbearing. Yet men and women are still socialized to perform their traditional roles . . . In the decades ahead, as the socialization of boys and girls and the experience and expectations of young men and women grow steadily more androgynous, the differences in work place behavior will continue to fade. At the moment, however, we are still plagued by disparities in perception and behavior that make the integration of men and women in the work place unnecessarily difficult and expensive. (Schwartz, 1989, pp. 66-67)

The fact that women continue to maintain primary responsibility for child rearing makes many feminists and many employers uncomfortable. Still data are very clear that women, both those who are employed and those who are not, spend much greater portions of their time than men do on homemaking and child-rearing responsibilities (Blau & Ferber, 1986; Shelton, 1992).

This statement is true even though many fathers are becoming increasingly involved with their children. Evidence from time diaries is sketchy, but there is clear evidence both that time spent by males in household work is increasing and that men's time is far more likely to be spent on child care related activities than on other household chores. Yet Lamb's research (1987), which outlined various child care responsibilities being taken on by fathers, suggests that much of the increase in time spent by fathers on child care has been in direct interaction with and supervision of children. Little change has been noted in parental involvement in planning and organizing a child's day. Therefore ultimate responsibility for child care remains nearly exclusively female. "In this respect, it appears that fathers are still pinch hitters or part-time players rather than regulars" (Furstenburg, 1988, p. 209).

Lamb (1987) maintained that four factors are important in explaining variation in the extent of paternal involvement in child rearing: (a) motivation (the extent to which the father wants to be involved), (b) skills and self-confidence, (c) social support (particularly from the mother), and (d) institutional practices. Indeed, employment practices, as opposed to policies, often make it more difficult for men than for women to balance work and family demands. For example, in a 1986 study, the New York research group Catalyst surveyed 384 large corporations. It found that although over one third of these firms offered unpaid leave time to fathers, only nine firms reported that fathers actually had taken advantage of the policy because, despite their policies, almost two thirds of the companies did not consider it reasonable for men to take any parental leave whatsoever. In fact, 41% of the firms with parental leave policies did not sanction their use for men. One southern manufacturer reported to Catalyst, "If a man requested a leave for this purpose, his career would take a dive" (Trost, 1988, p. B1).

Lamb argued that favorable conditions in all four of these areas will be necessary to increase fathers' involvement in the lives of their children. Until such conditions prevail, dominant social institutions and practices will continue to send the message that parenting is women's work.

Child Care as a Career Issue

Dilemmas faced by working parents in balancing work and family responsibilities are growing. The baby boom generation is at the peak of its child-rearing years. The question of availability of good quality, affordable child care is now an issue for the middle class. As with many past social policy issues, this class association brings child care into the mainstream.

Because parenting remains a predominantly female activity, a major issue affecting employed mothers is the provision of child care. The child care industry in the United States is growing rapidly but remains largely diverse and informal, "with most of the burden for finding, arranging, maintaining, and rearranging care falling on the employed mothers themselves" (Zill & Rogers, 1988, p. 47). Research has shown a relationship between child care and women's labor force decisions. A recent literature survey by Rachel Connelly (1991) found that child care costs reduce the probability that a mother will participate in the labor force.

Child care services are the fourth largest expenditure category for families with children, exceeded only by food, housing, and taxes (Kahn & Kamerman, 1987). Estimates of total child care expenditures range from $11 billion (U.S. Department of Commerce, 1987) to $20 billion annually (Kahn & Kamerman, 1987).

Not surprisingly, child care has become a popular topic among policy makers and researchers. During the 1988 presidential campaign, both candidates advocated some federal role in the provision of child care services, and the 1992 campaign included debate over family leave policy. A number of states have established task forces to study appropriate policy roles in child care. Also more and more private employers are becoming involved in child care (Burud, Aschbacher, & McCroskey, 1984; Fernandez, 1990; Kahn & Kamerman, 1987; U.S. Department of Labor, 1988). The *Wall Street Journal* now runs a regular work and family column highlighting innovative corporate practice.

In 1988 the Department of Labor estimated that 26 million of the 64 million families in the United States had children under 14 years of age. There were 12.8 million two-earner married couple families with 8.8 million children under age 6 and another 12.3 million children between ages 6 and 13. There were also 3.5 million single mothers in the labor force who had 1.8 million children under age 6 and 3.4 million children between ages 6 and 13. And 70% of working mothers worked 35 or more hours per week (U.S. Department of Labor, 1988).

Child care services typically are provided in one of three settings: the child's own home, family day care homes, or child care centers. Estimates vary as to the distribution of children among these modes. The most recent (1988) Census data (U.S. Department of Commerce, 1992) show that 28% of preschoolers were cared for in their own home, 37% in another home, and 27% in an organized child care or school facility. The remaining 8% were cared for by their mothers while they worked, either at home or elsewhere. The primary child care arrangement for over three fourths of children aged 5 to 14 was school. Secondary arrangements for these children included care in the child's home (24%), care in another home (15%), and organized child care for school facilities (6.9%). Also 7% of these school-aged children were reported to have cared for themselves before and after school, and no care arrangements were reported for 42% of school-aged children.

Of the preschoolers who were cared for in their own home, just over half (15% of all preschoolers) were cared for by their fathers. Grandparents cared for 5.7% of those preschoolers, other relatives for 2.2%, and nonrelatives for 5.3%. Of the 37% of preschool children cared for in someone else's home, 8% were cared for by grandparents, 5% by another relative, and 24% by a nonrelative.

The percentage of preschoolers cared for primarily by their fathers was 19% for children of married mothers but only 2% for unmarried mothers. The later group used grandparents 16% of the time, compared with only 3% of the time for married parents. Although relative care is still an important part of child care arrangements, particularly for infants and toddlers, it is declining and will continue to decline as the number of willing grandparents diminishes.

Even though use of formal group care for preschoolers is not the most popular form of care, it grew from 13% in 1977 to 27% in 1985 and is expected to continue to grow. Full-time working mothers used care outside the home more than part-timers and were also more likely to use formal care.

Of the 19 million employed women with children under age 15, 4.4% reported losing time from work in the last month as a result of failure in child care arrangements. The probability of losing work time decreased as children aged.

Presumably because of the large incidence of relative care, only 40% of women reported paying for child care services in 1988. Median payment for full-time and part-time workers was $54 per week, which represented 7% of total family income.

Child Care and RGWW Women

To determine the child care preferences of women in this current study, a supplemental questionnaire was distributed to participants in January 1988. The questionnaire was an insert in that month's newsletter and was sent to the 494 respondents to the original survey. Respondents to this additional inquiry returned 193 surveys.

The survey included three sections. Section 1 was for those who had no children, Section 2 was for those who had children but who had never employed child care services while working, and Section 3 was for women who had used employment-related child care services.

Of the total 193 respondents, 65 (33.7%) reported having no children; 21 (10.9%) had children but had not used employment-related child care; the remaining 107 (55.4%) had consumed child care services at some point in their careers.

The respondents were slightly younger and slightly better educated than the total sample. These respondents included 13 doctors, 5 lawyers, 15 PhDs, 60 MAs, and 51 college graduates. There were 16 business owners, 53 managers/administrators, and 93 professionals. In income, 11 of them made over $60,000 per year, 47% made less than $25,000, but over 87% had combined annual family income in excess of $40,000.

Nearly 60% of the respondents were under age 40, and almost 20% were under age 30. Also 51 had at least one child under age 12, 28 had two or more, and 5 had three children under age 12. Just 67% were married, and 13% were divorced. Only two were African American.

Of the 65 who had no children, 17 stated they planned to have children in the future, and 12 were undecided about having children. Concerns about child care do not appear to be important in the child-bearing decision: Only 22.5% of those responding to the question rated anticipated problems with child care as extremely or very important, whereas 61% thought it was important.

Of the women who had children but did not use child care, over half (11 of 21) had chosen to wait for their children to reach school age before entering the labor force.

Half of the 107 women who said they had used child care were currently using it. The previous years for which child care was used ranged from 1943-1960 to 1986-1987. Also 19 of the respondents stopped using child care more than 10 years ago.

There was significant variation in the number of hours of child care consumed each week. The range was 7 to 70 hours. The mean number of hours was 40.9; the median and the mode were both 45 hours. Ten respondents consumed 30 or fewer hours per week, while 17 reported more than 50 hours. Unfortunately no question was asked about part-time and full-time employment. Presumably the individuals consuming less child care either worked part-time or needed only before- and after-school care.

Table 7.1
Child Care Use by Professional Women

	Infants	Toddlers (12-30 months)	Pre-School (2.5-5)	School Age
Spouse	37	32	27	24
Other Relative	34	30	27	24
Neighbor	16	12	6	18
Friend	24	24	15	13
Day Care Home	35	43	37	21
In-Home Care	35	32	28	28
Day Care Center	7	19	41	20
Other	1	2	4	4

NOTE: n = 107.

Child Care Preferences

Respondents were asked to identify the different modes of child care they had used for children of different ages. The age groups were infants, toddlers (12 to 30 months), preschoolers (2.5 to 5 years), and schoolchildren (see Table 7.1). Respondents then were asked to identify the mode of child care they found most satisfactory for children in each age category.

Most respondents reported they had tried several modes of child care. The most common mode for infants was spouse care (37), followed very closely by day care homes and in-home care (35 each) and by care by a relative other than a spouse (34). Friends (24) and neighbors (16) also were mentioned. Institutional care, either nonprofit or for-profit centers, was not a popular mode for infants.

Interestingly this diversity in the use of different forms of child care is also reflected in the modal preferences for infant care. Although 37 respondents reported using spousal care for their infants, only 11 of them stated they found this to be the most satisfactory mode. The most

Table 7.2
Preferred Child Care Mode by Professional Women

	Infants	Toddlers (12-30 months)	Pre-School (2.5-5)	School Age
Spouse	11	9	5	10
Other Relative	14	11	6	13
Neighbor	6	3	0	9
Friend	9	11	6	8
Day Care Home	21	27	20	10
In-Home Care	26	22	20	23
Day Care Center	2	20	24	10
Other	1	1	1	1

NOTE: n = 107.

popular mode for children under 1 year of age was in-home care (26), followed by the day care home (21), and care by another relative (14).

For toddlers the day care home was the most satisfactory alternative (27), as well as the most commonly used (43). Care by the spouse, a relative, and in-home care were the next most often cited choices.

It is with preschool-aged children that care in a day care center becomes more common: 41 women reported having used day care centers, and 24 preferred them, making institutional care the most popular choice. Day care homes and in-home care were also popular alternatives for preschoolers. Care by spouse or other relative was fairly common, but most mothers appear to prefer a situation in which the child is involved with other children.

For school-aged children, in-home care was the most commonly used choice (28), followed by spousal and other relative care (24 each). In-home care was by far the preferred mode, possibly due to the ease of transporting children between home and neighborhood school.

The most common modes of summer care were in-home care (28) and organized recreational activities (30). Mothers also reported these to be the most satisfactory arrangements.

Child Care Costs

According to survey results, full-time child care typically is priced by the week, while part-time care is charged hourly. Nineteen women reported hourly rates that ranged from no cost to $5.00. The mean was $2.04, and the median and mode $2.00. Fifty-four respondents reported weekly fees that ranged from $0 to $250. The upper figure is extremely high and probably represents live-in help that carries responsibilities beyond child care. An alternative explanation is that the respondent erred and reported care costs for more than one child, or monthly, instead of weekly costs. Despite this extreme value (and the single report of zero expenditure), the mean value was $57.82, the median $53.50. The most often reported weekly expenditure was $60, followed closely by $50, figures that are consistent with survey of income and program participation data (U.S. Department of Commerce, 1992) that show a 1988 national average weekly child care payment of $54.

Desirable Qualities of Child Care

The survey listed seven reasons for selecting a child care provider and asked respondents to rate their importance from *not at all important* (1) to *very important* (5). Quality of staff was by far the most important characteristic sought in a day care provider. Over 91% of the respondents reported it to be very important, and another 7% found it to be somewhat important. No one rated quality of staff as unimportant.

Respondents also ranked flexibility of hours and variety of activities, followed by educational content, as somewhat important. It was somewhat surprising that the latter characteristic did not rate higher, particularly with this population. One reason may be that no distinction was made for age of child in this question. Educational content is significantly less important for infants, toddlers, and school-aged children than it is for preschoolers. Another possible explanation is that the parents in the sample treat preschool education separately from child care and that a number of the children attend separate preschools for a few hours per day. A third explanation is that concerns about education are incorporated into concern for staff quality, which was rated extremely important.

Although none of the factors on the list was considered to be unimportant, cost came closest to being ranked unimportant, with one quarter of respondents indicating neutrality on this issue. However, 17% of those responding indicated that cost was very important.

Attractiveness of facility was rated as very important by 12% of respondents, while 15% thought it was unimportant, and 43% expressed neutrality.

Referral Methods

Respondents used a fairly wide range of methods for finding child care. They most often used friends, followed by co-workers, neighbors, and relatives as sources of information. Information and referral agencies have been used by over one fourth of the women.

Travel Time

Of those answering this section, 60% reported spending extra travel time for child care. The mean time was 30.5 minutes, the mode 30 minutes, with a range from 5 minutes to 90 minutes per day.

Career Consequences

The survey included two open-ended questions concerning the mother's perceptions of the impact of day care on her career and with her employers attitudes toward her day care arrangements. Responses to the first question were divided fairly evenly between comments about the limitations that parenting places on career advancement and about the importance of dependable, quality child care in maintaining on-the-job concentration and in protecting career advancement. The first set of responses is consistent with Felice Schwartz's contention that the majority of women "want to pursue serious careers while participating actively in the rearing of children . . . [and] most of them are willing to trade some career growth and compensation for freedom from the constant pressure to work long hours and weekends" (Schwartz, 1989, p. 70).

Several women commented that the state of motherhood, rather than questions of child care, concerned them. Responses included the following:

The fact of having children and arranging care has limited what I expect from myself right now. I have chosen to work flex-time and thus am not moving up at all.

Having children definitely affects my productivity and ability to work overtime.

I don't feel that day care "arrangements" are a factor as much as the fact that I have children at all. This prevents me from traveling, which I know is a hindrance to me.

I don't think day care affected my productivity. I think having a child did. I have always chosen child over job, so I have not gone as far in my job as might have been possible. But I'm glad I made that choice.

This final statement brings out another often-stated view: that participants consider family more important than career. Many respondents reported very favorable child care arrangements but still noted that parenthood limited their ability to accept promotions, positions that required travel and long hours. No one really expressed any regret at this situation, and several stated that their family came first, period.

When children were small, it was difficult to attend outside civic functions that were expected on the job.

The children are the most important—much more important than career hoopla. It is easier to go to work and do a good job if you have full confidence that your children are fine!

Am no longer mobile—a career change must always mean good day care and environment for my son. But that is a sacrifice I'm willing to make—I understood that he is more important to me than career.

I currently would like a different job but can't get too serious about looking because I don't care to take my children out of the center we currently use. I feel I'd be more productive in another job, but I think of my children first—I can wait a few more years.

Decreased hours to have time with kids—but by choice, not necessity.

Some participants went so far as to say they would not work at all if they could not find acceptable child care, and many commented they had worked part-time or in flexible jobs until their children were old enough to take care of themselves.

> I had great child care, so I never had to worry while I was at work. Without such a nice arrangement, I probably would have had to quit teaching.

> If I did not find good care, I simply would not work. That's the bottom line.

> I "marked time" by teaching until the children were old enough to care for themselves, thus delaying graduate school for ten years. Others were far ahead of me in my chosen field.

> By choice, my career was put on hold until my children were in school full time.

> I kept a job with flexible hours after my husband died—as this made child care lots easier—that was more important at that time than career.

One interesting finding is that many of these women seem to accept primary responsibility for child care as their own. This sense of responsibility is reflected in their expression of gratitude for good quality child care.

> I have been fortunate. Without this kind of support I could not have been comfortable pursuing a career, and building a business.

> Fortunately . . . I have family members who can come to the rescue.

> I was incredibly lucky to have the same great live-in housekeeper for 23 years. I would have done almost anything to have kept from losing her.

> I was lucky. I found friends and people who became friends to provide one-on-one care.

> I have complete peace of mind after I kiss my two sons, ages two and four, good-bye. For this balance, I am immensely grateful.

> I tried to simply "low-key" any problems I had with child care at work and around colleagues. Fortunately, my children were healthy.

These responses lend themselves to another observation. Schwartz (1989) pointed out that in the future, as the experiences of young men and women become more similar, their workplace behavior also will become more similar. Although evidence is anecdotal, a larger than expected number of respondents (11 of 91) mentioned that their husbands were involved in child care responsibilities. It is also worth noting that words like *lucky* and *fortunate* are conspicuous. This gratitude is less an indication of these fathers' involvement than recognition that paternal responsibility for child care is still relatively uncommon.

This is also my husband's situation as we share all time off equally, depending on our schedules and work load.

Worked only part time, 3:00-11:30 p.m., after kids were all in school. Kids got home at 4:00 p.m. Husband at 5:00 p.m.

I was fortunate. My husband's work was closer to home than mine, so he had more of the problems with day care and he was very supportive.

Luckily, my spouse takes my child in the a.m. So I can go in early.

I took sabbatical leave while my sons were two and three and a half years old (in Japan four months). Husband (also on sabbatical leave) remained in the states and with help of baby-sitter during week was the provider for child care.

Employers and Child Care

The second open-ended question asked the respondents how they thought their employers perceived the relationship between their child care arrangements and their productivity. Somewhat surprisingly, the answers to this question generated significantly more positive than negative responses. Only 15 of 79 who answered had any strongly negative things to say about their bosses' attitudes. Another 15 declared "I am the boss" in one form or another.

There were, however, some unsupportive employers:

My employer always reminded us that our "job" should come first—before our families. Productivity was always measured and child care problems were no excuse for poor attendance or low productivity.

They expect [child care] to be my problem which I will handle in such a manner as to not affect work.

In general, my male bosses have not been aware or considerate of my work needs related to child care and perceived my lack of desire for excessive overtime as lack of job commitment.

While my boss appears to understand Dr. appts. and such, I think it [is] something he thinks about in "the back of his mind," and he would rather I didn't miss work for those reasons.

I am in a career measured by time spent and energy put forth and to look preoccupied with children is not respected . . . I will be forced to work late occasionally or give up the career.

Nevertheless the vast majority reported no problem with their employers' attitudes toward child care. However, a more careful review of the answers identified an interesting pattern. The reason that few problems were reported was not so much that employers were supportive of child care responsibilities as that these mothers kept their child care responsibilities from interfering with their work. Most of the respondents accepted, either voluntarily or by force, the separation of work and family. They saw solutions to day-to-day care as individual, rather than structural, in nature.

I've always tried my best to devote my full-time attention to work at work and home at home.

I think my boss forgot that I had a child. Except for childbirth, I never missed a day due to illness; child's or mine.

I believe arrangements are important so as not to interfere on a regular basis with general day-to-day work.

It is important to prove my capability of handling the situation by being responsible.

I doubt they ever noticed, since it didn't affect my work.

They never give it a thought and just assume I'll take care of it. They are hardly aware I have a child.

At that particular time, to my employer, I think he might have had to stop and think to decide if I had children.

Except for being extremely tired for years, I do not feel I suffered.

Although the majority of responses were in this vein, there were also some very positive statements about employers' attitudes toward participants' child-rearing responsibilities:

They were very understanding.

Positive and smooth.

Excellently.

Very positively; employer was concerned that I have quality child care for my children.

I feel my direct supervisor is supportive of working mothers and the state provides family sick day if needed.

I was fortunate—my employer was well aware that the flexibility made my productivity better as well as making it possible to have the children cared for. First "she" then later "he" knew that I was dedicated both toward doing my best . . . and as a mother.

Very satisfactory. Fortunately, I had great support systems.

Conclusions

Problems created by the conflict between work and family have been discussed in numerous articles (Blau & Ferber, 1986; Crosby, 1991; Kamerman & Kahn, 1981; Pleck, 1985; Snyder, 1987). A major factor in a family's ability to ease this work-family tension is its ability to find and pay for adequate child care. It appears that most of the mothers responding to this supplemental questionnaire demand high quality child care, and many expressed a high level of satisfaction with their child care arrangements. Problems of lack of availability, poor quality, and questionable dependability were rare.

Participants in this study demonstrated wide variation in preferred modes of child care. Because cost was not a significant factor for this population, the obvious conclusion is that parents differ on the type of care they want for their children. Employers and policy makers would be well advised to keep this variation in mind when developing benefit packages that include child care. There are several examples of successful on-site child care programs, but viable on-site child care accommodations usually are restricted to large companies with a relatively homogeneous work force. Most parents do not seem to want their very young children in a day care center.

On the one hand, participants in this study agreed that good quality, dependable child care enhances worker productivity. On the other hand, parents of young children want to be able to respond to family needs, as well as to employment demands. That desire requires employers to be more flexible than they have been in the past. Whether there should be a "mommy track" and a "daddy track" or generally more flexible employment structures for all workers remains to be seen.

Clearly employers are being forced to involve themselves in the private lives of their employees at an ever accelerating pace (Bennett, 1989). Only one sixth of the new entrants to the labor force in the United States through the year 2000 will be white males (Hudson Institute, 1987). Shortages of skilled labor will force employers to compete for nontraditional workers in previously unheard of ways. The demand for labor will ensure that women of childbearing age stay in the labor force. At the same time, our political and economic institutions depend on well-educated, well-socialized, well-nourished, and well-nurtured children.

> Work remains the primary role for all adults and a central ethic. It seems likely that unless it becomes possible for adults to manage work and family life without undue strain for themselves and their children, society will suffer a significant productivity loss in the labor market and economy and perhaps an even more important loss in the quantity and quality of future generations (Kamerman, 1984, pp. 60-67).

In the future, employers will be unable to demand that work and family be kept separate. The notion that parenting is solely a private responsibility with no social costs or benefits is dying rapidly. Parenting is a difficult and time-consuming endeavor. In the future, parents will need more help both from employers and from government. Recent federal policy changes that increased child care subsidies and require employers to provide family leave reflect the strength of public opinion on these issues. The information in this study suggests that, if assisted by appropriate support mechanisms and quality child care, parents will better fulfill both their family and their career responsibilities.

References

Bennett, A. (1989, May 8). As pool of skilled help tightens, firms move to broaden their role. *Wall Street Journal,* p. B1.

Blau, F. D., & Ferber, M. E. (1986). *The economics of women, men, and work.* Englewood Cliffs, NJ: Prentice-Hall.

Burud, S. L., Aschbacher, P. R., & McCroskey, J. (1984). *Employer-supported child care.* Dover, MA: Auburn House.

Connelly, R. (1991). The importance of child care costs to women's decision making. In O. M. Blau (Ed.), *The economics of child care* (pp. 87-117). New York: Russell Sage.

Crosby, F. J. (1991). *Juggling.* New York: Free Press.

Fernandez, J. P. (1990). *The politics and reality of family care in corporate America.* Lexington, MA: Lexington.

Fuchs, V. R. (1989). Women's quest for economic equality. *Journal of Economic Perspectives, 3,* 25-41.

Furstenburg, F. F. (1988). Good dads—bad dads: Two faces of fatherhood. In A. J. Cherlin (Ed.), *The changing American family and public policy* (p. 209). Washington, DC: Urban Institute Press.

Hudson Institute. (1987). *Workforce 2000: Work and workers for the 21st century.* Washington, DC: U.S. Department of Labor.

Kahn, A. J., & Kamerman, S. B. (1987). *Child care: Facing the hard choices.* Dover, MA: Auburn House.

Kamerman, S. B. (1984). Child care and family benefits: Policies of six industrialized countries. In R. Genovese (Ed.), *Families and change: Social needs and public policies* (pp. 60-67). New York: Praeger.

Kamerman, S. B., & Kahn, A. J. (1981). *Child care, family benefits, and working parents.* New York: Columbia University Press.

Lamb, M. E. (1987). *The father's role.* New York: John Wiley.

Moen, P. (1992). *Women's two roles.* New York: Auburn House.

Pleck, J. H. (1985). *Working wives, working husbands.* Beverly Hills, CA: Sage.

Schwartz, F. N. (1989). Management women and the new facts of life. *Harvard Business Review, 71,* 65-76.

Shelton, B. A. (1992). *Women, men, and time.* New York: Greenwood.

Snyder, N. M. (1987, March). *The growing demand for family policy.* Paper presented at the 48th National Conference of the American Society for Public Administration, Boston, MA.

Trost, C. (1988, November 1). Men, too, wrestle with career-family stress. *Wall Street Journal,* p. B1.

U.S. Department of Commerce. (1987). *Who's minding the kids? Child care arrangements: Winter 1984-85.* Washington, DC: Author.

U.S. Department of Commerce. (1992). *Who's minding the kids? Child care arrangements: Fall 1988.* Washington, DC: Author.

U.S. Department of Labor. (1988). *Child care: A workforce issue* (Report of the secretary's task force). Washington, DC: Author.

Zill, N., & Rogers, C. (1988). Recent trend in the well-being of children in the United States and their implications for public policy. In A. J. Cherlin (Ed.), *The changing American family and public policy* (pp. 31-115). Washington, DC: Urban Institute Press.

8 Career Women's Leisure: Challenges and Realities

A participant told us that during the 6 months prior to responding to the survey, the issue of greatest concern to her was "meeting people and developing friendships and balancing my life so it is not all work" and that the most pleasant, happiest, or most meaningful thing that had happened to her and to her daughter during the past 6 months had been "each making a new friend." Her response echoes those of many respondents who seek "balance" but who have limited time to invest in leisure. Women's search for balance is often conducted in the context of pressures like those expressed by another participant, who would warn college students: "If you do something well, people will be surprised; it will be a fluke. Learn to do everything better than the men you work with. Work harder."

Marcia McCoy's survey of career women's leisure attitudes and activities provides evidence that women are working harder and playing less than their male counterparts and that much of their leisure is work related. Results of her survey confirm her concern that, for women in this study, "the more you make, the more you

173

work." She further discovered that women have many constraints on opportunities for leisure, in addition to time constraints and role demands. Constraints include "woman's double burden," consisting of professional demands and home and family responsibilities; unclear boundaries between women's work and leisure; and what one might call the "masculinization of leisure," associated with male domination of sports and adventure. McCoy also discovered that a surprisingly high percentage of women's leisure is solitary and passive.

McCoy's conclusions confirm the prediction of John Robinson, director of the Americans' Use of Time Project at the University of Maryland, quoted in *Megatrends for Women,* that "the new status symbol of the 1990's will be time" (Aburdene & Naisbitt, 1992, p. 98). This study encourages us to consider our definitions and experiences of leisure, as well as the ways work, family, organizational, and social structures might be redesigned to help us all create more balance in our busy lives.

MARCIA L. McCOY

Since World War II, increasing numbers of women have pursued paid employment outside their homes; the increase has been greatest among women between the ages of 35 and 54 (Deem, 1986). Today a majority of the women in this country are employed (Gideonse, 1984; Rybczyn-ski, 1991). These women are single, married, divorced, or widowed, and are childless or have children of all ages. They work in all levels of employment, from menial jobs to high-income prestigious careers.

Much attention has been given recently to these employed women (especially women in the professions and in dual-career marriages) and the impact of their paid employment on society, their careers, their children, their marriages, and on their own physical and mental health. Many important aspects of women's careers have been examined.

A common focus of investigation has been on how employed women integrate their career roles with their family roles. Hall and Hall (1978) found that women tend to employ three distinct styles in coping with conflicts between roles. The woman who employs *reactive role behavior* engages in implicit acceptance of all role demands and attempts to meet all of them. Adopting this style might involve scheduling and organizing time and activities more effectively, working harder to meet all role demands, reprioritizing time and activities (e.g., cutting out all personal and leisure time), or using no conscious strategy to cope with role demands and strain. Not surprisingly, women who use this style have reported very low levels of happiness and satisfaction.

The woman who employs the style of *role redefinition* may negotiate with role senders (the persons demanding or expecting some type of behavior from the employed woman) for the purpose of altering roles to make them more compatible with other responsibilities and interests. Strategies included in this behavior style include engaging in collaborative problem solving with role senders (e.g., spouse, boss, children) and delegating various household and child care chores to other family members or hiring outside help.

The woman who employs the style of *personal reorientation* may alter her own attitudes toward roles and role expectations for herself, doing what she finds most important personally, regardless of traditional role expectations of society. Strategies in this behavior include separating roles, overlooking or ignoring less important roles, and viewing self-fulfillment and personal interests as valid sources of role demand.

To find time for themselves, women often must make a conscious effort to schedule that time. Rapoport and Rapoport (1972) described this conscious effort at finding leisure as conserving "health and energy deliberately as a human resource" (p. 225). For professional women surveyed by Gray (1983), considering their own personal interests as very important was significantly related to satisfactory coping with role demands. Lieber (1980) found, in surveying a sample of married professional women with children, that these women reported the coping strategy of making time "for wife and husband alone, mother and each child alone, and me—by myself" (p. 160).

Very little research attention has been given to the role of leisure in women's lives, regardless of employment status, although making time for leisure and personal fulfillment is regarded as a crucial coping strategy for many employed women (Colley, 1984; Deem, 1982; Shank, 1983). Women and men tend to perceive leisure differently (Deem, 1986; Hargreaves, 1989; Iso-Ahola, 1979) and have differential access to leisure. Leisure research, however, has tended to focus on men's leisure and to assume that women's leisure matches this "norm," or to ignore women's leisure entirely (Colley, 1984; Deem, 1986).

What, exactly, is leisure? There are almost as many definitions as there are definers of leisure. According to Neulinger (1981), "the term, *leisure*, is very much like the term, *intelligence*: everybody uses but hardly anyone can agree on what it means" (p. 30). However, three common elements are found in most definitions of leisure:

1. Emphasis on leisure as discretionary time. This is the "free" time left over after one has fulfilled subsistence and existence needs (e.g., job and household chores).
2. Emphasis on leisure as discretionary activity. For an act to be considered as leisure, it must be freely chosen, rather than being a necessity or obligation.
3. Emphasis on leisure as a state of mind. Leisure involves intrinsic motivations and satisfaction; that is, one engages in leisure because it is inherently satisfying (Haywood, Kew, & Branham, 1989; Iso-Ahola, 1980; Kelly, 1982; Neulinger, 1980, 1981).

For the purposes of this study, leisure is defined as the activities one chooses to do in one's free time for purposes of pleasure, relaxation, self-fulfillment, or social value.

Many leisure researchers (cf. Deem, 1986; Green, Hebron, & Woodward, 1987; Hargreaves, 1989; Iso-Ahola, 1979) have found that women and men have different perceptions and definitions of leisure. Women are more likely to define an activity as a leisure activity if it is not related to work (i.e., paid work or unpaid domestic work). For men, low work-relation also defines leisure, but only if the activity is chosen freely during their free time. In other words, work and freedom influence women's perceptions of leisure independently (if it is not work, it is leisure whether it is chosen freely or not), while these two factors affect men's perceptions interdependently. This phenomenon can be explained in terms of the socialization process in this culture. Women typically are socialized in a dependent role (to be dependent both on men and on other people) and thus usually are expected to remain at home to care for their families. When they do work outside the home, wives' jobs often are viewed as less important than husbands' jobs. In addition, employed wives usually are expected to continue their assigned role of primary responsibility for the home and family. Because women often work harder than others are aware of (holding two jobs as wage-earner and homemaker), they generally are tired of working and are more likely than men to perceive and appreciate an activity as being leisure (Green et al., 1987; Iso-Ahola, 1979).

Leisure opportunities for both genders are limited by sex-role socialization and by traditional norms for appropriate male and female leisure activities. Employed women and men, however, seem to have differential access to leisure time and activities. Men, more than women, generally have more discretionary time for leisure and find it easier to "indulge *of their own free will* in leisure activities" (Hargreaves, 1989, p. 136). Sex-typing of leisure activities is pervasive, with women's participation in leisure outside the home tending to be quite low and usually family centered (Colley, 1984; Deem, 1986; Green et al., 1987). In addition, expectations of family and friends, as well as other obligations, place greater limits on women's leisure than on men's (Deem, 1986; Shank, 1983). Overall, women's access to leisure is constrained, in ways that men's leisure is not, by a wide variety of mechanisms of social control, including more rigid assumptions about what constitutes appropriate leisure behavior for women, women's responsibility for most (if not all) child care and domestic work, and control by male partners of women's access to disposable income and time for leisure. In our male-dominated culture, the most compelling constraint on women's leisure both inside and outside the home may be fear of male violence, in the form of sexual assault and harassment, rape, and other forms of physical violence (Deem, 1986; Green et al., 1987; Hargreaves, 1989).

In addition to these external constraints, the degree to which a multiple-role woman adheres to traditional roles at home will affect her leisure. A woman employed outside the home who feels she must maintain full responsibility for managing the household, in addition to the time and effort she spends on her job, will find her discretionary time drastically reduced, if not entirely eliminated. According to Shank (1983), it is common for a woman to find that

> employment does not diminish her sense of responsibility to care for and nurture spouse and children, it increases it. . . . The insidious guilt that is frequently experienced by working mothers often results in attempts to make up for this time away by giving extra special time to her children. In other words, her time becomes their time, and she winds up last in line for nurturance. (p. 65)

For women in our society, goodness equals service; that is, a woman's worth traditionally has been defined by how well she fulfills her role of serving her family and others. Women still tend to feel selfish or guilty if they perceive themselves as failing to meet their obligations and responsibilities to others, particularly to family members (Green et al., 1987; Piotrkowski & Repetti, 1984). For many employed women, the needs and expectations of family are considered to be more important than their own needs for personal time, leisure, and self-nurturance.

Beyond the above internal and external constraints on women's leisure, the low value that society places on "women's work" comes into play. In our culture, leisure has always been viewed as a reward for hard work, particularly work that has high social value. The traditional role for women—that of wife and mother—has been stigmatized and devalued as not being "real work," "real work" being, traditionally, what men do outside the house (Hargreaves, 1989) and "women's work" being seen as having low social value. Hence women who are full-time mothers and/or homemakers commonly are referred to as "not working." Women in this role tend to be less inclined and rarely encouraged to reward themselves with leisure for the work they do (Deem, 1986; Shank, 1983). And when a woman does "real work" for pay outside the home, it is most often in addition to her traditional job at home. According to Marsden (1982), employed women tend to reduce substantially their leisure time and activities in order to maintain the household, while their husbands tend to increase by very little (if any) the time they spend at domestic work. As a result, an employed woman tends to have very little time for herself and her leisure.

Free time to enjoy leisure is particularly precious to employed women (Neulinger, 1981). Although men have constraints on their leisure, too, women's leisure is significantly more limited. Because of societal and personal expectations and constraints, women often must make deliberate efforts to gain even a small amount of leisure time.

The above issues have been discussed thus far in terms of employed women in general. How do these issues apply to women who are professionals or are otherwise involved in careers, as opposed to employment viewed as "just" a job? According to Cherpas (1985), a career is characterized by "a large investment of time and energy in job training, high personal salience, substantial ego involvement, and a continuous developmental quality where advances in responsibility, power, pay and status accrue over time" (p. 616). Occupations that are typically considered to be professional careers include physician, lawyer, university professor, scientist, engineer, and other PhD level positions, as well as architect, business owner or executive, journalist, administrator, and manager.

The professional woman who has received the most attention is the married professional woman, especially the "dual-career" wife. Dual-career couples have been the focus of a good deal of investigation since the early 1970s, when Rapoport and Rapoport (1972) coined the phrase and described the dual-career family as one in which both heads of the household pursue a professional career by choice and at the same time maintain a family life together.

Most of the constraints on women's leisure discussed above are particularly salient for married professional women, especially those who have children living at home. Having children means more time tied up with domestic responsibilities for both parents. A majority of the research into the division of domestic work such as household maintenance and child-rearing, however, indicates that wives still have primary responsibility for home and children (Bird, 1979; Bryson, Bryson, Licht, & Licht, 1976; French, 1992; Green et al., 1987; Piotrkowski & Repetti, 1984; Presser, 1982; Shainess, 1980; Yogev, 1981, 1983) even if outside help is hired (Bryson et al., 1976; Shainess, 1980). One result of this uneven division is that professional women with children are forced to sacrifice their personal and leisure time (Bird, 1979; Iso-Ahola & Mannell, 1985; Piotrkowski & Repetti, 1984; Presser, 1982).

The constraints on leisure time of married professional women with children at home are clear; what about single professional women with children at home? Very little research has focused specifically on single professional women with or without children. Single working mothers of all occupations and career levels make up 90% of all single heads of households (Shank, 1983). Also the proportion of divorced professional women is higher than the proportion of divorced professional men and the proportion of the general population who are divorced (Gray, 1983). Many of these divorced professional women have children living at home. Families headed by single mothers are generally far behind husband-wife families economically, because of the "absence of adult male work hours at the higher male wage" (Brown, 1982, p. 119). Although a single professional woman with children typically would earn more than a single nonprofessional mother, for example, the relatively limited income of a single professional woman and mother places important constraints on her leisure activities. She is less able to afford child care and household help than a dual-career mother, which results in even less personal time and more strain (Shank, 1983).

Professional women, married or single, with or without children at home, experience a number of external and internal constraints on their leisure time. What implications does this experience have for their emotional and physical health? The double day of professional women can be very costly (Quarm, 1984). Between their first job (the career) and their second job (the home, their second workplace), women put in an excessive number of working hours. Although each role by itself can involve a great deal of stress, fatigue, and emotional vulnerability, the combination of roles often compounds negative consequences (de Koninck, 1984). A professional woman with children, for example, may feel guilty and anxious about neglecting her parental role and may attempt to resolve this dilemma by trying to be a "superwoman," without taking any time for herself or for self-nurturance. This approach often results in physical, mental, and emotional stress and ill health (Shank, 1983).

Even though career women with or without families have little free time, personal time spent on their own leisure is very important. Rather than contributing to the problem of role overload, leisure very often is an important coping strategy for professional women (Gray, 1983; Hall & Hall, 1978; Lieber, 1980; Rapoport & Rapoport, 1972). For example, various types of physical exercises are popular leisure activities that can be beneficial in a number of ways. Exercise promotes short-term coping in terms of stress management and enhanced feelings of confidence and physical well-being. In addition, improving and maintaining one's physical health are long-term benefits that are effective aids for coping with other aspects of role overload. According to Shank (1983), "leisure experiences are related to a person's sense of identity, self-concept, and the creation of a meaningful life" (p. 66) and should be made an important part of women's lives.

Leisure Time

The leisure survey focused on the leisure activities of career women, how much time they spend at various leisure activities, and whom they choose as companions for leisure activities. I also asked participants to list activities they engaged in most often and those in which they would like to engage more often. Because some of the 494 women in this sample reported jobs that were not considered to be professional, only the responses of the 439 women with professional roles were analyzed. Demographic profiles of the smaller group of 439 professional women are very similar to those of the larger sample of 494 women.

Although the survey respondents were asked to indicate how much time they spend engaging in the various leisure activities in a week, analysis of the data revealed that most of the women reported the amount of time they spend when they do the activities. Many of the leisure activities in the survey are not necessarily activities in which the women would engage every week or even on a less regular basis; that is, many are strictly seasonal activities (e.g., skiing, camping) or usually are done only rarely (e.g., traveling, visiting an art museum). Thus the times reported are not necessarily the amount of leisure time the women have in a "regular" week, but represent leisure time in general.

The women reported a very wide range of total leisure times, from 10 minutes to 273.5 hours. The mean leisure time was 48.5 hours, which supports the conclusion that the reported leisure times are not weekly leisure times.

Single women reported more leisure time (56.7 hours, on the average) than did married women (44.4 hours). Single women were more likely than married women to live alone and had more freedom to plan and spend their leisure time as they please (Woodward & Green, 1988).

Not surprisingly, women with children at home reported less leisure time than women with no children at home (41.8 hours, compared with 54.2 hours). Women who are mothers with children at home very likely are spending what could be leisure time at parenting, caretaking, and household tasks. Although no statistically significant interaction was found between motherhood and marital status, examination of the leisure times of married and single mothers and women without children revealed that married mothers have the least leisure time. I had expected that single mothers would have the smallest amount of leisure time. It seems, however, that the presence of a husband, rather than increasing the leisure time of mothers by sharing household and parenting tasks, actually decreases the mothers' leisure time. This finding supports Green and Hebron's (1988) assertion that living with a male partner means less independent leisure and less time for leisure of any type, for women, because of increased domestic workload.

A linear relationship was found between leisure time and age, with women in their 20s reporting the highest amounts of leisure time. Again it appears that having a spouse reduces leisure time; only about half (53%) of these youngest women were married, compared to 69% of the women above age 30, who had less leisure time than the youngest women. The younger women who are married may hold less traditional values concerning domestic tasks (taking care of home and spouse) than the married women in the higher age groups, and therefore have more time available for leisure. In addition, women aged 40 and above are more likely to be at the peak of their careers, spending much more time at work-oriented activities.

Women with annual individual incomes of less than $30,000 reported more leisure time than did women earning more than $60,000. Possibly more women in the lower income brackets are working less than full-time; spending less time at work would allow more time for leisure. The women earning less may also be less likely to conceptualize their work as career oriented; they may work at jobs with less opportunity or expectation for overtime work (e.g., working late and on weekends, bringing work home). Presumably more women at the higher income levels are such professionals as lawyers, doctors, and business owners; these careers often require more time at work than the usual 40 hours per week. This statement may be an illustration of the expression, "the more you make, the more you work."

Range of Activities

The leisure activity reported by the largest proportion of the sample was watching television programs or taped programs on a VCR. Almost

90% of the women engaged in this activity. About the same number of women reported they read a newspaper, magazine, or career-related journal for leisure. These two activities, along with shopping, eating out at a restaurant, and reading books, were engaged in by at least 75% of the sample (see Table 8.1).

Not surprisingly, the most commonly reported leisure activities are those that are most convenient in terms of time, energy, expense, planning, and materials required. The activities reported by smaller proportions of the sample seem to require more planning, time commit-ment, and expense. The less common activities also seem to involve personal taste and preference; many of these activities are less popular with the general adult public (e.g., meditation, certain sporting and recreational activities). In addition, the more commonly reported leisure activities are more likely to be engaged in alone than are the less popular activities. The career women in the sample may be selecting leisure activities that allow them to enjoy some time to themselves, or they may consider certain types of activities to be easier, more enjoy-able, or relaxing when pursued alone. Perhaps some of the women would like to do some activities with someone else, but are unable to find a companion. Perhaps they do some of the activities alone out of convenience; when they have a small amount of time in which to do some leisure activity, other people may not be available to join them or they find that their time for leisure disappears before a companion is available.

When the sample was divided into subgroups based on marital status, motherhood, and age to compare activities reported by at least 50% of each subgroup, no differences were found between any of the subgroups and the entire sample; the most popular activities of the sample as a whole were the same activities and in about the same ranked order as those reported by approximately half of each subgroup. Some minor differences were observed between some of the subgroups themselves, based on an elective criterion of at least 15% difference between subgroups. For the most part, however, the women in the subgroups chose very similar leisure activities.

Married women ($n = 225$, 77.33%) were more likely to report they engage in sexual activities as leisure than were single women ($n = 65$, 43.9%). This finding is not particularly surprising in that the married women are somewhat more likely than the single women to have available partners. Similarly mothers with children at home ($n = 152$, 74.9%) were more likely to report sexual activities as leisure than

Table 8.1
Relative Popularity of Leisure Activities

ACTIVITY	N	%	ACTIVITY	N	%
1. Watch TV or VCR	387	88.2	27. Play cards or board games	116	26.4
2. Read newspaper, magazine or journal	380	86.6	28. Go to a library	112	25.5
3. Shopping	360	82.0	29. Child's school activity	100	22.8
4. Eat out	339	77.2	30. Take photographs or home movies	100	22.8
5. Read a book	335	76.3	31. Play a musical instrument	96	21.9
6. Aerobic activities	297	67.7	32. Exercise class	96	21.9
7. Listen to stereo	291	66.3	33. Travel	94	21.4
8. Sexual activities	290	66.1	34. Work out	92	21.0
9. Organization meetings/activities	256	58.3	35. Attend sports events	92	21.0
10. Visit friends or relatives	255	58.1	36. Go to a club or bar to drink or dance	88	20.0
11. Go to church	247	56.3	37. Do crossword or jigsaw puzzles	84	19.1
12. Socialize on the phone	236	53.8	38. Visit museum or art gallery	83	18.9
13. Outdoor gardening or yardwork	235	53.5	39. Attend a lecture	76	17.3
14. Go for a walk or drive	201	45.8	40. Play golf, tennis, racquet/handball	75	17.1
15. Socialize in the home	199	45.3	41. Read aloud	63	14.4
16. Raise houseplants	185	42.1	42. Boat or fish	52	11.8
17. Take a nap	171	39.0	43. Camp, hike, backpack	48	10.9
18. Go to movies	171	39.0	44. Picnic	48	10.9
19. Play with, train, or care for a pet	164	37.4	45. Meditate or do yoga	43	9.8
20. Do a craft hobby	162	36.9	46. Play a team sport	33	7.5
21. Take hot bath/sauna/jacuzzi/hot tub	161	36.7	47. Ski	32	7.3
22. Relax	152	34.6	48. Other	26	5.9
23. Write letters to friends	140	31.9	49. Collect stuff	20	4.6
24. Volunteer work	133	30.3	50. Bowl	20	4.6
25. Attend live performance	131	29.8	51. Play video games, pinball, or pool	11	2.5
26. Gourmet cooking or baking	126	28.7			

women without children ($n = 138, 58.5\%$). Again availability of partners may be a factor; 81.8% of the mothers were married, compared with 53.0% of women without children.

Women aged 20 to 29 reported some leisure activities in higher percentages than did women in other age groups. These women were more likely to go shopping, eat out, and visit friends or relatives than women in the other age groups. Women aged 20 through 49 were more likely to engage in sexual activities as leisure and go to movies than were women aged 50 and above. For these types of activities, at least, the women under 50 appear to be more active than women 50 and over. Otherwise the leisure activities of women in the various subgroups are much more similar than they are different. Apparently age was not a major factor in the choice of leisure activities. One might expect that the women over 50 would be less active than the younger women for various health reasons. This presumption is not supported by the data, however, which show no significant differences between age groups in reported health status.

Leisure Companions

Family members commonly were chosen as leisure companions, especially by women with families (spouse and/or children living at home). These women, who comprised about 75% of the sample, have "built-in" leisure companions, people at home who are often readily available for many leisure activities, such as watching TV, eating out, doing yard or garden work, or engaging in sexual activities. Many women with families may choose certain activities such as attending church, traveling, or going to children's school activities because of family members' involvement; sharing leisure time with family may be a major purpose of pursuing such activities.

Single women with no children at home, on the other hand, were much less likely to choose family as companions for leisure activities. The family members they do share their leisure with are probably their family of origin, or for some, grown children or grandchildren. These types of family companions tend to be less readily available for at-home activities or "spur of the moment" activities. The single women were much more likely to share their leisure with friends, if they choose a companion.

The activities most often pursued with friends, such as eating out, shopping, playing golf, tennis, or racquetball, going to movies, or attending live performances or clubs are almost all socially oriented and usually are pursued outside the home. Interestingly, less than half (45.8%) of the sample reported eating out with friends, which was the most popular activity done with friends as companion choice. This smaller group of women sharing their leisure with friends are mostly the single women in the sample, who appear to be more connected with a network of friends than are married women.

Regardless of age, marital status, or motherhood, the women reported pursuing about half of their leisure activities alone. Single women pursued more activities alone than married women, and nonmothers pursued more activities alone than did mothers. Many of the most popular activities pursued alone are those generally not intended to be shared with others, such as reading or taking a nap or a bath. It seems that many of the women chose these activities because of their relaxing, solitary characteristics. These women also may have chosen to pursue some leisure activities alone for more external reasons: A partner may not be readily available, or potential partners may not be interested in the activity.

Co-workers were not commonly chosen as leisure companions and were chosen as companions by more than 10% of the women for only two activities. Some of the women ate out with co-workers, presumably during lunch breaks from work. Co-workers also were chosen as companions when going to organization meetings and activities; it is likely that these women were peers belonging to the same professional organizations. Less commonly, the women socialized with co-workers, inviting them to their homes, talking with them on the telephone, or going out to clubs or bars, probably after work. Outside of these social activities, the women did not share leisure with their co-workers, especially activities engaged in at home or activities of a more personal nature. It appears that these women, at least in terms of leisure, were keeping their professional lives and their personal lives separate.

Most Frequent and Most Desired Activities

I asked our participants what leisure activity they did most often and the reason that activity attracted them. If the women responded to these open-ended questions with more than one activity or reason, I used only the first response in my analysis. Almost all of the activity responses were the same activities as previously listed. I categorized others by type of activity (e.g., sports, dance, music, family, education, work, religious activities). The women's reasons for choosing these activities fell into 15 categories (see Table 8.2).

Almost all of the participants ($n = 405$, 92.3%) responded to this survey item. Two thirds of the women reported the five most common activities: reading a book (20.7%), watching TV or VCR (14.1%), doing aerobic activities (13.8%), reading a newspaper, magazine, or journal (12.3%), and doing craft hobbies (5.4%). All of these activities were engaged in alone by most of the women, except for watching TV, which they did with family members (see Table 8.3).

Participants reported choosing these activities because they are relaxing, convenient, educational, and healthy. They require little or no effort and are conveniently available within the home. These relaxing activities are good strategies for coping with the double day of professional women. The women also do aerobic activities to relax, but primarily for health and appearance. Interestingly, almost as many women reported doing aerobic activities ($n = 56$) as watching TV ($n = 57$).

The most frequent activities are solitary activities. Recall that the women commonly engaged in other activities alone. These findings suggest that many career women may be somewhat isolated from social support networks outside their families. On the other hand, time alone may be inherently more attractive to women with spouses and/or children at home.

I also asked participants to list the leisure activity they wish they could pursue more often, with whom they would engage in the activity, and why they would choose the activity. Again I used only the first response given, if more than one activity or reason was provided.

Most of the women ($n = 398$, 90.7%) answered this item. The activities the women said they would like to pursue more often were somewhat different from the activities they pursued most often (see Table 8.4). The women said they would like to do aerobic activities (18.1%), play golf or tennis (8.3%), travel (8.3.%), do craft hobbies (8.3%), and read a book (8.0%). They would play golf or tennis with friends, travel with family members, and read, do aerobic activities, and do craft hobbies alone. For these last three activities, the women gave about the same reasons as in the previous item. They reported they would like to play golf or tennis for the exercise and challenge involved. Their primary reason for wanting to travel more often was to see new places and people and to enjoy new experiences.

Most of the desired leisure activities the women reported require more physical activity and are more socially oriented than the activities they pursued most often. These are activities they may have been unable

Table 8.2
Reasons Given for Leisure Activities

BODY	• Health • Weight control • Exercise • Wish to improve appearance • Physical self-improvement
EASE	• Convenient, readily available • Easy to do, passive • Requires little or no energy or thinking • Requires no special equipment or preparation
ENERGY	• Challenge, excitement, stimulation • Competition
ENJOY	• Pleasure, enjoyment, satisfaction • Fun, entertainment • Enjoy something inherent about the activity
ESCAPE	• Change of pace/environment/mind set • Taking mind/time off of work and responsibilities
MIND	• Desire to keep up with current events • Educational, intellectual, enlightening
NEED	• A need for the activity (e.g., exercise or shopping)
NEW	• Seeing new places • Meeting people • Experiencing new things
OUTSIDE	• Being outside, enjoying outdoors
PEOPLE	• Companionship, closeness, intimacy, interaction • Time with family or friends • Something inherent about the people involved
RELAX	• Relaxing, calming • Peace, quiet, serenity
RESULT	• Creativity • Enjoy the result • Constructive, productive, useful
SELF	• Time for self, solitude • Self-expression • Self-enrichment or benefit • Spiritual renewal
STRESS	• Stress management, tension reduction

Table 8.3
Leisure Activities Done Most Often

ACTIVITY	REASONS	N	%
1. Read a book	Relax	29	34.5
	Mind	24	28.6
(*n* = 84)	Escape	15	17.9
	Self	7	8.3
	Ease	5	6.0
	Enjoy	4	4.8
2. Watch TV or VCR	Ease	23	40.4
	Relax	15	26.3
(*n* = 57)	Enjoy	7	12.3
	Escape	6	10.5
	People	5	8.8
	Mind	1	1.8
3. Aerobic activity	Body	26	46.4
	Relax	8	14.3
	Stress	8	14.3
(*n* = 56)	Energy	5	8.9
	Enjoy	3	5.4
	Outside	3	5.4
	Ease	1	1.8
	Escape	1	1.8
	Self	1	1.8
4. Read a newspaper	Mind	22	44.0
	Relax	16	32.0
	Ease	8	16.0
(*n* = 50)	Enjoy	2	4.0
	Escape	1	2.0
	Self	1	2.0
5. Craft hobbies	Relax	11	50.0
	Result	9	40.9
	Ease	1	4.5
(*n* = 22)	Escape	1	4.5

Table 8.4
Leisure Activities Desired More Often

ACTIVITY	REASONS	N	%
1. Aerobic activity	Body	40	55.6
	Relax	8	11.1
(n = 72)	Need	7	9.7
	Stress	4	5.6
	Outside	3	4.2
	People	3	4.2
	Self	3	4.2
	Energy	2	2.8
	Enjoy	1	1.4
	Escape	1	1.4
2. Play golf or tennis	Body	11	33.3
	Energy	9	27.3
	Enjoy	5	15.2
(n = 33)	Outside	5	15.2
	People	1	3.0
	Relax	1	3.0
	Self	1	3.0
3. Travel	New	20	60.6
	Escape	4	12.1
	Enjoy	2	6.1
(n = 33)	Mind	2	6.1
	Relax	2	6.1
	Energy	1	3.0
	Outside	1	3.0
	People	1	3.0
4. Craft hobbies	Result	21	63.6
	Enjoy	4	12.1
	Relax	3	9.1
(n = 33)	Self	2	6.1
	Energy	1	3.0
	Escape	1	3.0
	People	1	3.0
5. Read a book	Mind	11	34.4
	Relax	10	31.3
	Self	5	15.6
(n = 32)	Enjoy	2	6.3
	Escape	2	6.3
	Ease	1	3.1
	Other	1	3.1

to pursue because of time constraints. In addition, some of these activities require a substantial time and financial commitment, planning, or equipment and space.

Many factors limit the leisure time and activities of career women, primarily constraints inherent in having a career or a family (and especially the double day of women who have both). Even so, the career women in the sample seemed to engage in a somewhat well-rounded assortment of leisure activities, with a strong emphasis on sedentary, relaxing activities that are easy to do and require little or no expense, planning, or time commitment. The women did many of the more popular activities at home, with family members, or alone.

Although the women in this study chose their leisure activities with time and convenience in mind, it seems they did have an understanding of the value of leisure in their lives, especially in terms of relaxation and stress management. Thus they could accomplish more than one goal at once. They could meet their needs for relaxation in ways they enjoyed, without having to spend much time or effort in the process.

Leisure can contribute in many important ways to career women's lives in terms of physical, as well as emotional, well-being. Through leisure, women can realize many benefits. They can manage stress, relax, learn, socialize, improve and maintain physical health, enjoy spending time alone or with their companions, and most importantly, nurture themselves.

References

Aburdene, P., & Naisbitt, J. (1992). *Megatrends for women*. New York: Random House.

Bird, C. (1979). *The two-paycheck marriage: How women at work are changing life in America*. New York: Rawson, Wade.

Brown, C. V. (1982). Bringing down the rear: The decline in the relative economic position of single-mother families. In A. Hoiberg (Ed.), *Women and the world of work* (pp. 109-127). New York: Plenum.

Bryson, R. B., Bryson, J. B., Licht, M. H., & Licht, B. G. (1976). The professional pair: Husband and wife psychologists. *American Psychologist, 31*, 10-16.

Cherpas, C. C. (1985). Dual-career families: Terminology, typologies, and work and family issues. *Journal of Counseling and Development, 63*, 616-620.

Colley, A. (1984). Sex roles and explanations of leisure behavior. *Leisure Studies, 3*, 335-341.

de Koninck, M. (1984). Double work and women's health. *Canada's Mental Health, 32*, 28-31.

Deem, R. (1982). Women, leisure and inequality. *Leisure Studies, 1,* 29-46.

Deem, R. (1986). *All work and no play? The sociology of women and leisure.* Milton Keynes, UK: Open University Press.

French, M. (1992). *The war against women.* New York: Summit.

Gideonse, S. (1984). Government response to working women and their families: Values, the policy-making process, and research utilization. In K. M. Borman, D. Quarm, & S. Gideonse (Eds.), *Women in the workplace: Effects on families* (pp. 1-32). Norwood, NJ: Ablex.

Gray, J. D. (1983). The married professional woman: An examination of her role conflicts and coping strategies. *Psychology of Women Quarterly, 7,* 235-243.

Green, E., & Hebron, S. (1988). Leisure and male partners. In E. Wimbush & M. Talbot (Eds.), *Relative freedoms: Women and leisure* (pp. 37-47). Milton Keynes, UK: Open University Press.

Green, E., Hebron, S., & Woodward, D. (1987). Women, leisure and social control. In J. Hanmer & P. Maynard (Eds.), *Women, leisure, and social control* (pp. 75-94). Atlantic Highlands, NJ: Humanities Press.

Hall, F. S., & Hall, D. T. (1978). Dual careers: How do couples and companies cope with the problems? *Organizational Dynamics, 6,* 57-77.

Hargreaves, J. (1989). The promise and problems of women's leisure and sport. In C. Rojek (Ed.), *Leisure for leisure: Critical essays* (pp. 130-149). New York: Routledge.

Haywood, L., Kew, F., & Branham, P. (1989). *Understanding leisure.* London: Hutchinson.

Iso-Ahola, S. E. (1979). Basic dimensions of definitions of leisure. *Journal of Leisure Research, 11,* 28-39.

Iso-Ahola, S. E. (1980). Toward a dialectical social psychology of leisure and recreation. In S. E. Iso-Ahola (Ed.), *Social psychological perspectives on leisure and recreation* (pp. 19-37). Springfield, IL: Charles C. Thomas.

Iso-Ahola, S. E., & Mannell, R. C. (1985). Social and psychological constraints on leisure. In M. G. Wade (Ed.), *Constraints on leisure* (pp. 111-151). Springfield, IL: Charles C. Thomas.

Kelly, J. R. (1982). *Leisure.* Englewood Cliffs, NJ: Prentice-Hall.

Lieber, E. K. (1980). The professional woman: Coping in a two-career family. *Educational Horizons, 58,* 156-161.

Marsden, L. R. (1982). The relationship between the labor force employment of women and the changing social organization in Canada. In A. Hoiberg (Ed.), *Women and the world of work* (pp. 65-76). New York: Plenum.

Neulinger, J. (1980). Introduction. In S. E. Iso-Ahola (Ed.), *Social psychological perspectives on leisure and recreation* (pp. 5-18). Springfield, IL: Charles C. Thomas.

Neulinger, J. (1981). *The psychology of leisure* (2nd ed.). Springfield, IL: Charles C. Thomas.

Piotrkowski, C. S., & Repetti, R. L. (1984). Dual-earner families. *Marriage and Family Review, 7,* 99-124.

Presser, H. B. (1982). Child care use and constraints in the United States. In A. Hoiberg (Ed.), *Women and the world of work* (pp. 295-304). New York: Plenum.

Quarm, D. (1984). Sexual inequality: The high cost of leaving parenting to women. In K. M. Borman, D. Quarm, & S. Gideonse (Eds.), *Women in the workplace: Effects on families* (pp. 187-208). Norwood, NJ: Ablex.

Rapoport, R., & Rapoport, R. N. (1972). The dual-career family: A variant pattern and social change. In C. Safilios-Rothschild (Ed.), *Toward a sociology of women* (pp. 216-244). Santa Barbara: John Wiley.

Rybczynski, W. (1991). *Waiting for the weekend.* New York: Viking.

Shainess, N. (1980). The working wife and mother: A new woman? *American Journal of Psychotherapy, 34,* 374-386.

Shank, J. (1983). Self-nurturance through leisure: An issue in the counseling of dual-career women. *Women and Therapy, 2,* 63-68.

Woodward, D., & Green, E. (1988). "Not tonight, dear!" The social control of women's leisure. In E. Wimbush & M. Talbot (Eds.), *Relative freedoms: Women and leisure* (pp. 131-146). Milton Keynes, UK: Open University Press.

Yogev, S. (1981). Do professional women have egalitarian marital relationships? *Journal of Marriage and the Family, 43,* 865-871.

Yogev, S. (1983). Dual-career couples: Conflicts and treatment. *American Journal of Family Therapy, 11,* 38-44.

9

Is Alcoholism
the Cost of Equality?
Career Women and Alcohol

Are women who aspire to roles previously occupied by men likely to succumb to the "equal opportunity disease" of alcoholism? Are those who make dire predictions that women who replace homemaking and care-giving roles with careers trying to protect women "for our own good," or are they making thinly disguised attempts to gain social control of women they would exclude from circles of male power? Is the work world a male-defined culture in which alcohol consumption is an accepted part of symbolic interaction? Is a woman expected to "drink like a man," or to act like a lady? Is drinking by a woman in a professional setting viewed as drinking by a man in a professional setting would be viewed? Are women conscious of the ways their decisions to drink or abstain affect their career opportunities for advancement?

These are just a few of the questions concerning women's alcohol use that have been the research focus of Elsie Shore since the beginning of her career as a psychology professor and researcher. In this study she considers career women's perceptions of the role of alcohol in their social and professional lives with a research design that helps her examine the validity of the recurrent warning that women may be vulnerable to alcoholism as we aspire to professional roles previously reserved for men. If these warnings barely disguise the motives of those who would gain the social control of women by diverting our attention from our professional achievement goals, we need to be aware of the duplicity of those who would protect us "for our own good." If, however, career women do experience distinct risks in our use of alcohol in social and professional roles, we need to be better informed so that we may take appropriate precautions, on our own behalf, and on behalf of the peers with whom we make policy and appropriate interventions.

Shore's study confirms that career women are more likely than noncareer women to drink, that women's drinking is viewed more negatively than men's drinking, and that there is an inverse ratio between this study's career women's income and drinking. She found career women in this study to be slightly more likely to drink than expected, in comparison with national norms, but the study does not confirm the possibility that career women experience heightened risk of excessive drinking that dire predictions posit. Shore's analysis does point out areas of potential problems with alcohol, including relationships with male peers and supervisors whose behavior may increase career women's risks for alcohol-related accidents. Shore's study of negative outcomes of drinking is statistically reassuring, while offering areas of concern for women who choose to drink and for those of us who exercise responsibility for creating a healthy working culture. She concludes that women's involvement in the design of policies and programs pertaining to prevention and intervention makes consideration of alcohol an area of both personal and professional responsibility.

ELSIE R. SHORE

After years of being ignored by policy makers, researchers, and the public, women's use of alcohol recently has become a subject of concern and study. To a large extent, this attention coincides with changes brought about by the women's movement and focuses on the working woman. The concern is that women who work outside the home, especially those holding high-level business or professional positions, will be at greater risk for the development of alcoholism or other negative effects of alcohol use than are women in other roles (Gomberg, 1977; Wilsnack, 1978). Although research on women has been increasing in recent years, the assumption that access to positions of power and autonomy brings with it alcoholism predates attempts to document the relationship (e.g., Whitehead & Ferrence, 1977).

A number of factors have been proposed as reasons for increased alcoholism and alcohol-related problems among women working outside the home. Research on sex-role identification problems has produced conflicting evidence (Beckman, 1978; Scida & Vannicelli, 1979; Wilsnack, 1973, 1974) and has largely been abandoned. Others have conceptualized role issues in terms of overload and the stress produced when a woman tries to fulfill the obligations of many roles, some of which conflict in their demands on her time and energy (Parker, Parker, Wolz, & Harford, 1980; Wilsnack & Cheloha, 1987).

In many business environments, norms and expectations regarding drinking have been linked with the development of alcohol problems (Trice & Sonnenstuhl, 1988). Women workers will be exposed to these norms and may be expected to conform to them (Cosper, 1979; Johnson, 1982). Even if she is not given an overt or covert message, as a new member of the group the woman may feel that adoption of the existing attitudes and behaviors will help her become an accepted part of the work community. In addition, in some fields it is not unusual to conduct business over drinks, and it might be considered as bad practice to abstain while a potential customer, client, or colleague is drinking. The woman employee also might be expected to use alcohol to facilitate business transactions. Shore (1985b) found that both male and female managers and professionals were unclear about the norms for alcohol use by women. Such lack of clarity, or ambivalence, has been linked with the development of alcohol problems (Mizruchi & Perrucci, 1962; Noel & McCrady, 1984; Ullman, 1958).

Although attitudes toward women who drink remain more negative than attitudes toward men who drink (Gomberg, 1988; Sandmaier, 1980), there is greater acceptance of women's drinking today than in the past. Drinking in public, with or without a male escort, also is more accepted. The tendency to postpone marriage and the high divorce rate mean that more women are single. Socializing among single people more often occurs outside the home, in clubs, bars, and restaurants. As a result more women are in places where drinking is expected, and more of them are driving to and from these places.

Many hypotheses have been offered to explain the expected rise in alcoholism and alcohol-related problems among women, but the rise itself has yet to be documented. Research studies instead indicate that women's drinking has changed very little in the last 20 years, especially concerning the prevalence of heavy drinking (Fillmore, 1984; Roman, 1988; Wilsnack, Wilsnack, & Klassen, 1984).

Roman suggested a possible important link "between employment and normative/social drinking rather than between employment and problem drinking" (1988, p. 9). Hingson, Mangione, and Barrett (1981) found that the drinking rate among employed women in Boston ranged from 47% to 58%, and Parker, Kaelber, Harford, and Brody (1983) reported that 89% of the employed women in their Detroit sample drank. Almost all (96.6%) of the 147 business and professional women studied by Shore (1985a) drank at least infrequently.

The Research Group on Women and Work (RGWW) survey contained questions that measure subjects' drinking and assess some of the factors thought to influence it. In this way we might see whether there is support for the admonition that alcoholism is "the dark side of female emancipation" ("Cost of equality," 1980, p. 1).

Table 9.1
Quantity-Frequency of Consumption

	N	%
Abstainer	52	11.5
Light (<2 drinks per day)	369	81.6
Moderate (>2, <5 drinks per day)	22	4.9
Heavy (>5 drinks per day)	9	2

Alcohol Consumption

To measure quantity and frequency of alcohol consumption, the women were asked how often they drank wine, beer, and liquor and how much they usually drank of each beverage at one time (Jessor, Graves, Hanson, & Jessor, 1968). Responses were converted into ounces of absolute alcohol consumed per day. (One ounce of absolute alcohol is equivalent to two standard drinks.) In Table 9.1 respondents' consumption is divided into four categories; abstainer, light (.001 to .999 oz absolute alcohol), moderate (1.000 to 2.499 oz), and heavy (2.500 or more oz). The majority of the women reported levels of consumption that place them in the light range of consumption.

The vast majority of the women in this group (88.5%) drank at least once a year. Surveys in the United States indicate that, in the general population, a considerably larger proportion of women abstain from alcohol (Roman, 1988; Wechsler, 1978). Studies of working women, however, show rates comparable to those found in the RGWW study (Parker et al., 1983; Shore, 1985a).

The smallest group is that of heavy drinkers, the group most likely to contain problem drinkers and alcoholics. Thus, in this sample, the presence of a majority of drinkers is not accompanied by a large number of heavy drinkers. This finding might mean that predictions concerning risk of alcoholism related to the overall number of female drinkers are not supported. It should be noted that these data are cross-sectional and cannot address the question of whether heavy drinking is increasing among business and professional women. To investigate this question, longitudinal data are needed.

Because the overwhelming majority of the women in this study are light drinkers, this group dominated in various subgroup breakdowns. Only minor differences based on marital status are found, with a bit less abstention among divorced women and more moderate drinking among married women. Except for a slightly larger group of moderate drinkers ($N = 10$, 10.6%) among administrators, breakdown by type of job yielded no differences.

Women in their 40s reported greater consumption than the other age groups. The average consumption in this group was 0.50 oz of absolute alcohol, as compared with 0.29 oz among 30- to 39-year-olds, and 0.18 oz among women in their 20s. This is an unusual finding, as most studies report higher consumption among younger women, compared with older women.

A positive correlation was found between consumption and number of children. This relationship does not take into account the age of children or whether they are living at home. Many of the women in the sample had adult children not living with them. Thus the finding that level of consumption increases as number of children increases should not be seen as evidence that women with child care responsibilities are drinking more than those without such tasks. The finding may be correlated to participants' ages. In this sample, older women, who are more likely to have completed their families, drank more than younger women, who may not have begun or completed childbearing.

A small, but statistically significant, correlation was found between individual income and consumption. The correlation was inverse; that is, as income increased, consumption decreased. In studies of more varied populations, consumption tends to increase with increasing affluence. The income range in this group was much more limited, however, and the finding may reflect variation within a middle to upper-middle-class sample.

Negative Consequences

In many ways the amount of alcohol a person drinks is less important than her reasons for drinking and the effects alcohol has on her life. The women in our sample were asked to indicate how often in the last 6 months alcohol was used in certain ways and produced a variety of consequences.

As expected, the number of negative consequences was significantly related to level of consumption. On the average, abstainers endorsed .08 items on the scale; light drinkers, .55 items. The averages for moderate and heavy drinkers were 1.68 and 1.00 items, respectively.

The most frequently endorsed items (Table 9.2) reflect alcohol use for mood alteration: to become less depressed, blue, or sad; to ease pain, sleep, or forget problems. Here our sample does not differ from the general population in that this type of use has been found to occur more frequently among women than among men (Gomberg & Lisansky, 1984). Unfortunately, use for these personal reasons has been linked to the development of problems with alcohol.

It is in the next two consequences that we may be seeing the development or exacerbation of new dangers to women. Business and professional women may experience more occasions in which they might drive after drinking or ride with an intoxicated driver than might women without careers. Work-related drinking situations, including social occasions connected to work, usually require transportation to and from the event. Except in the largest metropolitan areas, buses or taxis often are scarce or unavailable.

The issue of riding with an intoxicated driver is not new to women, as they long have been passengers in cars driven by drinking husbands and boyfriends. It can be difficult to get the keys from an intoxicated spouse. How much more difficult must it be for a woman to refuse to ride with her boss, supervisor, or client?

Role Overload and Drinking

As stated earlier, some social analysts have expressed concern that the multiple roles taken on by working women would contribute to the development of alcohol problems. The RGWW survey asked two questions that could be conceptualized as measures of role overload or conflict. In the first, subjects were asked "How many hats do you wear?"; 11 roles, including homemaker, wife, student, club member, and financial manager, were listed as responses to this question, and space was provided for additional roles. No statistically significant correlation was

Table 9.2
Negative Consequences of Alcohol Use

Use/Consequence	Reported at least once in last six months	
	N	%
Drink to become less depressed, get rid of "blue" or sad feelings	116	23.8
To ease physical pain, get to sleep	93	19
To forget problems at home or at work	91	19
Passenger in a car driven by someone you felt was high or drunk	73	15
Drove a car when you felt drunk or high from drinking	61	12.5
Drank while on medication not to be mixed with alcohol	37	7.6
Drinking interfered with homemaking	34	7
Got drunk/high in situation in which it would have been better to stay sober	26	5.3

found between number of roles and alcohol consumption. The correlation between number of roles and negative consequences approached significant levels ($r = -.07$, $p = .06$). The relation was inverse, with negative consequences decreasing as number of roles increased.

The women also were asked to list all of the organizations to which they belong. No significant correlation was found between number of organizations and alcohol consumption, but a statistically significant inverse relation was found between organization memberships and negative consequences. As number of organization memberships increased, number of negative consequences decreased.

Early hypotheses and popular impressions about role demands and alcohol use are not supported by these data. The data do provide support for a more recent national study (Wilsnack & Cheloha, 1987) that found that role *deprivation* was correlated with problem drinking. A busier life actually might offer fewer opportunities for heavier drinking, as well as a sense of fulfillment that leaves fewer reasons for alcohol abuse. In addition to filling time and providing personal satisfaction, active membership in organizations may expose the woman to greater public scrutiny and, thus, inhibit excessive drinking.

The Drinking Context

Researchers have spoken of "social inducement" as important to understanding women's drinking. Being in the company of drinkers may lead a woman into drinking and, perhaps, into abusive drinking. In addition, various contextual factors might promote or inhibit drinking.

Each participant was asked to rate the drinking of her spouse and her best friend. The level of consumption of both of these people was significantly related to the woman's consumption and to negative uses/consequences. The relations were positive; that is, the woman's drinking and negative consequences increased with increases in spouse's and friend's drinking.

The women were asked how often in the last 30 days they were in settings where other people were drinking, whether or not they themselves were drinking. Greater frequency in drinking settings was positively correlated with both consumption and negative consequences.

One hundred women (20.9%) responded affirmatively when asked whether drinking is permitted or expected as part of the job. This group experienced a higher number of negative consequences of drinking than did those for whom on-the-job drinking was not permitted or expected.

To investigate this relation further, individual negative uses/consequences were studied. As indicated in Table 9.3, driving while intoxicated and riding with an intoxicated driver were reported more frequently by women permitted or expected to drink. This finding seems a logical relation in that on-the-job or job-related drinking occurs outside the home and sometimes away from the office and, therefore, requires return transportation to home or office. This finding highlights the importance of job characteristics and company policies in exposing or protecting employees from harm.

Table 9.3
Negative Consequences of On-the-Job Drinking

Consequence	Drinking Permitted / Expected			
	YES		NO	
	N	%	*N*	%
Driving while impaired	20	20	39	10.4
Passenger of impaired driver	22	22	51	13.6

Conclusion

All warnings about the potentially dire consequences of women's attempts to expand their roles and rights must be evaluated in the context of a long history during which such warnings were designed to keep women from realizing their individual potential or participating fully in society. Even statements that appear to be scientific must be scrutinized for their political content (Fillmore, 1984; Morrissey, 1986). In this study I compared the predictions and theories about working women's drinking to their own reports. A large number of the career women in this sample drank alcoholic beverages, but their level of consumption was light. Women in the business world may feel free to drink and may think they should drink in order to be accepted, but they also may be influenced by norms that promote differential rates of consumption for males and females. In other words, a woman may feel she should drink "with the boys," but should still drink "like a lady."

This is not to say that women do not become alcoholic or that alcohol should not be viewed by women as the potentially dangerous drug that it is. This also is not to say that there will not be an increase in alcohol problems among business and professional women in the future. Women must be considered in efforts to prevent and treat alcohol abuse, but a future that includes substance abuse should not be assumed because a woman has chosen to enter the world of work.

At the same time, this study highlights the importance of the drinking environment as an influence on women. The woman with a spouse or best friend who drinks heavily may find herself joining in this dangerous behavior, perhaps simply because she is in more drinking situations than a woman whose spouse or friends do not drink as much. The woman who is permitted or expected to drink as part of her job is more likely to do so, thereby exposing herself to the dangers of such behavior. Among the dangers are driving while intoxicated and riding with an intoxicated driver. The latter area has received less attention than other areas of concern for drinking women, but it actually may pose a growing threat to their lives.

The importance of the norms and expectations of the business environment as influences on women's drinking and its consequences suggests an area for prevention (Noel & McCrady, 1984). Employers need to consider both the formal policies and the informal norms of their companies. Changes in policies and norms can make the work environment better for both men and women and reduce the health care and productivity costs of alcoholism and alcohol-related problems. Instead of expecting women to exhibit behavior that has been documented to be unhealthful, we might learn more healthful and safer behaviors from them and transform our workplaces.

References

Beckman, L. J. (1978). Sex-role conflict in alcoholic women: Myth or reality? *Journal of Abnormal Psychology, 87,* 408-417.

Cosper, R. (1979). Drinking as conformity: A critique of sociological literature on occupational differences in drinking. *Journal of Studies on Alcohol, 40,* 868-891.

Cost of equality? As women's roles grow more like men's, so do their problems. (1980, January 14). *Wall Street Journal,* pp. 1, 22.

Fillmore, K. M. (1984). "When angels fall": Women's drinking as cultural preoccupational and as reality. In S. C. Wilsnack & L. J. Beckman (Eds.), *Alcohol problems in women: Antecedents, consequences, and intervention* (pp. 7-36). New York: Guilford.

Gomberg, E. (1977). Women, work, and alcohol: A disturbing trend. *Supervisory Management, 22,* 16-22.

Gomberg, E. L. (1988). Alcoholic women in treatment: The question of stigma and age. *Alcohol and Alcoholism, 23,* 507-514.

Gomberg, E. S. L., & Lisansky, J. M. (1984). Antecedents of alcohol problems in women. In S. C. Wilsnack & L. J. Beckman (Eds.), *Alcohol problems in women: Antecedents, consequences, and intervention* (pp. 233-259). New York: Guilford.

Hingson, R., Mangione, T., & Barrett, J. (1981). Job characteristics and drinking practices in the Boston Metropolitan area. *Journal of Studies on Alcohol, 42,* 723-738.

Jessor, R., Graves, T. D., Hanson, R. C., & Jessor, S. L. (1968). *Society, personality, and deviant behavior: A study of a tri-ethnic community.* New York: Holt, Rinehart & Winston.

Johnson, P. B. (1982). Sex differences, women's roles, and alcohol use: Preliminary national data. *Journal of Social Issues, 38,* 93-116.

Mizruchi, E. H., & Perrucci, R. (1962). Norm qualities and differential effects of deviant behavior: An exploratory analysis. *American Sociological Review, 27,* 391-399.

Morrissey, E. R. (1986). Power and control through discourse: The case of drinking and drinking problems among women. *Contemporary Crises, 10,* 157-179.

Noel, N. E., & McCrady, B. S. (1984). Target populations for alcohol abuse prevention. In P. M. Miller & T. D. Nirenberg (Eds.), *Prevention of alcohol abuse* (pp. 55-94). New York: Plenum.

Parker, D. A., Kaelber, C., Harford, T. C., & Brody, J. A. (1983). Alcohol problems among employed men and women in metropolitan Detroit. *Journal of Studies on Alcohol, 44,* 1026-1039.

Parker, D. A., Parker, E. S., Wolz, W. M., & Harford, T. C. (1980). Sex roles and alcohol consumption: A research note. *Journal of Health and Social Behavior, 21,* 43-48.

Roman, P. M. (1988). *Women and alcohol use: A review of the research literature.* Rockville, MD: U.S. Department of Health and Human Services.

Sandmaier, M. (1980). *The invisible alcoholics: Women and alcohol abuse in America.* New York: McGraw-Hill.

Scida, J., & Vannicelli, M. (1979). Sex-role conflict and women's drinking. *Journal of Studies on Alcohol, 40,* 28-44.

Shore, E. R. (1985a). Alcohol consumption rates among managers and professionals. *Journal of Studies on Alcohol, 46*(2), 153-156.

Shore, E. R. (1985b). Norms regarding drinking behavior in the business environment. *Journal of Social Psychology, 125,* 735-741.

Trice, H. M., & Sonnenstuhl, W. J. (1988). Drinking behavior and risk factors related to the workplace: Implications for research and prevention. *Journal of Applied Behavioral Science, 24,* 327-346.

Ullman, A. D. (1958). Sociological backgrounds of alcoholism. *Annals of the American Academy of Political and Social Science, 315,* 48-54.

Wechsler, H. (1978). Introduction: Summary of the literature. In National Institute on Alcohol Abuse and Alcoholism, *Alcoholism and alcohol abuse among women: Reesearch issues* (pp. 3-31). (Research Monograph No. 1, DHEW Publication No. ADM 80-835). Washington, DC: Government Printing Office.

Whitehead, P. C., & Ferrence, R. G. (1977). Liberated drinking: New hazard for women. *Addictions, 24,* 36-53.

Wilsnack, R. W., & Cheloha, R. (1987). Women's roles and problem drinking across the lifespan. *Social Problems, 34,* 231-248.

Wilsnack, R. W., Wilsnack, S. C., & Klassen, A. D. (1984). Women's drinking and drinking problems: Patterns from a 1981 national survey. *American Journal of Public Health, 74,* 1231-1238.

Wilsnack, S. C. (1973). Sex role identity in female alcoholism. *Journal of Abnormal Psychology, 82,* 253-261.

Wilsnack, S. C. (1974). The effects of social drinking on women's fantasies. *Journal of Personality, 42,* 43-61.

Wilsnack, S. C. (1978). Introduction: Current status and research needs. In National Institute on Alcohol Abuse and Alcoholism, *Alcoholism and alcohol abuse among women: Research issues* (pp. 163-186) (Research Monograph No. 1, DHEW Publication No. ADM 80-81). Washington, DC: Government Printing Office.

10 Leadership or Empowerment? Reframing Our Questions

Carol Wolfe Konek's study of leadership values further elucidates themes evident in earlier chapters. Participants' attitudes toward their professional lives, leadership aspirations, and sense of social responsibility suggest that one woman's definition of a *professional woman* applies to many: "One who gives 100% of herself to her job—takes opportunities to grow in knowledge and skills—is willing to learn—treats others with respect—can be aggressive yet feminine—accepts challenges." Konek's results reveal at least one source of a tendency seen repeatedly throughout the study: the sense that the sacrifice and struggle of career women's lives are worth the rewards. These women seek responsibility and leadership opportunities; they are highly motivated; and they express a commitment to a social vision that expands leadership beyond professionalism.

Perhaps most interesting for the study as a whole, however, is the participants' nontraditional understanding of leadership and its relationship to sanctioned power. Consistent with feminist scholarship on women's leadership values, they see leadership as a personal opportunity that may or may not relate to existing structures. They see power as a personal attribute, rather than as a limited resource to be tapped or hoarded. They express comfort with ambition and see no inconsistency between the exercise of power and femininity. Their attitudes suggest that career women may not seek to change the structures in which they participate, so much as to circumvent those structures. Having been excluded from the traditions of work, career women have learned to define new traditions for themselves, with greater emphasis on relationships and social responsibility, and to live and work accordingly.

CAROL WOLFE KONEK

When I try to recall the moment I first became interested in women's leadership, I see myself surrounded by a group of faculty women and administrators in a boardroom on our campus, mapping the location of women in the entire university, and plotting strategies for our inclusion in all areas of university life. I was excited to be included in this subversive activity, for I was a part-time lecturer in composition who, as a re-entry, part-time student with four young children, once had been so alienated from student life that I had studied in my car rather than in the library.

My inclusion in this mapping ceremony meant that the faculty women accepted me, that they were diminishing status divisions by which we were separated, and that our mutual analysis of the organizational pyramid of the university would have far-reaching implications for all of us. That night in the boardroom, we mapped our absence in the structure of our university. We planned for our inclusion, as students, faculty, and administrators, in enrollment in all classes, departments, and colleges, in access to traditional and nontraditional careers, in salary and sabbatical benefits, in promotion and tenure, in curriculum planning and content, and in both student and university governance. We were so exhilarated by this empowering experience, we even decided to ask a clerk of one of our legislators to obtain a copy of the state budget, which, although a matter of public record, was kept secret by convention, protecting the "privacy" of our colleagues whose salaries were unknown to any but their chairs, deans, and central administrators.

The subversive activity of that night in the boardroom helped me see that I was not on the organizational chart, although I recall a woman's observation that "women are the lines between the boxes on the chart." It seems even now that I started my career in a hole under the mythical career ladder and that, without my connection with these women, I might never have reached the bottom rung of the ladder.

This mapping ceremony coincided with my invitation to team-teach a women's studies class with Annette TenElshof, an associate dean in student affairs, who, after having learned of a new program being started at San Diego State University, launched our women's studies program with a few "experimental," interdisciplinary classes taught by "volunteers." Looking back on my journey from the parking lot, to that boardroom, to the administrative and teaching positions I now hold, and to my work with the Research Group on Women and Work, I realize that this experience in empowerment provided a metaphor for my career and for my realization that women working in collaboration could change everything forever. When I first heard a woman say, "The personal is political," I believed her.

Strategies for Sharing Power

I, like many other women who have worked to empower ourselves and others in the second wave of feminism, have transformed our philosophy of leadership. In the beginning, we were dismayed that so few bright, talented women found access to sanctioned leadership roles. Then we were concerned that women were underrepresented at the top of every organizational pyramid we could find. As we sought to increase the representation of women in those pyramids, we considered the individual, androgynous "traits" of leadership, studied the structures and processes of sanctioned and informal power in organizations, and worked at acquiring and teaching these "traits" and gaining access to leadership ladders within existing structures of power. At that time, many of us held liberal feminist beliefs about individual rights and the desirability of sharing equal opportunity with males. As we worked to eradicate sexist language, socialization, and role expectations, many of us wished to replace sexism with androgyny (Heilbrun, 1973), believing we could find new ways of sharing power that inevitably would change organizations as women's inclusion transformed organizational culture. Gradually activists became concerned that if the organizational women were shaped to the goals and values of the organization, we might fail to reshape organizations. It became apparent to many feminists that organizations had greater power to change women than women had to change organizations unless women intentionally brought their experience to bear on the structures of work and power.

Whereas feminist leadership theory in the 1970s often focused on the similarities between male and female leadership values, feminist writers and activists in the 1980s increasingly identified distinctive values from "women's culture" that would not only make positive contributions to the workplace but also ultimately transform society. Women who had been admonished to compensate for their lack of training in team sports and the military by schooling themselves in competitive values associated with male culture (Harragan, 1977; Hennig & Jardim, 1977; Trahey, 1977) now found themselves encouraged to appreciate the distinctiveness of values learned from women's culture (Ferguson, 1984; Gilligan, 1982; Helgeson, 1990; Morgan, 1989; Ruddick, 1989). Feminist theorists were less likely to posit the attainment of androgyny as our ultimate goal and increasingly valorized women's essential traits, sometimes veering toward separatist positions as we deconstructed male myths as they were replicated in organizational paradigms.

By the 1990s feminist theorists were increasingly sensitized to the "politics of location" and postmodernist reflections that all analysis functioned at the praxis of race, ethnicity, class, gender, sexual orientation, and ableness, with the concomitant understanding that inclusion could only be posited on respect for and commitment to diversity (Fine, 1984; Lather, 1988; Pearson, 1989; Stenstad, 1988). As we systematically began to seek out and listen to voices of previously silenced women from all over the globe, we increasingly saw the tyranny in our own privilege. The interconnectedness of all forms of domination and submission became increasingly apparent to feminists, with profound implications for global, national, organizational, and individual power relationships.

Constrictive Power

Patriarchy and bureaucracy have become almost synonymous in feminist discourse, signifying disconnection, separation, alienation, compartmentalization, and constriction. Robin Morgan reflected:

> If I had to name one quality as the genius of patriarchy, it would be compartmentalization, the capacity for institutionalizing disconnection. Intellect severed from emotion. Thought separated from action. Science split from art. The earth itself divided; national borders. Human beings categorized: by sex, age, race, ethnicity, sexual preference, height, weight, class, religion, physical ability, ad nauseam. (Morgan, 1989, p. 51)

A consideration of historical antecedents of constrictive definitions of power helps us realize how anachronistic concepts of domination seem in reference to contemporary organizational and social life:

> Power over other persons . . . is exercised when potential power wielders, motivated to achieve certain goals of their own, marshal in their power base resources (economic, military, institutional or skill) that enable them to influence the behavior of respondents by activating motives of respondents relevant to those resources and to those goals. (Burns, 1979, p. 18)

Much of management theory has perpetuated notions of the legitimization of patterns of dominance of leaders and submission of followers.

Models of constrictive power are predicated on assumptions that power is to be limited, to be restricted by those whose roles are sanctioned (Table 10.1). Although concepts of constrictive power have been modified by human relations theorists in the direction of egalitarian leadership values, male adult development often was defined as a process moving from dependence to independence, with autonomy being the most advanced stage of development (Erickson, 1978; Kohlberg, 1984; Levinson, 1978). A study that can be used to document the individualistic leadership behaviors of executives at the top of corporate pyramids reveals that *Fortune* 500 CEOs, by and large, have short-term goals, and value individual gains over corporate loyalty or long-term social benefits (Maccoby, 1976).

Table 10.1
Constrictive Group Assumptions

1.	Groups are inevitably hierarchical in structure.
2.	Some group members are superior to others.
3.	Superior group members rise to positions of authority by virtue of expertise, influence, and charisma.
4.	Natural leadership emerges due to innate traits of those predestined to lead.
5.	Power is limited, and, as a scarce resource, should be guarded, hoarded, or restricted.
6.	Energy must be controlled and directed by the person in authority.
7.	The expression of power is diminshing to both the individual and the group.
8.	Groups must conserve resources of energy, knowledge, action, and association to be powerful.
9.	Groups with competitive infrastructures are able to achieve cohesion when competing with other groups.
10.	Individuals are at their optimum when competing with other members of the group.

Although they often failed to assess adequately the power dynamics of race, ethnicity, class, and gender, theorists in humanistic psychology, management, and social change theory, in focusing on egalitarian group processes, helped provide foundations for liberal feminist leadership theory. For instance, Maslow (1962) described the self-actualizing individual as having broad, integrative, and inclusive concerns for others' maturation. Rollo May (1972) described developmental stages of social power from exploitative power, predicated on the threat of violence, through *manipulative power,* defined as "power over," through *competitive power,* defined as "power against," through *nutrient power,* defined as "power for," to *integrative power,* defined as "power with." Burns (1979) described *transforming leadership* as occurring when one or more persons engage with others in such a way that leaders and followers raise one another to higher levels of motivation and morality. Although human relations theorists made important contributions to the democratization of leadership, their analysis often was limited by a failure to critique the cult of individualism that undergirds male development theory and that is projected onto constructions of the organization.

Developmental theorists are likely to see individuals moving through role or structure constraints to more holistic perspectives. Hagberg (1984) hypothesized that individuals pass through stages of externally and organizationally oriented power stages before moving on to internally and globally oriented power stages—beginning with powerlessness, characterized by manipulation; power by association, characterized by dependence on supervisors; symbol-dependent perception of power; power through self-reflection with resulting influence; visionary power, characterized by empowerment of others; and power by gestalt, associated with wisdom, characterized by service, ethics, acceptance, and powerlessness (pp. 251-256). Pearson's developmental theory (1989) posits a model of archetypal progress in which the individual experiences a journey from roles as innocent to orphan to martyr to wanderer to warrior to magician, experienced as a state of wholeness and abundance (pp. 20-21). The more advanced stages of both of these developmental theories are characterized by transcendence of individualism to a state of experienced connectivity or generativity. Although human development theorists reject definitions of power that are constrictive, and seek to reconstruct definitions of power we might describe as generative, andocentric theorists construct adult maturity as individualistic, while gynocentric theorists construct adult development as connective.

Generative Power

Feminist discourse abounds with the metaphors of connection characterized by a kind of generative power that values process over position and that generates power as it distributes responsibility, functions, and rewards. According to much feminist discourse, women's culture often is characterized by connection, inclusion, community. Robin Morgan (1989) valorized feminist culture when she noted: "If I had to characterize one quality as the genius of feminist thought, culture, and action, it would be connectivity. In its rejection of the static, this capacity is witty and protean, like the dance of nature itself, characterized by noticing, exploring, making connections" (p. 53).

Morgan extended principles outlined in Gilligan's (1982) study of women's moral decision-making strategies in which Gilligan distinguishes between male and female moral decision-making strategies predicated on the principle that women strive to protect relationships, rather than emulating men's dominant strategy of attempting to protect principles and that women's morality may arise from the experience of connection and be conceived as a problem of inclusion rather than of balancing claims.

Belenky, Clinchy, Goldberger, and Tarule (1986) discerned principles of connectivity and collectivity in their study of women's learning and cognitive modes, which led them to hypothesize:

> Webs and nets . . . suggest a complexity of relationships and the delicate interrelatedness of all so that tension and movement in one part of the system will grow to be felt in all parts of the whole. In the complexity of a web, no one position dominates over the whole. Each person—no matter how small—has some potential for power; each is always subject to the action of others. (p. 178)

Discomfort with hierarchy may result in willingness to discount, displace, or subvert its structures and to replace bureaucratic or sanctioned power with perceptions of agency and association that transcend and transform relational processes into generative, or empowering, leadership. Generative leadership empowers through processes that are inclusive, accepting of diversity, reciprocal, creative, nurturing, supportive, and open. It accommodates the possibility that "women may express their influence through affiliation, rather than expressing it through power 'over' others" (Miller, 1976, p. 116), that "women may be more inner-directed in assessing their own achievement without reference to that of others" (O'Leary, 1977, p. 94), that women may tend

Table 10.2

Generative Group Assumptions

1.	Empowering groups are inclusive.
2.	Empowering groups are open to diversity of members.
3.	Empowering groups set more goals than constrictive groups and allow for diversity of goal setting.
4.	Groups that maximize exchanges with the contextual system are empowering to members and are characterized by vitality.
5.	Empowering groups generate leadership opportunities for the individuals in the groups.
6.	The group sanctions power and responsibility for both new and experienced group members.
7.	Groups with visionary, global objectives are more energized than parochial groups with constrictive goals.
8.	The expression of energy generates energy.
9.	Community enhances self-realization and self-expression.
10.	Nurturance and support are self-renewing.
11.	Power increases as it is shared and distributed.
12.	All parts of a system respond to the empowering behavior of one or all of its members.
13.	Growth is natural.

to minimize the authoritative exercise of power and to maximize subordinate autonomy (Hennig & Jardim, 1977), and that women may tend to structure in horizontals and in webs, while men structure organizations in hierarchies (Kanter, 1977) (Table 10.2).

In considering the way women experience and express their sense of connectivity within hierarchical organizations, professions, and careers, we must keep in mind that "women may be less willing to challenge or even to acknowledge the hierarchical distribution of power because they experience shared leadership in horizontal rather than vertical leadership structures [as] common forms of feminine experience" (Bunch, 1986, p. 132).

Emergent feminist theories of leadership emphasize a focus on transforming competition into collaboration and connection. These theories point out that patriarchal power is viewed in feminist discourse as constructed as "power over," while contemporary feminist constructions of power might include "power to" or "power with" (Eisler, 1987; French, 1981; Rollo May, 1972). For women, power is likely to be viewed as relational, consensual, and contextual, rather than as hierarchical or structural. Power is less likely to be attributed only to those with sanctioned roles by those who experience power as a process that can transform society through acts arising from the identification of collective interests of even those who are defined as powerless (Janeway, 1980). Innumerable contemporary feminist scholars are engaged in efforts to teach maternal thinking (Ruddick, 1989), to form a partnership society (Eisler, 1987), to bring "connective knowing" to bear on decision making (Belenky et al., 1986), and to reassert the value of relationship over principle in moral decision making (Gilligan, 1982).

Some feminists considering leadership opportunities proclaim that they do not merely "want a piece of the pie," but "want to change the recipe of the pie" (Brocke-Utne, 1987). Spokespersons for many of the diverse feminisms express intentions of "flattening the hierarchy" and of adopting cooperative, rather than competitive, leadership strategies in professional and community roles, emphasizing the need for influencing the reconstruction of organizations and redefining the distribution of power within those organizations.

Shapes of Power

If women's perceptions of organizational structures and experiences of empowerment are distinctive, emergent research theories and methodologies may be limited in the ways inquiries about women's empowerment are shaped. Studies that compare women and men may be predicated on male-defined values, aspirations, and organizational perspectives. A study of psychosexual differences in male and female patterns of belief substantiates male emphasis on the concurrence of pride and glory, and female emphasis on containment and transformation, and documents a pattern of male belief that enhancement leads to deprivation, and of female belief that deprivation leads to enhancement (Robert May, 1980). Women may consider the achievement of a collective or connective view of success as an expression of their sense of individual responsibility. Yet it is possible that women's valuing of achievement that includes affiliation may reflect a sense of social responsibility congruent with concepts of "power to" and "power with" styles of leadership.

Leadership theories predicated on the assumption of individuation as the goal of normal adult development may misconstrue women's leadership values and activities. Conclusions based on studies of the adult development of male subjects, such as those of Erikson, Kohlberg, and Levinson, to mention only a few, may misconstrue women's leadership values and behaviors. Studies that ignore the "integry" or connective activities of holding the parts of a system together may cause women's contributions to power structures to be invisible (Boulding, 1987, p. 16). Studies documenting success avoidance in women, when based on the creation of arbitrary dichotomies between affiliation and achievement, may underestimate the importance of the integration of achievement with affiliation for women (Gilligan, 1982). Achievement and attribution studies occasionally have been used to explain women's inadequacy, rather than their sense of responsibility to others (Gilligan, 1982). "Studies of attribution theory which document women's willingness to accept blame for failure, while refusing to accept credit for success may have underestimated the importance to women of linking affiliation and achievement" (O'Leary, 1977, p. 102).

Kathleen Iannello (1992) considered the possibility that hierarchy and its concomitant focus on control and domination has been a historical stage of organizational development (p. 45) when she distinguished between hierarchical and nonhierarchical assumptions and noted: "Power is associated with the notion of controlling others, while empowerment is associated with the notion of controlling oneself. Therefore, within organizations based on empowerment, members monitor themselves. In organizations based on power, there must be an administrative oversight function" (pp. 44-45). Self-empowering processes are likely to be found in vertical organizations, such as that Jardim described as "a centrar-chy . . . a flat structure with relationships of greater equality and lesser status [where] titles aren't as important [and] performance ranks above position; people above things; closeness above distance; direct access above the more traditional series of filters than that in hierarchies that divide subordinates from superiors" (Jardim, 1993, p. 28).

These theorists share their perception of what we can describe as *generative power,* power that multiplies as it divides, power that is abundant and reciprocal, power that is generated in relationship, a power too dynamic to move from the top down or even to be diagrammed on an organizational chart.

Such theories are not without feminist critics, however. On the one hand, such efforts to reconstruct leadership may be categorized with other "maternalist" or "essentialist" theories that are viewed as resulting in the exaggerated valorization of traditional feminine values, permitting the co-option of feminist progress (Segal, 1987). On the other hand, these efforts at reconstructing leadership may be an effort to resolve leadership dilemmas that enabled women to discount and marginalize their own contributions to professional and social organizations and causes. Such philosophical efforts may represent feminist intentions of restructuring organizations to include and act on values previously considered to be feminine. Additionally such efforts may represent a more serious scholarly effort to reconstruct masculinity than is undertaken even by the most thoughtful advocates of human relations management theory.

Concepts of feminist leadership theory that reconstruct the concept of *power over* and substitute alternative concepts of *power to, power with* (Rollo May, 1972), *power for* (Miller, 1976), and *power of* ask us to form new metaphors for individual and collective power. This process involves relocating power and revisioning the active exercise of responsibility. Elizabeth Janeway (1980) described a process by which the powerless can come to disbelieve in the myths of the powerful and, by coming together and learning to engage in unorthodox thinking, can experience the replacement of individualism with community, whereupon the realization and expression of collective power have a transformative effect on the structure of power. An application of Janeway's theory to women's potential for creating change suggests that hierarchies would be flattened if women were to collectively withdraw their belief in myths of dominance and their complicity in submission. Organizations would change if women were to engage in unorthodox thinking resulting in the reconstruction of organizational interactions into patterns more reflective of their values. When we consider the potential for using our inclusion in previously hierarchical structures to create a transformative effect on those structures, we assume that we must find new ways of articulating our values in order to exercise our leadership in social responsibility while preserving our personal and professional integrity and our function of "integry." We assume that we must understand the values women hold in relationship to leadership and to power.

An expressed goal of many feminists, and women who aspire to leadership roles are inevitably nontraditional women, if not self-defined feminists, is to "flatten the hierarchy" or, as Eisler (1987) suggested, to "replace the hierarchy of status with an hierarchy of actualization" (p. 106), which implies a shift from an organization-centered paradigm to an individual-centered paradigm. As feminist theorists seek new egalitarian definitions of power, we must deconstruct andocentric concepts of the nature of authority and responsibility. We must critique "trait" definitions of leadership and structural allocations of power. We must posit a model of generative leadership values that would bring synergy to individual, organizational, and social values.

New Shapes of Power

In her comparison of hierarchical and nonhierarchical paradigms, Iannello asserted: "Power is associated with controlling others, while empowerment is associated with controlling oneself. Within organizations based on empowerment, members monitor themselves. In organizations based on power, there must be an administrative oversight function" (Iannello, 1992, p. 44).

In her exploration of the possibility that organizational power is most effective when shaped in vertical, rather than horizontal, organizational structures, Ferguson (1984) noted: "Bureaucratic discourse both creates and reflects the masculine notion of the subject, then posits that version of subjectivity as universal. But women's experience provides a vision of human relatedness and autonomy in which subjectivity is rooted in but not reduced to social relations" (p. 204).

Ferguson's (1984) attempt to posit an "alternative vision of collective life, one based on the concrete life experience of women" (p. 212) is premised on her acknowledgment that "power within bureaucracies is not change-making power. The organizational forms and discourse of bureaucratic capitalism institutionalize modes of domination that recreate the very patterns of oppression that feminism arose to combat" (p. 203).

Women's experience and expression of power may not correspond to the structures men create and maintain. Women may experience leadership as expressive, active, and perceptual. In these respects, institutionalized structures may not appear to correspond to women's "cultural" modes of expression and valuing. When women recognize barriers they are unwilling to challenge or transform, they may reframe their issues by defining alternative systems of satisfaction. For instance, women (e.g., RGWW participants in the study in Chap. 4) who do not expect assistance with their career advancement from their supervisors may accept their alienation from that particular source of affirmation, while compensating for this disadvantage by reframing their expectations and redefining success. We must not assume that because such women are not appreciated at work, they do not appreciate work. We must consider evidence that rewards and satisfaction may not correspond to the hierarchical organizational chart that has become such a dominant representation of organizational life, that even the most sophisticated social analyst may believe its shape and compartmentalization actually distributes and limits power.

Strategies for overcoming internalized sexism often include learning new ways of seeing. Elise Boulding (1987) described *social imagination* as "the capacity to visualize the present in fresh ways and to visualize the not-yet in positive ways" (p. 116). In her peace work with those she sees as victims of "imaginative illiteracy," Boulding nurtures creativity, engagement, and diversity. She believes that "the future, like history, is created by acts of imagination which inspire social action in the direction of the imagined" (p. 116). In teaching us to look forward, Boulding's instructions parallel those of Meridel LeSueur (personal communication, September 1980, Wichita State University), who instructed us that "ours is a society which dismembers" and that we must take corrective action by "learning to re-member." LeSueur's version of re-membering would involve us in reconnecting a fragmented and distorted body of knowledge, as well as healing the impaired body politic. In creating the future and in understanding the past, feminists are engaged in thinking connectively, in revisioning the past and the future, and in taking coherent, responsible action.

Women working in organizations they see as male-defined (as RGWW participants in Chap. 2 reported) are challenged to find new ways of defining and distributing power. Because the concept of *leadership* evokes ideas of one person ahead of others, set apart from others, over others, more knowing than others, it is not surprising that feminist discourse has focused increasingly on concepts of *empowerment*. Such shifts correspond to efforts to "de-center" subjectivity and to arrive at a "multi-vocal" way of seeing and being that expands inclusion and that nurtures diversity.

Helgeson (1990), in an exploration of women's distinctive nonhierarchical leadership styles and collaborative form of decision making, attributes differences in women's style, in part, to the role of women's reliance on voice over men's reliance on vision. She concluded that women create organizations

> where authority is not imposed from the top down in hierarchical fashion, [but] in a web structure, where talent is nurtured and encouraged rather than commanded, and a variety of interconnections exist, influence and persuasion take the place of giving orders. The lines of authority are less defined, more dependent upon a moral center. Compassion, empathy, inspiration, and direction—all aspects of nurturance—are connective values, better communicated by voice, by tone, than by vision. (pp. 224-225)

Diversity of inclusion and participation flattens hierarchies with multivocal expressions of experience from many locations of race, ethnicity, class, religion, gender, sexual orientation, and ableness. The right to discover one's voice is coming to be viewed as an educational right by theorists like Fine, who studied silence and voice in a public school and concluded:

> Much more could be done if all educators saw politics as inherent and the giving of voice as essential to the task of education. To not mention racism is as political a stance as is a thorough-going discussion of its dynamics; to not examine domestic violence bears consequences for the numerous youths who have witnessed abuse at home and feel alone, alienated in their experience, unable to concentrate, so that the effects of the violence permeate the classroom even—or particularly—if not named. (Fine, 1984, p. 136)

Just as Fine listened to the silence of children to develop what would correspond to Boulding's (1987) social imagination to construct an alternative empowering system in which voice is generated, Pearson (1989) saw the confluence and synchronicity of social movements that give rise to alternative structures of power:

> While the macrocosmic community clings to the old ways and responds to growing fragmentation by trying to enforce them on others, microcosmic communities are changing: workplaces, neighborhoods, associations, network. The political processes of the environmental, peace and feminist

movements, for instance, are radically different from that of conventional politics. (p. 152)

Sen and Grown (1985), arguing that "a crisis now affects both the world economic system and the structures through which the majority of the world's populations reproduce themselves (the process by which human beings meet their basic needs and survive from one day to the next) (p. 43), analyzed a global imperative for women and development:

> Democratization of organizations and widening of their membership base is essential since it distributes power and diffuses hierarchy, explicit assertion and commitment to an ethic that rejects personal aggrandizement, with respect for the many voices of our movement, for their cross-fertilizing potential, for the power of dialogue, for the humility to learn from the experiences of others. (pp. 88-87)

Individuals who, despite their sanctioned existence in organizational pyramids, participate in relational circles of interaction, belief, and influence, may be simultaneously overcoming internalized and institutionalized barriers to empowerment.

Studies of leadership predicated on the assumption that perception follows form (that participants in an organizational structure adhere to organizational premises of the organizers) are inevitably limited. When the discussion is reframed, when the analysis becomes woman centered, rather than organization centered, as this study attempts, the possibility arises that career women may experience empowerment incidentally, relationally, and expressively, as functions of their own self-definition. They may experience empowerment holistically, in ways that transcend career-specific or organizationally defined limitations.

In considering apparent contradictions between women's perception of institutionalized sexism and internalized empowerment, we may benefit from constructing an analogy between sexism and racism. Bell Hooks (1990), in her essay "Radical Black Subjectivity," pointed to the power implicit in renaming oneself as subject and in reframing concepts of power and identity. Hooks advocated that

> confrontation with difference which takes place on new ground, in that counter-hegemonic marginal space where radical black subjectivity is seen, not overseen by any authoritative Other claiming to know us better than we know ourselves. . . .

> In an essay on counter-hegemonic cultural practice, I named marginality
> as a site of transformation where liberatory black subjectivity can fully
> emerge, emphasizing that there is a definite distinction between that
> marginality which is imposed by oppressive structure and that marginality
> one chooses as a site of resistance, as location of radical openness and
> possibility. (p .22)

The value of marginality is affirmed by Josette Feral (1985), a French
feminist, in her essay "The Powers of Difference" with her explanation
that "choosing marginality (with an emphasis on the margins) in order
to designate one's difference, a difference no longer conceived of as an
inverted image or as a double, but as alterity, multiplicity, heterogene-
ity" (p. 91). Stenstad (1988) also affirmed the marginal perspective,
explaining that "the practice of thinking at the boundary transforms our
thinking; it transforms us. The transformative experience of anarchic
thinking is perhaps one of its most subversive effects. It is a powerful
way to clear out lingering internalizations of patriarchal presupposi-
tions" (p. 90).

Whereas *anarchy* is customarily a pejorative concept, suggestive of
terroristic upheaval, Stenstad's anarchic thinking is similar to Boulding's *social imagination* and Janeway's *distrust* in its insistence on a
new way of thinking in original, creative, and constructive ways that
heal separation and compartmentalization and that disrupt the structure
of domination and submission. Stenstad saw this way of thinking
outside the ruling structure as "making strange . . . to decenter the
familiar, the taken-for-granted, the true, the real" (1988, p. 98) resulting
in the "opening up of a space for non-divisive other-ness, for difference,
for a multiplicity of voices, which makes anarchic thinking crucially
important to feminist thinking . . . a thinking and praxis which will
genuinely differ from that allowed for and legitimated by patriarchy"
(p. 99). This occupation of the margins creates new ways of seeing that
transform language and generate "new words springing from the very
woman who refuses to appropriate man's words and their implicit
founding values, while she chooses to re-invent her relationships with
society" (p. 93), a process that engages her in "rethinking society," in
remembering "her innermost divisions in the present" so that she may
undertake "the difficult task of creating the conditions whereby the
future of difference will no longer mean a difference of futures" (p. 94).
Constructs of wholeness, community, and diversity would "redistribute
throughout all of society . . . helplessness, passivity, need, and longings

for care . . . [now] projected onto disabled women" (Asche & Fine, 1992, p. 171), as well as engendering a vision of wholeness based on a multidimensional vision of the world allowing for ambiguity and variety (Collins, 1982, p. 366).

In learning to see that the "personal is political," women began to see similarities in their life experiences and to see that "relationships with men . . . were governed by certain unequal distributions of power— educational, economic, social, political and physical" (Collins, 1982, p. 362) and that these structures could be transformed into a pluralistic world [resulting from] a holistic ethic which affirms singleness within community, diversity within unity, the validity of both/and rather than either/or (p. 367). Yet, diversity results in unity only when consciousness is articulated and formulated in policies of social justice within society's organizations. Charlotte Bunch (1986) observed that "too often feminists have used the 'personal is political' to define all of our personal desires and problems as political. But the personal and political circles overlap only as we incorporate political analysis and identity into our personal lives and action" (p. 84). "If women are creating a new society . . . using intellect, intuition, politics, magic and art to restructure existing institutions and invent new ones . . . working quietly, persistently, vigorously" (Cheatum & Powell, 1986, p. xix), it is important that we listen to the voices of those whose empowerment may complicate and enrich previous constructs of leadership.

Purpose of the Study

It is important to define women's leadership in a way that recognizes women's values and reflects women's experience. It may be helpful to substitute descriptive for comparative studies of leadership values if we are to take a new look at the assumptions we hold about women's contributions to society and to their professions. For the purpose of this study, I sought to construct items to reflect participants' inner values, rather than organizational expectations. I sought to allow for the possibility that empowerment might be viewed as relational, reciprocal, consensual, contextual, and actualizing. I assumed that women who have positive influences on others, who receive positive responses from others, and who are free to exercise their talents would have a sense of their own power. I therefore formulated questions that encouraged participants to look at their sphere of influence from a process perspective.

I constructed items on leadership aspirations, achievement motivation, affiliation, achievement, activism, and on personal, professional, and social responsibility. I attempted to avoid posing dichotomies between values, "slanting" the items in the direction of self-esteem, rather than self-deprivation, and focusing on inner perceptions and motives, rather than on externally defined roles and expectations.

I designed this study to assess participants' attitudes toward leadership without perpetuating the notion that power is only structural or that leadership is only sanctioned in the formal organization. I designed items to accommodate the possibility of generative constructs of leadership, allowing that participants might have leadership experience within and beyond their professional roles, that they might see leadership as relational and reciprocal, and that they might express their leadership aspirations in social, professional, and personal realms of activity.

Analysis of Results

I asked participants to respond to 39 generative leadership items on a Likert scale. Descriptive statistics were completed initially by using data from 494 cases. Frequencies on these items were cross-tabulated and correlated by using Pearson's r's with demographic data, including age, marital status, income, and educational level. Results of this process resulted in few statistically significant or interesting results, suggesting that the topics covered in these items might be related thematically. To test this possibility, responses to the 39 items also were analyzed by factor analysis using orthogonal rotation. Salient loadings were defined as any loadings with an absolute value of .35 or greater. Thirty-four items loaded on to three factors, which were labeled Leadership Aspirations, Social Responsibility, and Professional Enhancement.

Leadership Aspirations

Results of the factor analysis reveal participants in this study to be highly committed to the pursuit of leadership opportunities. Results indicate active, intentional, enthusiastic leadership behaviors and attitudes (see Table 10.3). The loading of the first factor reveals participants' determination to create their own leadership opportunities, to

Table 10.3
Salient Factor Loadings: Leadership Aspiration (Factor 1)

I am active in seeking leadership opportunities.	.71801
I intend to move into increasingly challenging and responsible roles.	.70935
I seek leadership opportunities in most areas of my life.	.68818
I look forward to growing in leadership effectiveness.	.65063
I enjoy increasing my influence and responsibility.	.64616
I am pleased to be asked to serve as a group leader.	.61820
I enjoy thinking about my professional advancement and future goals.	.57664
I think I could contribute to effective management in any organization.	.56666
My parents gave me exceptional responsibility.	.55905
I am dissatisfied when I do not have responsibility and recognition.	.49204
I /do not/ identify with the leaders in any group or organization.	.47971
I prefer to design original strategies in my work.	.44094
Leadership in volunteer or social groups is a professional asset.	.41382
If encouraged to do so, I would /not/ gladly seek public office.	.41300
I am inspired by seeing others in leadership roles.	.39953
People often look to me for advice and inspiration.	.39308
I am a positive role model to women seeking leadership opportunities.	.36749
Leaders /do not/ have qualities that set them apart from other people.	.35091

move toward challenge, responsibility, and effectiveness. Eighteen items
loaded on to the Leadership Aspirations factor "I am active in seeking
leadership opportunities" have a coefficient of .71801. Items loading on
to this factor also confirm the pursuit of responsibility, challenge, and
influence in most areas of participants' lives, as indicated by items such
as "I intend to move into increasingly challenging and responsible
roles," with a coefficient of .70935, and "I seek leadership opportunities
in most areas of my life," "I enjoy increasing my influence and responsibility," "I am pleased to be asked to serve as a group leader," "I enjoy
thinking about my professional advancement and future goals" (with

coefficients from .68818 to .57664). All of these show intentionality and willingness to act on leadership aspirations.

Participants revealed themselves to be in active pursuit of leadership opportunities in their personal and professional roles. They revealed positive regard for their own effectiveness in their response to "I think I could contribute to effective management in any organization" (.56666). Participants identified early acceptance of responsibility in their agreement with the statement "My parents gave me exceptional responsibility" (.55905) and with the statement "I am dissatisfied when I do not have responsibility and recognition" (.49204). Respondents seemed to balance the intention of "seeking increasingly challenging and responsible roles" and to integrate responsibility, challenge, and recognition. The weight of this factor indicates that participants have positive leadership aspirations in all of their roles. Even as they expressed high personal aspirations, they acknowledged their responsibility to others.

Other items loading on to this factor support the possibility that respondents may see leadership in relational and social, rather than structural, terms. "I [do not] identify with the leaders in any group or organization" (.47971), "I prefer to design original strategies in my work" (.44094), "Leadership in volunteer or social groups is a professional asset" (.41382), "If encouraged to do so, I would [not] gladly seek public office" (.41300), and "I am inspired by seeing others in leadership roles" (.39953) suggest that respondents may discount access to traditional power structures or roles. Additional items loading on to this factor suggest an inclusive, equalitarian approach to leadership. "People often look to me for advice and inspiration" (.39308), "I am a positive role model to women seeking leadership opportunities" (.36749), and "Leaders [do not] have qualities that set them apart from other people" (.35091) are items contributing to the weight of the Leadership Aspiration factor.

The Leadership Aspiration factor is not, however, without ambiguity. Three items that initially were expressed in positive terms loaded on to this factor with the direction reversed. "I identify with the leaders in any group or organization," "If encouraged to do so, I would gladly seek public office," and "Leaders have qualities that set them apart from other people" all contributed negative loadings to the Leadership Aspirations factor, suggesting that participants may reject identification with the leader of any group or organization because they may believe power is distributed more equally than hierarchically, or they may identify only with leaders with certain admirable attributes. Participants may not be interested in public office and may be too self-directed to permit others to urge them to do so, or they may have leadership goals that are professional or social, rather than political. It is also possible that these items support the concept of process-centered, rather than structurally defined, leadership values. It is also possible that their leadership aspirations are more diffuse, more social, or less formal than conventional expectations might suggest.

The Leadership Aspirations factor is the strongest factor in the analysis. Items loading on to this factor are all congruent with generative leadership values, including aspirations, achievement, and affiliation. The profile of respondents emergent in this factor reveals a high degree of motivation and intentionality and an exceptionally active orientation to generative leadership opportunities.

Social Responsibility

Participants expressed a marked degree of social responsibility in the 11 values that load on to the second factor (see Table 10.4). "I must do work that is consistent with my social vision," the strongest loading item on this factor, has a coefficient of .63878. "Leadership experience in volunteer/social groups is a leadership asset," the second loading factor, has a coefficient of .61675. "I frequently think of the way my work relates to larger social issues" has a coefficient of .60615. These items show the willingness of participants to look beyond professional roles to see their leadership activities and aspirations as having social impact and to acknowledge that leadership skills are related to broader than professional contexts. The next item on this factor, "Society will be more responsible to the needs of everyone when more women are leaders," has a coefficient of .59127. (It is interesting to note that this item significantly [.0000] distinguished feminists from nonfeminists, with 79.4% of feminists and only 47% of nonfeminists in agreement with this concept. This response suggests that women who do not consider themselves as feminist may not see the goals of feminism as social progress.) "I hope to be known for making important social contributions," has a coefficient of .58476.

"Leadership skills can be taught and learned," "Most people can benefit from being included in decision making," "I trust others to know what is right for themselves," "I am inspired by seeing others in leadership roles," and "People seem to enjoy working with me to

Table 10.4
Salient Factor Loadings: Social Responsibility (Factor 2)

I must do work which is consistent with my social vision.	.63878
Leadership experience in volunteer/social groups is a leadership asset.	.61675
I frequently think of the way my work relates to larger social issues.	.60615
Society will be more responsible to the needs of everyone when more women are leaders.	.59127
I hope to be known for making important social contributions.	.58476
Leadership skills can be taught and learned.	.56603
Most people can benefit from being included in decision making.	.55003
I learn from superordinates and subordinates.	.54436
I trust others to know what is right for themselves.	.47102
I am inspired by seeing others in leadership roles.	.46899
People seem to enjoy working with me to achieve goals.	.44259

achieve goals" have coefficients from .56603 to .44259. These items, again, express inclusive, hierarchy-flattening assumptions about the reciprocity of power. "Leadership skills can be taught and learned" can be read as a refutation of the "trait" concept of leadership and acceptance of the importance of skill and experience. "I trust others to know what is right for themselves" suggests an egalitarian idea of leadership. "I am inspired by seeing others in leadership roles" poses ambiguity; women may benefit from mentoring, but they also may be disempowered by too much admiration for those in traditionally sanctioned leadership roles.

Whereas leadership aspirations and achievement items cluster into the strongest factor, items measuring social conscience, service, and inclusion cluster into the second factor. The second factor, Social Responsibility, reveals respondents' commitment to a social vision that expands leadership beyond professionalism. Both the first and second factors include items that can be interpreted as egalitarian and connective values described by theorists who advocate shared decision making as empowerment. Apparently these aspirants to power acknowledge the strong connective values described by theorists who advocate the construction of leadership in accordance with generative principles.

Table 10.5
Salient Factor Loadings: Professional Enhancement (Factor 3)

I am/not/ drained and depressed by the demands of my work.	.60522
I am /not/ uncomfortable with my own power.	.57514
I do /not/ feel I would have to sacrifice femininity in seeking power.	.46213
I am comfortable when I think of moving into more responsible roles.	.46088
My work energizes me so that I enjoy the rest of my life more.	.45288
I am /not/ diminished by others' exercise of leadership.	.42902

Professional Enhancement

Factor three, Professional Enhancement, indicates participants' positive attitudes toward their professional lives, supporting an integrative perspective on roles (see Table 10.5). "I am [not] drained and depressed by the demands of my work" (.60522) and "My work energizes me so that I enjoy the rest of my life more" (.45288) both affirm the role of work in the lives of participants. "I am [not] uncomfortable with my own power" (.57514) and "I am comfortable when I think of moving into more responsible roles" (.46088) suggest acceptance of ambition. "I do [not] feel I would have to sacrifice femininity in seeking power" (.46213) indicates a lack of significant gender role conflict over the exercise of power. In addition to the expression of high leadership aspirations and socially responsible, or connective, values, these participants expressed an integrative view of professional and personal power.

On the basis of the prevalence of the "role conflict" myth for professional women, this factor is particularly interesting. It also may shed some light on the source of the self-reliance expressed in earlier parts of the study. Participants see their lives enhanced by their work and by the leadership accomplishments of others. Although this is the third of three strong factors, it is nevertheless an indication of the high motivation, professional and personal affirmation, and role integration of the respondents.

Profile of Participants' Perceptions

The profile of participants' perceptions of leadership that emerges from the factor analysis is congruent with emergent feminist leadership theory. Participants in this study are committed to seeking empowering experiences. Their perceptions are more consistent with generative than with constrictive expectations regarding power. They strive to make contributions congruent with a social vision and with a strongly defined sense of social responsibility and professional enhancement. This evidence supports the concept of leadership as "power with," "power for," and "power to," rather than "power over." This part of the study focused on leadership as process, rather than as a component of structural position. The participants expressed strong connective values and commitment to social responsibility. They expressed connective values relative to the sharing of power, to the empowerment of others, and to social concerns.

This leadership profile gives us a view of highly motivated, conscientized women. It is important to ask the questions: Leadership to what ends? What will be the social effects of the exercise of this leadership? Will these women who express such strong leadership aspirations and such strong social responsibility direct their efforts to causes that ultimately will advantage women? Will their participation in leadership processes result in the reconstruction of social structures that do not currently reflect the inclusive, egalitarian values these participants hold?

As we develop inclusive, process-centered theories of leadership, we need to be increasingly sensitive to the ambiguities inherent in holding apparently contradictory values. We need to define leadership in ways that enable us to express egalitarian values and to behave in reciprocal ways that preserve and enhance connection. We need to move beyond constrictive to generative constructions of power that support the full expression of individual potential.

We can express power in a process congruent with ideas of social responsibility, while accepting our individual responsibility for constructing cultural, social, organizational, and political policies that reflect and realize our deepest values. If we only see our power as existing primarily in relationships, and if we exercise it primarily in informal webs and networks, we can, by implication, avoid the social imperative of reconstructing those institutions that, historically, have prohibited or discounted women's participation, diminishing the significance of so many lives and distorting organizational structures of power.

Principles of equality, inclusion, reciprocity, and democracy are congruent with leadership aspirations, social responsibility, and professional and personal enhancement. When we regard equality as a human right, rather than as a female privilege, we will find that we have achieved greater congruence between our personal beliefs and our political actions.

Other contributors to this study explore the apparent contradiction posed by participants' recognition of inequality and simultaneous unwillingness to confront and change social and organizational structures. Considering process paradigms of power allows us to think of ways in which the power of these participants will manifest itself in their roles and their social interaction. Perhaps these women experience empowerment in phases evolving from personal experience to social generalization, moving from relational to structural expressions of power.

Anne Wilson Schaef, in developing a model of what she described as women's "levels of truth," pointed out that the farther along one is on the levels of truth continuum regarding a particular concept, the better able that person will be to understand the concept itself and the levels of others in regard to the concept (Schaef, 1981). She also observed that two adjacent levels of truth may give the appearance of dualism when viewed statically, rather than as processes. It is possible that the apparent ambiguities revealed by this study are related to acceptance of values that are apparently incongruent but that ultimately may move toward consistency. If these participants realize their leadership potential while acting on egalitarian values, it is possible that the collective well-being of women will become a social imperative for women themselves. It is possible that, although the feminism of the participants is defined in terms of individual rather than collective goals, through the conscious articulation of collectivist feminist goals, they eventually will insist on structural change.

It is important to think of women's leadership experience and beliefs as evolving. It is important to think of the existence of conflicts between coexisting, seemingly mutually exclusive beliefs as the source of tension and conflict that will result in growth and expansion. Historically, conventional concepts of leadership predicated on the maintenance of existing structures of power were inadequate to the needs of individuals and inappropriate to the attainment of the highest human ideals in social life. It is unlikely that the full participation of women can be accommodated by existing belief and structural systems. The realization of principles of inclusion and equality in male-oriented work structures may be transforming for women, for those structures and the men in them, and for society. Participants in this study intend to realize leadership potential. That realization has the potential for social transformation.

References

Asche, A., & Fine, M. (1992). Beyond pedestals: Revisiting the lives of women with disabilities. In M. Fine (Ed.), *Disruptive voices: The possibilities of feminist research* (pp. 139-171). Ann Arbor: University of Michigan Press.

Belenky, M. F., Clinchy, B. M., Goldberger, N. R., & Tarule, J. M. (1986). *Women's ways of knowing: The development of self, voice, and mind.* New York: Basic Books.

Boulding, E. (1987). *The female world from a global perspective.* Bloomington: University of Indiana Press.

Brocke-Utne, B. (1987, July). *Why women's studies?* Plenary address, Third International Interdisciplinary Congress on Women, Dublin, Ireland.

Bunch, C. (1986). *Passionate politics: Feminist theory in action.* New York: St. Martin's.

Burns, J. M. (1979). *Leadership.* New York: Harper & Row.

Cheatum, A., & Powell, M. C. (1986). *This way day break comes: Women's values and the future.* Philadelphia, PA: New Society.

Collins, S. (1982). The personal is political. In C. Spretnak (Ed.), *The politics of women's spirituality: Essays on the rise of spiritual power within the feminist movement* (pp. 362-367). New York: Anchor Books.

Eisler, R. (1987). *The chalice and the blade: Our history, our future.* New York: Harper & Row.

Erickson, E. H. (1978). *Adulthood essays.* New York: Norton.

Feral, J. (1985) The powers of difference. In H. Eisenstein & A. Jardine (Eds.), *The future of difference* (pp. 88-105). New Brunswick, NJ: Rutgers University Press.

Ferguson, K. E. (1984). *The feminist case against bureaucracy.* Philadelphia: Temple University Press.

Fine, M. (1984). Silencing and nurturing voice in an improbable context: Urban adolescents in public school. In M. Fine (Ed.), *Disruptive voices: The possibilities of feminist research* (pp. 115-138). Ann Arbor: University of Michigan Press.

French, M. (1981). *Beyond power.* New York: Summit.

Gilligan, C. (1982). *In a different voice.* Cambridge, MA: Harvard University Press.

Hagberg, J. (1984). *Real power: Stages of personal power in organizations.* Minneapolis, MN: Winston.

Harragan, B. (1977). *Games mother never taught you.* New York: Rawson Associates.

Heilbrun, C. G. (1973). *Toward a recognition of androgyny.* New York: Knopf.

Helgeson, S. (1990). *The female advantage: Women's ways of leadership.* Garden City, NY: Doubleday.

Hennig, M., & Jardim, A. (1977). *The managerial woman.* New York, NY: Doubleday.

hooks, b. (1990). *Yearning: Race, gender, and cultural politics.* Boston: South End.

Iannello, K. (1992). *Decisions without hierarchy: Feminist interventions in organization theory and practice.* New York: Routledge.

Janeway, E. (1980). *Powers of the weak.* New York: Knopf.

Jardim, A. (1993). From hierarchy to centrarchy. *Women's Review of Books, 10*(5), 27-28.

Kanter, R. M. (1977). *Men and women of the corporation.* New York: Basic Books.

Kohlberg, L. (1984). *The psychology of moral development: The nature and validity of moral stages.* New York: Harper & Row.

Lather, P. (1988). Feminist perspectives on empowering research methodologies. *Women's Studies International Forum, 11*(6), 569-581.

Lenz, E., & Myerhoff, B. (1985). *The feminization of America: How women's values are changing our public and private lives.* Los Angeles: Tarcher.

Levinson, D. J., with Darrow, C. N., Klein, E. B., Levinson, M. H., & McKee, B. (1978). *The seasons of a man's life.* New York: Knopf.

Maccoby, M. (1976). *The gamesman: The new corporate leaders.* New York: Simon & Schuster.

Maslow, A. (1962). *Toward a psychology of being.* Princeton, NJ: Van Nostrand.

May, Robert. (1980). *Sex and fantasy: Patterns of male and female development.* New York: Norton.

May, Rollo. (1972). *Power and innocence: A search for the sources of violence.* New York: Norton.

Miller, J. B. (1976). *Toward a new psychology of women.* Boston: Beacon.

Morgan, R. (1989). *The demon lover: On the sexuality of terrorism.* New York: Norton.

O'Leary, V. E. (1977). *Toward understanding women.* Belmont, CA: Wadsworth.

Pearson, C. (1989). *The hero within: Six archetypes we live by.* New York: Harper & Row.

Ruddick, S. (1989). *Maternal thinking: Toward a politics of peace.* Boston: Beacon.

Schaef, A. W. (1981). *Women's reality: An emerging female system in the white male society.* Minneapolis: Winston.

Segal, L. (1987). *Is the future female? Troubled thoughts on contemporary feminism.* London: Virago.

Sen, G., & Grown, C. (1985). *Development, crisis, and alternative visions: Third world women's perspectives* (DAWN [Development Alternatives with Women for a New Era]). New Delhi: Institute of Social Studies Trust (ISST), S.M.M.

Spretnak, C. (Ed.). (1982). *The politics of women's spirituality: Essays on the rise of spiritual power within the feminist movement.* New York: Anchor.

Stenstad, G. (1988). Anarchic thinking. *Hypatia, 3*(2), 87-100.

Trahey, J. (1977). *On women and power.* New York: Rawson Associates.

11

The Future of Women and Careers: Issues and Challenges

CAROL WOLFE KONEK
SALLY L. KITCH
ELSIE R. SHORE

Career Women's Issues

Our collaborative study of career women helps the Research Group on Women and Work gain perspectives on issues affecting the aspirations and achievements of career women, as well as on challenges that will affect career women in the future. Analysis of our results, along with responses of our participants, persuade us that the combined research interests of our collaborating researchers provides a holistic view of several very important issues that reveal much about the quality of career women's working and personal lives. Our decision to focus our study within a framework with perceptions of feminism on the one hand and attitudes toward leadership on the other provided a political context within which we could view other perceptions of professional and personal life.

This political framework allowed us to look at issues that directly reflect the professional culture within which career women function, including their perceptions of the opportunity structure, experience with equality, equity, and discrimination, experience with supporting or indifferent relationships with supervisors, and responses to the challenges of a changing professional culture signaled by technological change. We also constructed a representation of the personal domain of our participants' lives by including perceptions of the challenges and limitations of dual-career marriages, responses to the dilemmas presented by child care responsibilities, as well as two interesting issues related to the intersection between personal and professional life and a possible measure of strategies for dealing with stresses in both: attitudes toward leisure and toward the use and abuse of alcohol. The confluence of our findings in these issues gives us a dynamic, provocative profile of career women's perspectives of issues and challenges.

Nancy McCarthy Snyder's analysis of demographic data of participants in this study supports the generalizability of this study. Wichita often is chosen to test-market new products because it is regarded as a typical middle-sized city with "middle American values." As in similar cities around the country, a large number of participants were in the mid years of their careers, with 38% in their 30s and 27% in their 40s. A large percentage of the participants were married. Also 36% of the participants were childless; 96% had some college; 56% were college graduates; almost 30% had master's degrees; and 16% held law, medical, or doctoral degrees. By only one measure, income, does our sample appear atypical. In 1987 the median income for full-time year-round women workers was approximately $17,000; three quarters of our sample earned over $20,000. Otherwise the participants were typical mid-career professional women of good educational backgrounds with above-average incomes.

Although Sally Kitch found that 64% of participants identified themselves as feminists and that more than 90% of feminists and nonfeminists supported equal educational opportunities and equal pay, she found that participants supported a very individualistic version of feminism in their definitions and responses to specific questions. Although 90% of participants recognized that sex discrimination exists in the workplace, 83% agreed that a woman's hard work will ensure her career success. Similarly, although large majorities of both feminists and nonfeminists agreed that the workplace is male oriented, 65% also agreed that career women must be prepared to compete on the same terms as men.

The concept of feminism has allowed these participants to recognize the structural difficulties for women in the world of work, but it has not persuaded them to adopt typically feminist solutions. Instead of envisioning class action suits or job actions, these respondents imagine transcending obstacles with individual effort. Instead of projecting their life values and priorities into the work world, they may seek to adapt themselves to its exigencies and mold themselves to the male-defined organizational model. The self-identified feminists preferred professional organizations for women, such as Women in Banking, to feminist organizations, such as the National Organization for Women or the National Women's Political Caucus. The data suggest that collective action and group identity have appeal to respondents primarily when they contribute to individual career success.

Participants in the RGWW study reported salary inequities. Flo Hamrick found that although younger women reported more salary inequity as compared with men in similar jobs than did older women, the majority of participants of all ages reported dissatisfaction with their salaries as compared with their own skills and experience. But even those who recognized that their salaries were inadequate when compared with men's did not identify the problem as salary discrimination. Only 30% of those who thought their salaries were unequal believed they had experienced such discrimination. Respondents who were satisfied with their salaries (and earned above-average salaries for the sample) expressed less support for collective action on behalf of women and were less likely to identify themselves as feminists than were respondents who were dissatisfied. In other words, Hamrick's data suggest that feminist identification is influenced, perhaps in large part, by a woman's level of material comfort.

Brooke Collison's study of supervisory relationships suggests that women in supervisory relationships are perceived as supportive of women, advancing the idea of mentoring as a career advantage. Yet Collison's data on participants' relationships with their supervisors suggest that supervisors are unlikely to be seen as part of a collective in which a woman can advance her career or increase her skills: 72% of participants saw their supervisors as being "fair," and they were more likely to see female than male supervisors as "assisting with advancement." Yet, regardless of the gender or helpfulness of the supervisor, older respondents tended not to identify their supervisors as important to their acquisition of skills or to their advancement, suggesting the possibility that women become somewhat alienated as they grow older or that women in the sample have learned, through experience and of necessity, to be independent. Younger workers were more likely to identify their supervisors as powerful, as sources of skill acquisition, and as "fair"—in short, to identify with them—as they moved in their careers. Older workers, on the other hand, tended not to see those values in their supervisors and expressed the belief that their success was dependent primarily on their own efforts. Although

Collison is unsure whether the older women have a more accurate picture of the work world than do the younger women, he concludes that age and experience reinforce self-reliance and skepticism about the benefits of alliances in the workplace.

According to Nancy Brooks's study, almost 64% of respondents were enthusiastic about high technology, with younger women expressing a higher degree of enthusiasm than older women. Yet, even in their approach to technology, participants revealed their independence and individualism. Although strongly supportive of high technology in their work, the women in our sample showed little interest in the interactive capabilities of modern technological processes. Although the participants expressed a high degree of enthusiasm for advances afforded by technological progress, only 15% used high technology for telecommunications, and only 9% used electronic mail. Participants were also more likely to learn about technology through self-study than through peer discussions, and they indicated that they value technology for its contribution to their individual efficiency and productivity. Electronic networking, admittedly a new idea at the time of data collection, was of little interest to the participants, suggesting that participants' adaptation of technology to their professional lives reinforces independence and individualism.

Wayne Carlisle discovered that the participants were more enthusiastic about the advantages of dual-career relationships than other studies have indicated. They reported that income level, self-esteem, respect, cohesion and equality in the relationship, and autonomy were major advantages. Perhaps because they valued their dual-career relationships, they were willing to tolerate the work overloads and stresses that accompany that life design in a work world organized for the one-career couple. Instead of seeking support from others in similar situations or seeking restructuring of the workplace, however, these respondents seemed to rely on their own coping behaviors. When asked how women might best prepare for dual-career lives, they suggested individual strategies including reading, thinking, and experimentation. Their collaborative strategies were primarily personal, such as negotiating responsibilities with their partners. Overall, they rated the disadvantages experienced in role conflict, career leveling, and societal pressure as low when compared with the advantages of increased self-esteem, income, and mutual respect in their dual-career relationships.

As Nancy McCarthy Snyder found, few participants who reported negative attitudes about the impact of child care responsibilities on their productivity, not because the employers were supportive, but because the mothers did not allow their parental responsibilities to impinge on their roles in the workplace. A significant majority reported they had never missed work because of child care problems, and only one fourth reported they had brought a child to work. The women in the sample clearly viewed parenting (and attendant child care arrangements) as a private familial responsibility that should not burden an employer. Yet respondents with children for whom child care was an important consideration also recognized that good quality, dependable child care enhances worker productivity. They wished that employers would accommodate the parents' needs for flexibility in responding to familial as well as employment demands.

Marcia McCoy's analysis of participants' view of leisure activities gives us a profile of women who have little time for leisure and who spend the majority of their scarce leisure hours in passive or isolated pursuits. All demographic subgroups reported doing about half of all leisure activities most often by themselves. Four of the five activities— reading books, watching TV, reading newspapers and magazines, and doing craft hobbies—are rather passive and solitary activities. Even aerobic exercise was frequently undertaken alone.

McCoy inferred from these data that participants may be such hard workers that they have reduced amounts of spare time and must grab leisure activities when and where they can, rather than have planned leisure activities that occupy a central and significant place in their lives. The activities also suggest that they can be "worked at" and may not provide much contrast to career activities as less toilsome pastimes might. Participants may engage in recreational activities alone because they do not see value in being with others or expending effort to attain companionship or a sense of community. In short, the rules for leisure mimic the rules for professional success.

McCoy also concluded that participants separated personal and professional activities to a surprising degree. In only two activities did more than 10% of the women report participating often with co-workers: eating out, and going to organization meetings and activities. Less commonly, women reported socializing with co-workers, such as inviting them to their homes, talking on the telephone, or going with them to clubs or bars. These data suggest that participants may tend not to be as socially connected to co-workers as their feminist identity might predict.

Elsie Shore found that although few participants reported drinking heavily or having problems with alcohol, a relatively large number had used alcohol to alleviate depression (24%), ease pain, get to sleep, or forget problems at home or at work (19%). Thus alcohol was used by at least some of these women as a device for escape, a passive and isolating way of coping. If these women viewed work-related stresses as a function of institutional constraints and inequities, would they might be less likely to become angry, rather than depressed, and to engage in collective action, rather than drink? The alcoholism rate among males in the American business world has been a source of concern for some time. The individualistic orientation may contribute to the dysphoria and loneliness that leads to abusive drinking in both genders.

Carol Wolfe Konek discovered that participants seek leadership opportunities in an intentional way, while accommodating egalitarian and inclusive values. Participants expressed positive, empowering values, including leadership aspirations, social responsibility, and professional enhancement. The leadership values with which they identify are congruent with leadership processes identified as feminist, especially concepts of *power with* and *power for,* rather than *power over.* The potential for the women in the sample to exercise generative, or empowering, leadership strategies is quite impressive: Indeed, it makes the lack of defined focus on structural and cultural change in the survey of feminist attitudes all the more puzzling.

Although participants intended to increase their influence and responsibility and actively to seek leadership opportunity, they might do so outside of the organizational structures in which we ordinarily look for social change. The participants expressed perceptions of their own empowerment that could transcend their role definitions. The empowerment profile indicates that participants in this study may view power as relational rather than structural and that they may not be focused on structural barriers they might be expected to work to remove. They may believe that their acceptance of increased influence and responsibility will have a transforming effect on society, or they may accept the inevitability of inequity. These women may see that exercising leadership for the attainment of social justice for oneself and others offers a way of exercising power and social responsibility simultaneously.

Perspectives on Responsibility

As the members of the Research Group on Women and Work began summarizing, analyzing, and comparing data, certain patterns became evident in participants' responses to the questionnaire. Implicit in many of those responses was the same devotion to individual effort and self-reliance that had appeared in their responses to feminism and feminist activism. For example, Carlisle discovered that participants took personal responsibility for handling the overload and stress of dual-career relationships. He found that they preferred to develop their own coping behaviors, rather than to seek support from others in similar situations or to effect the restructuring of a workplace designed for one-career couples. There also appeared to be a distrust for organizations and the people in them. For example, Collison discovered that participants did not rely on the mentoring of their supervisors for their own career advancement or skill acquisition. McCarthy Snyder's work demonstrated that mothers were coping with their child care problems by keeping them out of the workplace. They viewed parenting as a private familial responsibility for which employers have little or no responsibility. Wolfe Konek also discovered that the women in the study conceptualized power in relational, rather than structural, ways.

So striking were these patterns that the group decided to test for them directly. We attached three questions to the third questionnaire that went out to participants early in 1991. The questions asked respondents to rank solutions to the problems of balancing work and child care, of achieving occupational success, and of creating a better future for women.

Possible solutions for the problems of balancing work and child care ranged from themselves as the children's parents, to employers, to various levels of government, including the President of the United States (see Table 11.1). The mean rankings of these possibilities indicate that participants overwhelmingly saw themselves as having the most responsibility (ranked at 1.66) for achieving that balance. Employers (ranked at 4.24 and 7.05) came next, with day care providers (ranked 6.42 and 7.32) mixed in. Various levels of government (ranked at 7.49, 8.18, 8.33, 8.38, and 10.09) were seen as least responsible for providing solutions. Also relatively free of responsibility were grandparents (ranked at 8.47), probably because of participants' geographical mobility.

When asked to rank 15 factors according to their importance in contributing to their career success, participants ranked personal motivation to succeed and hard work the highest (at 1.79 and 3.66, respectively). Family and personal relationships came next (ranked at 4.97 and 5.59); mentors and bosses (ranked at 5.83 and 7.34) and teachers (ranked at 6.83) followed. Changes in law and public policy ranked near the bottom (at 11.03) (see Table 11.2). Female friends, though ranked

Table 11.1
Balancing Work and Child Care:
Who Should Be Looking for Solutions?

Rank	Choice	Mean
1	Parents	1.66
2	All employers	4.24
3	Managers of departments that have affected parents working in them	5.79
4	Day care associations	6.42
5	Companies with a large proportion of female employees	6.42
6	Managers of departments that have affected mothers working in them	7.05
7	Private day care centers	7.32
8	Social welfare organizations	7.49
9	State government	8.18
10	Federal government	8.33
11	City/County governments	8.38
12	Grandparents	8.47
13	President of the United States	10.09

only in the middle (at 8.41), rated higher than either female co-workers (at 9.52), male co-workers (10.21), or male friends (10.49). Professional organizations ranked much higher (at 8.94) than feminist organizations (at 13.20) in terms of their importance to careers, but even professional organizations were not ranked at the top.

Finally, when asked to rank factors according to their probable effect on improving conditions for the next generation, participants demonstrated the same preference for individual effort and self-reliance and the same relative distrust of structural change as they had exhibited on the other questions (see Table 11.3). They predicted that individual hard

Table 11.2
Ranking of Factors Affecting Occupational Success

Rank	Choice	Mean
1	Personal motivation to succeed	1.79
2	Hard work	3.66
3	Actions/attitudes of one's family	4.97
4	Personal relationships (spouse, significant other)	5.59
5	Mentors and role models	5.83
6	Influential teachers	6.83
7	Relationships with superiors, supervisors, bosses	7.34
8	Female friends	8.41
9	Membership in professional organizations	8.94
10	The women's movement	9.46
11	Female co-workers	9.52
12	Male co-workers	10.21
13	Male friends	10.49
14	Changes in laws and public policies	11.03
15	Membership in feminist organizations	13.20

work and know-how (ranked at 2.62, 3.17, and 3.56) would have a greater impact on career women's futures than would changes in the law (ranked at 5.17), structural change in the workplace (ranked at 5.19), or feminists' collective efforts (ranked at 5.69). At the bottom of the list were changes in men's attitudes (ranked at 6.37), about which these participants appeared very pessimistic. The lowest ranked choice is really an alternative to the question (ranked at 8.00). The respondents' rejection of the idea that the future will not be better for the next generation of women reveals an optimism about their own advancement.

These results demonstrate how thoroughly participants in the RGWW study had internalized concepts of individualism and self-reliance and

Table 11.3
Factors Making the Future Better for Women

Rank	Choice	Mean
1	Women have worked hard to advance themselves.	2.62
2	Women's participation in the workforce will have proved their value as workers.	3.17
3	More women will know how to succeed in the workplace.	3.56
4	More women will have the power to ensure that things are better for other women.	4.30
5	Laws will have made employers less likely to discriminate.	5.17
6	The workplace will have changed to meet women's needs.	5.19
7	The efforts of feminists will have improved conditions for women.	5.69
8	Men who have worked with women will understand that discrimination is wrong.	6.37
9	The future will not be better for the next generation of women.	8.00

how much more trusting they were of personal than of professional or public relationships. At the top of each list were individual efforts and responsibility. Parents are responsible for their own child care. The most important factor in a woman's occupational success is her personal motivation to succeed. The future will be better for women because they will have worked hard to advance themselves. Those who are closest—primarily family members and personal friends—are those most likely to provide support. Participants did not see government as a reliable source of solutions to personal problems or of strategies for career success. They did not anticipate legal solutions to problems in the future.

To understand fully the attitudes these rankings reveal, we must remember the historical moment in which they developed. We must recall the political atmosphere of the 1980s, when Americans were exhorted by their government to keep personal and family matters in the private sphere and not to rely on it or on any aspect of the public sector for solutions or support. It would be a mistake to interpret these results as eternal, although the endurance in American culture of a belief in the individual and of at least mild distrust of government (especially in the nation's heartland) suggests there may always be a strain of self-reliance in American views. Rather, given the extreme nature of the politics of the 1980s, it is probably best to see these results as evidence of the impact of political structures on individuals at particular times. In other words, the responses provided evidence that systems create the people they need in order to fulfill their systemic agendas. Government in the 1980s was becoming focused on the "common defense" to the detriment of attention to the "general welfare." The populace was focused on individual success and was somewhat alienated from a collective consciousness or even a sense of interdependence with those not closely connected to them. Competition was the watchword of the decade, and a competitive spirit resulted in many arenas.

For the women of the RGWW study, the messages had somewhat mixed results. On the one hand, the era's individualism produced a sense of personal empowerment that allowed women to develop an internal locus of control and to develop strategies for circumventing the system by creating alternative networks and relationships. On the other hand, a focus on the individual deprived women of the benefits of a collective orientation. That focus exacerbated the stress of balancing career and family needs, for example, and prevented the development of efficient, collective solutions to such widespread, structural problems as day care. It also allowed organizations to neglect career development activities, such as mentoring, that would have addressed women's needs in a structural and, therefore, enduring way. Without structural changes, the need for personally designed strategies for career success will continue to plague the next generation of working women.

If governments and public policy do set individual as well as official agendas, however, then a change in governmental policy may well produce a change in individuals. The national agenda is in the process of shifting from a capital-intensive military-industrial economy to a service-intensive response to crises in social infrastructures. The failure of militarism, both in communist and capitalist countries, has created the possibility for the emergence of new ways of defining community and commitment. With the advent in 1992 of an administration committed to connecting personal and political processes, women's attitudes toward government and law may well follow the new policies and priorities. Law may eventually seem an appropriate ally in the advancement of women. The president of the United States may yet be perceived as a partner in the struggle to balance work and family responsibilities. As policies such as family leave and health-care reform are implemented, employers and managers may become more important to career women looking for justice in the workplace and balance in their work and family responsibilities. Negative views of men may change simply because the power structure with which they historically have been associated will have become more supportive of the changes women need.

In sum, the political climate of the 1980s was at least partially responsible for the distance the RGWW women felt from collective, interdependent, or structural approaches to problems it had identified as personal. As society rethinks that label and many others, the adage of feminism—that the personal is political—may be newly embraced. Perhaps even feminism itself will be more openly embraced in the process.

Challenges for the Future

As predicted by the results and analysis of the original questionnaire, career women advocate working harder and better on an individual basis before they advocate seeking collective policy or legal changes. They place most of their faith in their ability to overcome the odds—even if they are built into the systems in which they live and work—and to achieve individual success. Although this belief may reflect participants' optimism and initiative, it also may interfere with their dedication to the eradication of injustice for others.

The optimism and dedication of participants is potentially a transforming force in society. Although the prevalence of individualism can be seen as undermining the possibility of a coherent social effect from feminism in the future, it is important to realize that women's analysis of their place in the world of work may be in a formative stage. Career women may, at present, simply be adapting to the predominant value system in which they still are regarded as outsiders who must prove themselves and in which they must succeed in order to survive.

We express our concern for the potential for collective action of our participants, and we also must admire the adaptability, the agency, and the optimism of the participants and wonder at their energy and dedication to their careers. It is clear that, for these participants, the benefits of pursuing careers outweigh its deficits, a fact that may weaken both their own resolve and their motivation for creating sweeping changes in working conditions for women.

This study suggests that career women are better able to see the political as personal than to see the personal as political. The researchers in this study cannot help but prefer that they would understand the equation both ways. If highly motivated career women directed their energies toward solving the problems they so consistently identify, organizations could be transformed and structural inequities in home and family organization would become antique.

The individualism of career women is a caution to us all. If each of us thinks she must work hard and adapt to systemic injustice in order to achieve success, then every woman who struggles by our sides must struggle alone. If we do not work to change a system that includes structural inequities, every woman who follows us, including our own daughters, must start over, alone. If we do not work to make our professions, organizations, and society more responsive to the needs of women, we may be unwittingly complicit with a system that underestimates women's worth and undervalues women's work.

We also empathize with the participants' anxiety about their own career success. We realize that, in addition to their ingrained individualism, career women may believe that the price of their inclusion and acceptance in the male-defined workplace is conformity to extant structures and mores. We also appreciate the fatigue that accompanies the "double burden" of work and family responsibilities. Indeed the enormous energy required to "have it all" with little assistance from employers and co-workers and too little assistance from spouses is itself a barrier to women's working on their on behalf.

Yet these career women may be mistaken in their belief that injustice can best be overcome by hard work and individual skill and commitment. History demonstrates how often those attributes have failed to advance the disadvantaged and how frequently they have been superseded by political or ideological considerations. The women factory workers who were fired after World War II, for example, did not lose their jobs because of incompetence. They were fired because employers and the government, who had so recently lured those same women into the labor force, suddenly decided that white male workers deserved their jobs.

The results of this study indicate how much work is left to do before women achieve equitable treatment and opportunities in the workplace. They also suggest that persistent problems for career women must be addressed in a holistic way—at home, at the health club, at work, in the government, and in relationships. The lessons of the past tell us that reluctance to work for structural change may cause a woman to underestimate the willingness of her colleagues, male and female, to engage in partnership strategies for the realization of social justice, and she may underestimate her capacity to influence the transformation of society. By recognizing the importance of taking collective action with other women, she may more fully realize her own potential.

Collaboration as Transformation

As we gathered together to share our interests in conducting research on women, members of the Research Group on Women and Work focused on two goals: (a) to learn more about the issues, perspectives, and challenges of career women, and (b) to learn more about working in collaboration. As we discussed processes for finding participants for our research, for formulating our individual surveys, for gathering and analyzing our data, and for sharing results with each other and with our participants, we realized that we were connecting responsiveness and responsibility. We realized that we would come to know each other and each other's disciplinary perspectives very well. We realized that we wanted to know, as well as study, the women who volunteered to participate in our ambitious and demanding project. As we reduced the distance between ourselves as researchers and our participants, we realized that our collaboration with our participants, as well as our collaboration with one another, was transforming our research strategies and philosophies.

As we set out to transform both institutional and disciplinary barriers to collaborative research, we realized that our project offered us opportunities for complicating, deepening, and connecting the formulation of our research topics and the interpretation of our research results. We realized that our departments were more comfortable with and more supportive of individual research on specialized topics. We knew from our training that we were expected to formulate and test narrowly conceived hypotheses on subjects whose consent was to be related to our promise to protect their anonymity and integrity but who were to be otherwise uninformed and uninvolved with regard to our findings. We knew that developing a collaborative, participatory model of research in which we asked participants to fill out several lengthy surveys on many aspects of their lives and work was a departure from conventional research methodologies with which our colleagues were comfortable. Responses of our colleagues gave us invaluable opportunities to re-frame our methodological assumptions and to process our reactions with one another. In addition, we all benefited from working with others with diverse disciplinary perspectives and methodological values.

Keeping our participants informed of our results as we were inter-preting them in the *Working Papers* newsletter publicized our project with participants who reacted to our survey, to researchers, and to each other. We received both solicited and unsolicited feedback from our participants, and more than once responded to their suggestions by including additional surveys in newsletters. We found that our interac-tion with participants in the study, both casual, and in some workshop settings, allowed us to understand some limitations in our theoretical approaches to our research topics. We saw our perspectives maturing and changing as we interacted with our fellow researchers, with our participants, and with our topics, giving a new dimension to the concept of interaction.

Working across disciplines was stimulating, frustrating, and enrich-ing. We found that our research questions and methodologies, our writing styles, and our analytical perspectives contrasted in amazing and evocative ways, and we found ourselves resisting the impulse to strive for a "univocal" editorial approach to our finished book.

We intend to continue analyzing issues and perspectives with partici-pants whose responses we share in this volume, and we invite our readers to replicate or modify this study for your own purposes. We include the questionnaire for the initial survey to facilitate this process. We invite responses from our readers and fellow researchers.

Code Number: _____

SECTION 1: ABOUT YOU

Age at last birthday _____   Race/Ethnic Group _____

Current marital status: Married _____   Single _____   Separated _____
Divorced _____   Widowed _____   Living as married _____

Ages of children living at home _____

Ages of children living away from home _____

Height _____   Weight _____

My health is: Excellent _____   Good _____   Fair _____   Poor _____

Education completed: Some high school _____   High school graduate _____
Some college _____   A.A./A.S. _____   B.A./B.S. _____
M.A./M.S. _____   J.D./LL.D. _____   M.D. _____   Ph.D./Ed.D. _____
Other _____

Individual income per year: (Please check)

_____ Below $5,000
_____ $5,000 - 9,999   _____ $10,000 - 14,999   _____ $15,000 - 19,999
_____ $20,000 - 24,999   _____ $25,000 - 29,999   _____ $30,000 - 34,999
_____ $35,000 - 39,999   _____ $40,000 - 44,999   _____ $45,000 - 49,999
_____ $50,000 - 54,999   _____ $55,000 - 59,999   _____ $60,000+

Joint income, per year, if applicable: (Please check)

_____ Below $5,000
_____ $5,000 - 9,999   _____ $10,000 - 14,999   _____ $15,000 - 19,999
_____ $20,000 - 24,999   _____ $25,000 - 29,999   _____ $30,000 - 34,999
_____ $35,000 - 39,999   _____ $40,000 - 44,999   _____ $45,000 - 49,999
_____ $50,000 - 54,999   _____ $55,000 - 59,999   _____ $60,000+

Would you call yourself: very young _____   young _____   middle aged _____
older _____   old _____

Job title: _____

Type of job: Administrative Business _____   Owner _____   Clerical _____
Managerial _____   Production _____   Professional _____   Sales _____
Other _____

How long have you been working at your present level? _____

How long has it been since you changed jobs or location of job? _____

How many women are at your place of work who are peers—that is, who are working
at roughly the same employment level? _____

How many women do you associate with regularly outside of your place of work who
are peers in terms of career or job? _____

SECTION 2: YOUR JOB AND JOB ISSUES

A. Dual-Career Couples

The definition of a dual-career couple for this research is a heterosexual couple with each partner working at least 20 hours per week in a professional-level career. If you are NOT in a dual-career relationship, please answer question 1 or 2. If you ARE, please begin at question 3.

1. If single, are the issues faced in a dual-career relationship a concern for you if you consider marriage?   Yes _____ No _____

2. If divorced, were dual-career issues a contributing factor in the divorce?
                                    Yes _____ No _____

   Comments:

3. What are the primary advantages of being in a dual-career relationship? Check all that apply.

   More equal balance of power   _____
   More autonomy   _____
   Greater cohesion due to shared experiences   _____
   Increased self-esteem   _____
   More income   _____
   Greater respect from partner   _____
   Other: _____

4. What are the primary disadvantages of being in a dual-career relationship? Check all that apply.

   Role conflict   _____
   Work overload   _____
   Slower or leveled career progress   _____
   Societal pressure/attitude   _____
   Little time left for relationships   _____
   Other: _____

5. What are your most effective ways of coping with the disadvantages?

   Partner encouraged to share workload   _____
   Hire housework help   _____
   Improve time management skills   _____
   Exercise   _____
   Locate support from others in similar situation   _____
   Leisure/relaxing activities given priority   _____
   Other: _____

6. How can women be more effectively prepared for the issues they will face in a dual-career relationship?

   Courses on dual-career marriages   _____
   Included in career advising system   _____

      Reading literature and advice on the subject   _____

      Employer provided advice and flexibility   _____

      Other: _____

7.   Did you interrupt your career to have/raise children?

                Yes _____   No _____

    If yes, for how long? _____   What effect, if any, did the interruption have on your career?

      Made a career change   _____

      Returned to education for new degree or refresher   _____

      Returned to same position   _____

      Lost responsibility and had to rebuild reputation   _____

      Other: _____

8.   In what ways does your partner contribute to child raising, housework, and directly to your career?

      Shares equally in all areas   _____

      Shares significantly but not equally   _____

      Helps with work-related entertainment   _____

      Gives emotional support and encouragement   _____

      Insignificant or no support   _____

B. Supervision

1.   In your present work setting:

    a.   Which of the following is the best description of your supervisor-supervisee situation:

        (1)   You are supervised by: male _____

                                            female _____

                                            no one _____

    b.   You supervise how many persons?

           female _____   male _____

2.   How satisfied are you with the quality of the supervision you receive?

	Agree				Disagree
My supervisor treats me fairly.	1	2	3	4	5
I learn my job skills from my supervisor.	1	2	3	4	5
My supervisor will help me advance professionally.	1	2	3	4	5

C. High Technology

For the purposes of this study, high technology is defined as work-related devices that interact with users through programming and/or electronic communication.

1.   Please check all of the high technology devices you use in your work:

    _____ Computer   _____ Telecommunications

    _____ Word processor   _____ Voice-messaging

    _____ Electronic mail   _____ Plotter

_____ Programmable telephone   _____ "Smart" typewriter
_____ Other (please list) _____

2. Please check all the tasks for which you use high technology devices at work:

_____ Communication
_____ Writing
_____ Recording and calculating numerical data
_____ Graphics
_____ Storing and retrieving information
_____ Other (please list) _____

3. How much formal and informal training time have you had for high technology devices (all devices)?

_____ more than 1 year   _____ 6-12 months   _____ 1-6 months

4. Please summarize the type of training you received to work with high technology.

5. How has your use of high technology influenced your work effectiveness?

_____ Positively   _____ Extremely varied influence
_____ Neutral   _____ Does not apply
_____ Negatively

6. What other machines did you work with (high technology or otherwise) before you obtained your current position?

7. How much access do you have to the technological devices in your workplace?

_____ Total   _____ Moderate
_____ None   _____ Restricted
_____ Does not apply

8. How much do technological skills influence salary and wages in your employment area?

_____ Strong influence   _____ Weak influence
_____ Moderate influence   _____ Extremely varied influence
_____ Does not apply

9. How do you currently feel about using high technology in your work? (Please check the best response.)

_____ Very enthusiastic and accepting   _____ Resistant
_____ Cautiously optimistic   _____ Very negative and rejecting
_____ Neutral

10. Please explain your understanding of the place technological skills have for your career path. How will your career advancement be influenced by high technology at work?

D. Sex Discrimination at Work

1. Have you experienced any form of sex discrimination in your work experience?

Yes _____ No _____

If yes, in what context did discrimination most frequently occur?

_____ Promotion   _____ Salary
_____ Responsibility   _____ Other
_____ Selection

Comments:

2. Have you discussed a sex discrimination matter with your employer?

Yes _____ No _____

With an appropriate government agency?

Yes _____ No _____

With a counselor?

Yes _____ No _____

With a family member or friend?

Yes _____ No _____

What advice would you give to female college students regarding preparation for potential discrimination experiences in the workplace?

E. What's Your Opinion?

1. Women can't get an even break in today's society.

_____ Strongly Agree   _____ Disagree
_____ Agree   _____ Strongly Disagree
_____ Undecided

2. Under present societal conditions there isn't much hope for success for bright, aggressive females.

_____ Strongly Agree   _____ Disagree
_____ Agree   _____ Strongly Disagree
_____ Undecided

3. The more successful a female becomes, the more likely she will feel alone.

_____ Strongly Agree   _____ Disagree
_____ Agree   _____ Strongly Disagree
_____ Undecided

4. a. How would you define the term *professional woman*?

b.   If this term applies to you, please tell us in which ways.

F. In the Workplace

If You Are an Employee:

1.   Do you think that your salary is commensurate with your skills and experience?

Yes _____   No _____

2.   If you are dissatisfied with your salary, what keeps you in your current job?

3.   Is your wage equal to that of men in your occupation doing the same or equivalent work?   Yes _____   No _____

4.   Please list up to five titles and a brief description of jobs that you believe are of similar value as your own to the organization for which you work. For each position you list, indicate sex of person(s) holding the job and approximate yearly salary.

Job Title and Description	Sex of Worker	Approximate Salary (per year)
_____	_____	_____
_____	_____	_____
_____	_____	_____
_____	_____	_____
_____	_____	_____

5.   a.   Are you presently seeking another position?

Yes _____   No _____

b.   If your salary were raised, would you stay in your current position or continue to seek another position and salary?

Stay _____   Seek _____

Please comment.

6.   What would you say is the most valuable contribution of the job that you and others who share your job title make to the organization for which you work?

7.   What would the company president (or comparable administrator) say is the most valuable contribution of the job that you and others who share your job title make to the organization for which you work?

8. Does your supervisor use a formal evaluation system to rate your job performance?
    Yes _____ No _____
    Please explain the procedure used.

If You Are (Also/Only) an Employer and/or Supervisor:

9. When determining the initial salary or level of salary raises for employees whom
    you hire or supervise, which of the following factors do you take into
    consideration? (Mark each according to the following scale of importance):

    1 = of primary importance   2 = important   3 = of moderate importance
    4 = slightly important   5 = unimportant

    _____ salaries of other employees performing identical work
    _____ salaries of other employees performing similar work
    _____ salaries of other employees performing dissimilar but equally valuable work
    _____ place of job in predetermined corporate or organizational hierarchy
    _____ educational background
    _____ previous experience
    _____ individual merit
    _____ personal factors (appearance, community contacts, age, etc.)
    Please elaborate:

    _____ Other:
    Please elaborate:

10. Do you use a formal evaluation procedure with which to rate employees'
    performance?   Yes _____ No _____
    Please explain the procedure used and why you chose it.

11. Additional comments?

G. Women and Leadership

Beside each of the following statements, indicate the extent to which you agree or disagree with the goal or principle it represents using the following scale.

1 = completely disagree   2 = partially disagree   3 = neutral
4 = partially agree   5 = completely agree

1	2	3	4	5	I try to be a positive role model to women seeking leadership opportunities.
1	2	3	4	5	I enjoy increasing my influence and responsibility.
1	2	3	4	5	I look forward to growing in leadership effectiveness.
1	2	3	4	5	I am dissatisfied when I do not have adequate responsibility and recognition.
1	2	3	4	5	I am uncomfortable when I think of moving into more responsible roles in my work.
1	2	3	4	5	I am active in seeking leadership opportunities.
1	2	3	4	5	People often look to me for advice and inspiration.
1	2	3	4	5	I consider myself to be a competent decision maker.
1	2	3	4	5	I often think I would have more opportunities if I were a man.
1	2	3	4	5	I feel my parents gave me more responsibility than other parents gave their children.
1	2	3	4	5	I often defer to others for advice and guidance.
1	2	3	4	5	I seek more responsibility than my job description requires.
1	2	3	4	5	My work energizes me so that I enjoy the rest of my life more.
1	2	3	4	5	I am drained and depressed by the demands of my work.
1	2	3	4	5	I enjoy thinking about my professional advancement and future goals.
1	2	3	4	5	I intend to move into increasingly challenging and responsible roles.
1	2	3	4	5	I prefer to design new strategies for completing tasks rather than follow conventional methods.
1	2	3	4	5	I identify with the leaders in any group or organization.
1	2	3	4	5	I frequently think about the way my work relates to larger social trends.
1	2	3	4	5	I must do work that is consistent with my social vision.
1	2	3	4	5	I hope to be known as a person who has made important social contributions.
1	2	3	4	5	I believe most people benefit from being included in decision making.
1	2	3	4	5	I trust others to know what is right for themselves.
1	2	3	4	5	I learn from superordinates and from subordinates.
1	2	3	4	5	People seem to enjoy working with me to achieve goals.
1	2	3	4	5	I am pleased to be asked to serve as a group leader.
1	2	3	4	5	I seek leadership experience in most areas of my life.
1	2	3	4	5	I feel leadership experience in volunteer or social groups is a professional asset.

1	2	3	4	5	I wish I had become aware of my leadership potential at an earlier age.
1	2	3	4	5	If encouraged to do so, I would gladly seek public office.
1	2	3	4	5	I think I could contribute to effective management in this or another organization.
1	2	3	4	5	Society will be more responsible to the needs of everyone when more women are leaders.
1	2	3	4	5	Children should be given more leadership training.
1	2	3	4	5	Leadership skills can be taught and learned.
1	2	3	4	5	Leaders have personal qualities that set them apart from other people.
1	2	3	4	5	I am uncomfortable with my own power.
1	2	3	4	5	I feel I would sacrifice my femininity were I to seek power.
1	2	3	4	5	I am inspired by seeing others in leadership roles.
1	2	3	4	5	I am diminished by others' exercise of leadership.

SECTION 3: YOUR ATTITUDES, KNOWLEDGE, AND USE OF ALCOHOL

1. Your Use of Alcohol.
    Answer questions A-F by filling in the number that best describes your use of alcoholic beverages.

    _____ A.   How often do you usually drink wine?

    1.   1 or 2 times a day
    2.   about 3 or 4 times a week
    3.   about 1 or 2 times a week
    4.   about 1 or 2 times a month
    5.   at least 1 time a year
    6.   less than 1 time a year

    _____ B.   When you drink wine, how much do you usually drink at one time?

    1.   a bottle or more
    2.   about half a bottle or about 5 glasses
    3.   3 or 4 glasses
    4.   1 or 2 glasses
    5.   less than one glass
    6.   never drink wine

    _____ C.   How often do you usually drink beer?

    1.   1 or 2 times a day
    2.   about 3 or 4 times a week
    3.   about 1 or 2 times a week
    4.   about 1 or 2 times a month
    5.   at least 1 time a year
    6.   less than 1 time a year
    7.   never

_____ D.   When you drink beer, how much do you usually drink at one time?

1.   7 or more bottles
2.   5 or 6 bottles
3.   3 or 4 bottles
4.   1 or 2 bottles
5.   less than 1 bottle
6.   never drink beer

_____ E.   How often do you usually drink liquor?

1.   1 or 2 times a day
2.   about 3 or 4 times a week
3.   about 1 or 2 times a week
4.   about 1 or 2 times a month
5.   at least 1 time a year
6.   less than 1 time a year
7.   never

_____ F.   When you drink liquor, how much do you usually drink at one time?

1.   7 or more drinks
2.   5 or 6 drinks
3.   3 or 4 drinks
4.   1 or 2 drinks
5.   less than 1 drink
6.   never drink liquor

During a social or other occasion (of 2 hours' duration) in which you are drinking, how many drinks can you have:

a.   before you feel the effects?   _____
b.   before you should not drive a car?   _____
c.   before you get drunk?   _____

2.   Your Life-Style

In the last 30 days, how often were you in settings where other people were drinking, even if you were not drinking?

_____ Daily or almost every day   _____ One to three times total
_____ Several times a week   _____ Not at all
_____ Once or twice a week

Is drinking permitted or expected as part of your job?

Yes _____   No _____

If Yes, is it acceptable NOT to drink on those occasions when others are drinking?

_____ Definitely acceptable   _____ Possibly unacceptable
_____ Possibly acceptable   _____ Definitely unacceptable
_____ I'm not sure how it might be viewed.

Choose the letter of the term that best characterizes the drinking habits of:

_____ (1) your spouse   _____ (2) your best friend

a.   abstainer   b.   light   c.   moderate
d.   heavy   e.   problem   f.   alcoholic

3. Attitudes and Effects

    Choose from the following categories the answer that fits best.

    1. Daily
    2. Four or more times each month
    3. One to three times each month
    4. One to three times in the last 6 months
    5. Not at all in the last 6 months

    Within the last 6 MONTHS, how often have the following occurred?

    _____ You had a drink or drinks with friends at a social occasion.

    _____ You had a drink or drinks to ease physical pain or help you get to sleep.

    _____ You felt that your drinking may hurt your chances for getting a job, a promotion, or other benefits at work.

    _____ You forgot to do something for your spouse or children when you had been drinking.

    _____ You drove a car when you felt drunk or high from drinking.

    _____ You were a passenger in a car driven by someone who you felt was high or drunk.

    _____ You had a drink or drinks to become less depressed or to get rid of "blue" or sad feelings.

    _____ You felt that drinking interfered with homemaking or chores around the house.

    _____ You felt that drinks made a party more festive.

    _____ You were told by someone at work that you should cut down your drinking.

    _____ You had a fight with a family member, friend, or someone at work when you had been drinking.

    _____ You had a drink or drinks while on medication that is not supposed to be mixed with alcohol.

    _____ You became less particular about your choice of sexual partners when you had been drinking.

    _____ You had a drink or drinks to forget problems at home or at work.

    _____ Your spouse/significant other told you that your drinking is causing problems in the relationship.

    _____ You were charged with driving under the influence (DUI).

    _____ You had an accident (auto, home, or other) when you had been drinking.

    _____ You developed or were treated for a medical problem that could be related to alcohol use.

    _____ You got drunk or high in a situation in which it would have been better to stay completely or mostly sober.

4. Alcohol Information Scale

    T   F   1. Alcohol is similar to food in that it must be digested.

    T   F   2. Alcohol affects coordination and balance but does not affect thinking ability.

    T   F   3. There is approximately the same amount of alcohol in a 1-ounce shot of 100 proof distilled spirits, a 4-ounce glass of table wine, and a 12-ounce can of beer.

    T   F   4. A cold shower, exercise, or coffee will help you sober up faster.

    T   F   5. What alcohol does for you depends, in part, on your mood before you start drinking.

    T   F   6. Beverage alcohol has a depressant effect on the central nervous system.

    T   F   7. Alcohol affects males and females differently due to hormonal differences between the sexes.

    T   F   8. One way to slow down the effect of alcohol is to dilute the drink.

    T   F   9. A mixed drink that is carbonated will make you intoxicated faster than a noncarbonated mixed drink.

    T   F   10. Women on "the pill" absorb alcohol faster than those not taking oral contraceptives.

    T   F   11. Having food in your stomach will slow down the rate at which alcohol is absorbed.

    T   F   12. Sweet mixed drinks produce worse hangovers than nonsweet drinks.

    T   F   13. A male and a female of the same weight can drink equal amounts of alcohol and experience the same effects.

    T   F   14. One way to slow down the rate of alcohol entering the bloodstream is to drink slower.

    T   F   15. Abusive or alcoholic drinking causes medical problems at the same rate for men or for women.

    T   F   16. The passage of time is the only cure for intoxication.

    T   F   17. A heavier person must drink more alcohol to become intoxicated.

    T   F   18. A woman should limit or stop drinking during pregnancy.

    T   F   19. Liquor that is 90 proof contains 45% alcohol.

5. Professional Situations: Please evaluate the following situations.

    A. Sara Hughes is trying to land a new account for her firm. She takes two representatives of the other company to dinner. During the course of the meal, she has three or four drinks. Sara and the others discuss the needs of the new account and the capabilities of Sara's firm to meet these needs.

          _____ How would you evaluate this behavior?

          1. Completely positive   4. Somewhat negative
          2. Somewhat positive   5. Completely negative
          3. Neutral

B. After a successful sales year, Linda Brinkley and the other sales representatives attend a celebration sponsored by their company. Linda is very pleased with her performance on the job. At the party she has a number of drinks. Although she doesn't do anything objectionable, it is obvious that she is somewhat drunk.

_____ How would you evaluate this behavior?

1. Completely positive   4. Somewhat negative
2. Somewhat positive   5. Completely negative
3. Neutral

C. Joyce Russell is a department manager. She is attending a "working lunch" with other department managers and their supervisors. During the meeting the others have a drink or two while Joyce has coffee. The group develops plans for the coming quarter and returns to the office.

_____ How would you evaluate this behavior?

1. Completely positive   4. Somewhat negative
2. Somewhat positive   5. Completely negative
3. Neutral

D. Ellen Vaughn is an attorney with a local law firm. She sometimes conducts business with clients over lunch. At such times she will have a drink at the start of the meal. Her luncheon meetings generally take from one hour to an hour and a half. She has found this to be a convenient and usually productive way to work with clients.

_____ How would you evaluate this behavior?

1. Completely positive   4. Somewhat negative
2. Somewhat positive   5. Completely negative
3. Neutral

E. Nancy Myers has been under a good deal of stress lately. Both her business and her children are having "growing pains," and seeing them through their crises is difficult and tiring. Nancy finds that having a few drinks takes her away from her problems for a while.

_____ How would you evaluate this behavior?

1. Completely positive   4. Somewhat negative
2. Somewhat positive   5. Completely negative
3. Neutral

SECTION 4: WHAT DO YOU THINK?

Beside each of the following statements, indicate the extent to which you agree or disagree with the goal or principle it represents, using the following scale.

1 = completely disagree   2 = partially disagree   3 = neutral
4 = partially agree   5 = completely agree

1   2   3   4   5   Men and women should receive equal pay for equal work.

1   2   3   4   5   All workers should receive comparable pay for work of comparable worth.

1	2	3	4	5	Most women have been subject to sex discrimination at some time in their lives, whether they know it or not.
1	2	3	4	5	Certain jobs should be reserved for women, just as certain jobs should be reserved for men.
1	2	3	4	5	Women's special duties in the family require them to commit less time and energy to their careers than men do.
1	2	3	4	5	Women's activist groups have helped improve things for working women.
1	2	3	4	5	Working women would be better off if feminist groups would discontinue their efforts to attain greater rights for women.
1	2	3	4	5	Women should be able to obtain education in any field and to enter any field in the work world.
1	2	3	4	5	In order to improve conditions for women with careers, vast changes will have to be made in the structure of the family.
1	2	3	4	5	A career woman's best friend is her housekeeper or baby-sitter.
1	2	3	4	5	A career woman's best friend is her nonsexist husband.
1	2	3	4	5	A career woman is better off if she never marries.
1	2	3	4	5	Career women should not expect to shirk their household responsibilities.
1	2	3	4	5	Career women have very little in common with full-time homemakers.
1	2	3	4	5	The biggest problem a career woman faces is the structure of the organization in which she works; most firms, companies, or institutions in today's society are not supportive of career women's needs.
1	2	3	4	5	Any woman who wants to succeed in her career had better be able to compete on the same terms as a man; asking for special consideration or support services because she is a woman is a big mistake.
1	2	3	4	5	Corporations, firms, and other institutions are under no obligation to offer support services for working women.
1	2	3	4	5	A woman who wants a career should choose not to become a mother.
1	2	3	4	5	The very structure of work in modern American society is male oriented; even women without families face obstacles as they pursue their careers.
1	2	3	4	5	When all is said and done, a woman will succeed in her career if she is willing to work hard for that success.

1.   Please define feminism as you understand it.

2. Do you consider yourself to be a feminist?

        Yes _____ No _____

3. a. If you have answered No, do you know any women who define themselves as feminists? Yes _____ No _____

   b. If you have answered Yes, please describe one of those women.

SECTION 5: YOUR LEISURE

A. Below is a list of activities you might choose to do for pleasure, relaxation, self-fulfillment, social value, or other reasons. Place a check to the left of each activity you do in your leisure time. To the right of each checked activity indicate how much time (in hours and/or minutes) you might spend at that activity in a week. Finally, check the people with whom you do the activity. You may check more than one.

FAM - family, including spouse   FR - friends   AL - alone
CO-W - co-workers

Leisure Activity	Total Time	With FAM	FR	CO-W	AL
1. Do an aerobic exercise (run, jog, walk, bike, swim, roller skate, jump rope, cross-country ski)	___	___	___	___	___
2. Go to an exercise class	___	___	___	___	___
3. Work out (lift weights, use an exercise machine, etc.)	___	___	___	___	___
4. Ski (water or snow)	___	___	___	___	___
5. Camp, hike, or backpack	___	___	___	___	___
6. Boat or fish	___	___	___	___	___
7. Play a team sport (e.g., softball, basketball)	___	___	___	___	___
8. Play golf, tennis, racquetball, or hand-ball	___	___	___	___	___
9. Bowl	___	___	___	___	___
10. Engage in a sexual activity	___	___	___	___	___
11. Watch TV programs or taped programs on a VCR	___	___	___	___	___
12. Go to movies	___	___	___	___	___
13. Attend sports events	___	___	___	___	___
14. Listen to stereo (radio, tapes, albums)	___	___	___	___	___
15. Play a musical instrument	___	___	___	___	___

Leisure Activity	Total Time	With FAM	FR	CO-W	AL
_____ 16. Attend a musical, theater, or ballet performance	____	____	____	____	____
_____ 17. Visit a museum or art gallery	____	____	____	____	____
_____ 18. Play video games, pinball, or pool	____	____	____	____	____
_____ 19. Play cards or board games	____	____	____	____	____
_____ 20. Work puzzles (crossword, jigsaw, etc.)	____	____	____	____	____
_____ 21. Read a book (fiction or nonfiction)	____	____	____	____	____
_____ 22. Read a newspaper, magazine, or a career-related journal	____	____	____	____	____
_____ 23. Read aloud	____	____	____	____	____
_____ 24. Go to a library	____	____	____	____	____
_____ 25. Take a hot bath, sauna, jacuzzi, or hot tub	____	____	____	____	____
_____ 26. Meditate or do yoga	____	____	____	____	____
_____ 27. Relax (e.g., sit and do nothing)	____	____	____	____	____
_____ 28. Take a nap	____	____	____	____	____
_____ 29. Go for a walk or drive	____	____	____	____	____
_____ 30. Play with, train, or care for a pet	____	____	____	____	____
_____ 31. Collect stamps, coins, memorabilia, etc.	____	____	____	____	____
_____ 32. Take photographs or home movies	____	____	____	____	____
_____ 33. Do a craft hobby (woodworking, weaving, painting, sketching, needlework, ceramics, etc.)	____	____	____	____	____
_____ 34. Do gourmet cooking or baking	____	____	____	____	____
_____ 35. Raise houseplants	____	____	____	____	____
_____ 36. Do outdoor gardening or other yardwork	____	____	____	____	____

Leisure Activity		Total Time	With FAM	FR	CO-W	AL
_____ 37.	Socialize in your home (for social rather than professional reasons)	____	____	____	____	____
_____ 38.	Visit friends or relatives	____	____	____	____	____
_____ 39.	Go to a club or bar to drink or dance	____	____	____	____	____
_____ 40.	Eat out at a restaurant	____	____	____	____	____
_____ 41.	Go on a picnic	____	____	____	____	____
_____ 42.	Write letters to friends	____	____	____	____	____
_____ 43.	Socialize on the telephone	____	____	____	____	____
_____ 44.	Do volunteer work	____	____	____	____	____
_____ 45.	Go to meetings or activities of any organizations to which you belong	____	____	____	____	____
_____ 46.	Go to church	____	____	____	____	____
_____ 47.	Attend a lecture	____	____	____	____	____
_____ 48.	Attend a child's school activity (sports event, concert, or program)	____	____	____	____	____
_____ 49.	Travel	____	____	____	____	____
_____ 50.	Go shopping (for clothes, groceries, household items, etc.)	____	____	____	____	____
_____ 51.	Other	____	____	____	____	____

B. What leisure activity do you do most often?

What is it about this activity that attracts you?

C. What leisure activity do you wish you could do more often, and how much time would you spend doing it in a week if you could?

With whom would you do this activity?

FAM _____   FR _____   CO-W _____   AL _____

What is it about this activity that attracts you?

SECTION 6: YOUR NEEDS AND INTERESTS

The Research Group on Women and Work (RGWW) hopes to serve as a resource for working women. For this we need the following information from you.

1. What is the most convenient way for you to receive information for your own use?

    _____ Newsletter articles   _____ Workshops held during the
    _____ Workshops held on the weekends   week
    _____ Audio- or videotapes   _____ Workshops held at night
    _____ Television programs   _____ University classes
    _____ Other

2. In the last 6 months, what has been the issue of greatest concern to you in any realm (i.e., work, home, family, personal) of your life?

3. Would you like to see this issue addressed by the RGWW?

    Yes _____   No _____

4. What other subjects would you like to see the RGWW address?

5. In the past 6 months, what has been the most pleasant, happiest, or most meaningful thing that has happened to you?

Thank you for completing this lengthy questionnaire. We hope that you have found it interesting. Please feel free to include below any other comments you might have.

SURVEY ON CHILD CARE

All readers please complete. If you have no children, complete Section I; if you have children but never used child care, complete Section II; and if you are currently using child care or if you used child care when your children were younger, complete Section III. The term *child care* will be used here to refer only to child care during working hours, rather than to baby-sitting for volunteer, leisure, social, or other activities.

SECTION I: Please answer if you do not have children.

1. Do you expect to have children in the future?

    Yes _____ No _____ Undecided _____

2. How important have anticipated problems with child care been in your decision to not have children or to postpone having children?

extremely important	_____
very important	_____
somewhat important	_____
not important	_____

SECTION II: Please answer if you have children but have never used child care.

1. Please check the statement that best describes your situation. (Check only one)

    _____ a.   I wanted to wait until my children were in school all day before entering the labor force.

    _____ b.   I would have entered the labor force sooner but was pressured by my spouse to wait until the children were older.

    _____ c.   I would have entered the labor force sooner but was pressured by others to wait until the children were older.

    _____ d.   I would have entered the labor force sooner but was unable to find acceptable child care.

    _____ e.   I was employed, and the children were cared for by my spouse or someone else within my household.

    _____ f.   Other, please specify _____

SECTION III: Please answer if you have children and have used child care.

1. Are you currently using child care?

    Yes _____ No _____

    If no, during what years (e.g., 1978-1986) did you use child care? _____

    If yes, how many hours per week? _____

2. Please check the type of child care that you have used. (Check all those that are appropriate to your experience.)

	infants (12-30 months)	toddlers (2.5 to 5 years)	preschool	school age
spouse	____	____	____	____
other relative	____	____	____	____
neighbor	____	____	____	____
friend	____	____	____	____
day care home	____	____	____	____
in-home care	____	____	____	____
nonprofit center	____	____	____	____
for-profit center	____	____	____	____
other	____	____	____	____

3. Which of the child care arrangements listed in the last question have you found
    most satisfactory?

    for infants   _____
    for toddlers   _____
    for preschoolers   _____
    for school-age children   _____

4. How much, on average, do you (or did you) pay per child for child care?
    _____ per hour or _____ per week

5. Have your child care arrangements required any extra travel in addition to your
    travel to and from work?
    Yes _____ No _____

6. Have you ever missed work due to lack of child care?
    Yes _____ No _____

7. Have you ever had to bring your child to work due to lack of child care?
    Yes _____ No _____

8. On a scale of 1 to 5, where 1 is *not at all important* and 5 is *very important,* how
    would you rate the following reasons for choosing a child care provider?

	Not at all Important				Very Important
Quality of staff	1	2	3	4	5
Flexibility of hours	1	2	3	4	5
Variety of activities	1	2	3	4	5
Educational content	1	2	3	4	5
Cost	1	2	3	4	5
Proximity/Access to child care during the day	1	2	3	4	5
Attractive facilities	1	2	3	4	5

9. What methods have you used to find child care arrangements? (Check all that apply.)

    _____ Co-worker   _____ Phone book
    _____ Previous day care provider   _____ Newspaper ad
    _____ Neighbor   _____ Child's school
    _____ Relative   _____ Church or synagogue
    _____ Friend   _____ Information and referral
    _____ Other   agency

10. How many times have you changed child care arrangements while your child was
    less than 6 years old?

    Oldest child _____ Second child _____ Third child _____

    Which of the following best explain the reasons for the change?
    (Check all that apply.)

    Care provider quit.   _____
    I need a provider closer to home.   _____
    I need a provider closer to work.   _____

My child is not happy with the care.   _____

I am not happy with the care.   _____

I need a care provider with more flexible hours.   _____

I need less expensive care.   _____

We moved.   _____

Other (specify): _____

11. What kind of summer care have you used for children between age 5 and 12? (Check all that apply.)

Center care   _____

Neighborhood family care   _____

In-home care by adult   _____

In-home care by teenager   _____

Self-care   _____

Other   _____

Which of these have you found most satisfactory?

_____

12. At what age did you regularly leave your child alone?

by self   _____

with siblings   _____

13. How do you perceive the overall effects of your day care arrangement on your career productivity? Please report its effects on career mobility, aspirations, outcomes, etc.

14. How do you think your employer perceives the relationship between your child care arrangements and your productivity?

Index

About the Contributors

Nancy A. Brooks is Associate Professor of Sociology at Wichita State University, where she specializes in the sociology of medicine and the sociology of technology. She has numerous professional publications, is co-editor of the book *Women and Disability: The Double Handicap,* co-author of the monograph *Framing the Artist: A Social Portrait of Mid-America Artists,* and co-author of *Carrying On: Humor in Families with Chronic Disease.* She has had multiple sclerosis for 27 years.

Wayne Carlisle, before his untimely death, was Director of Placement and Career Services at Wichita State University. In that capacity, he provided insight, guidance, and mentoring to women students and colleagues seeking career opportunities. He served a 3-year term on the Executive Board of the National Association of Student Personnel Administrators, exercised significant responsibilities with its regional association, served as Program Chair for the 1991 national conference, and on four occasions served as Chair of Career Services at national conferences. In 1990 he received the Fred Turner Award from the National Association of Student Personnel Administrators. The award is given to one individual annually who has given exceptional service to the association. Never before in its 73-year history had a Director of Placement and Career Services won this award.

Brooke B. Collison is Associate Professor of Counselor Education at Oregon State University, Corvallis. Prior to his tenure at OSU, he was a counselor-educator at Wichita State University. He is a past president of the American Counseling Association, was appointed by Governor Barbara Roberts to membership on the Oregon State Council on Vocational

Education in 1991, and serves as a member of the board of directors of the National Career Development Training Institute at the University of South Carolina, Columbia.

Flo Hamrick is a former Associate Director of the Office of Placement and Career Services at Wichita State University who is now a doctoral student in Higher Education with a concentration in Inquiry and Research Methodology at Indiana University. As a colleague of Wayne Carlisle, she often co-presented with him on topics of career advancement, gender and supervision, male-female mentoring, and workplace discrimination.

Sally L. Kitch is Director of the Center for Women's Studies and Professor of Women's Studies and Comparative Studies at The Ohio State University, Columbus. During most of the RGWW study, however, she was Director of the Center for Women's Studies at Wichita State University. Her research interests include feminist theory, women's literature and feminist literary criticism, and cultural theory as applied to both past and present social organizations. The historical focus of her work is reflected in her two recent books, *Chaste Liberation: Celibacy and Female Cultural Status* and *This Strange Society of Women: Reading the Lives and Letters of the Woman's Commonwealth,* each of which won a national women's studies award prior to publication. Although rarely as data based as her work with RGWW, her theoretical orientation does lead her to investigate a variety of subjects, including the gendered nature of war imagery, postmodern concepts of identity, and poststructuralist psychoanalytic approaches to African American women's literature.

Carol Wolfe Konek is Associate Professor in the Center for Women's Studies and Associate Dean of Fairmount College of Liberal Arts and Sciences at Wichita State University. Her most recent books are *Daddyboy: A Family's Struggle With Alzheimer's* and *Transformations: Voices of Women in Recovery.* She recently published literary non-fiction in *Affillia: A Journal of Women and Social Work, Frontiers: A Journal of Women's Liberation, Heresles: A Journal of Art and Politics, Feminisms,* and the *National Women's Studies Association Journal.* She currently is gathering narratives of women in gangs and is active in the global women's movement and in women's peace and women's health movements.

Marcia L. McCoy is currently a student in the Clinical Psychology doctoral program at the University of Kansas, Lawrence, where she teaches a human sexuality course in Psychology and a course on women and violence in Women's Studies. Her dissertation research is an investigation of the cognitive and situational factors influencing men engaging in gang rape on campus, particularly members of fraternities and athletic groups. Other research and teaching interests include rape prevention through education of men, resocialization of gender roles and attitudes about sexuality, and HIV/AIDS prevention through effective instruction and safer sex. She aspires to become a university professor engaged in a wide range of leisure activities, including restoring sports cars and building and flying airplanes.

Elsie R. Shore is Associate Professor of Psychology at Wichita State University, where she organized the Research Group on Women and Work to support her work on women and alcohol. She received her master's degree in Educational Psychology and Measurements and her doctorate in Clinical-Community Psychology from the University of Nebraska, Lincoln. Her research interests include women and alcohol and the prevention of alcohol-related problems. She has published her research in a variety of professional journals, including the *Journal of Studies on Alcohol, British Journal of Addiction,* and *Addictive Behaviors.*

Nancy McCarthy Snyder is Associate Professor in the Hugo Wall Center for Urban Studies at Wichita State University. She received her doctorate in Economics from Southern Illinois University, Carbondale. Her research has focused on income distribution policy, social welfare policy, and public finance. She has worked extensively with the state of Kansas in a number of capacities: as a member of the 1992 Kansas Commission on Education Restructuring and Accountability and as an evaluator of the Kansas Welfare-to-Work program, known as KanWork. She is currently on leave from WSU and is serving as Director of Research and Accountability for the Corporation for Change, an organization charged with planning, research, coordination, and evaluation of children and family policy in Kansas.